RADICALIZING LEARNING

RADICALIZING LEARNING

Adult Education for a Just World

Stephen D. Brookfield, John D. Holst

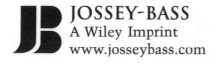

JOSSEY-BASS
A Wiley Imprint
www.josseybass.com

Published by Jossey-Bass
A Wiley Imprint
989 Market Street, San Francisco, CA 94103-1741—www.josseybass.com

Jossey-Bass books and products are available through most bookstores. To contact Jossey-Bass directly
call our Customer Care Department within the U.S. at 800-956-7739, outside the U.S. at 317-572-3986,
or fax 317-572-4002.

Jossey-Bass also publishes its books in a variety of electronic formats. Some content that appears in
print may not be available in electronic books.

Library of Congress Cataloging-in-Publication Data
Brookfield, Stephen.
   Radicalizing learning : adult education for a just world / Stephen D. Brookfield, John D. Holst.
      p. cm. —(The Jossey-Bass higher and adult education series)
   Includes bibliographical references and index.
   ISBN 978-0-7879-9825-7 (cloth)
   1. Adult education—United States.   2. Adult learning—United States.   3. Critical pedagogy—
United States.   I. Holst, John D.   II. Title.
   LC5251.B74 2010
   374'.015—dc22
                                                                        2010021299

Printed in the United States of America.
FIRST EDITION
HB Printing 10 9 8 7 6 5 4 3 2 1

The Jossey-Bass

Higher and Adult Education Series

Contents

PREFACE

As we were writing this book, two momentous events happened in the United States. The first was the meltdown of the banking and investment sector, some would say the near collapse of capitalism itself. The other was the election of the first biracial president. These two events intersected as President Obama attempted to regulate the operations of the financial sector (banks, insurance companies, and investment capital) and to reform the largely private health care system. Both these relatively mild attempts to curb the worst excesses of capitalism were met with a tide of criticism from the right, whose representatives quickly invoked the terms *socialism* and *socialistic* to condemn Obama's reforms. Their invocation was intended to show that Obama's proposals curbed individual freedom and went against the deep grain of liberty itself invoked so frequently as characterizing U.S. culture.

The two of us were alternately amused and bewildered by these criticisms. First, it was amusing to hear the term *socialism* applied to reforms designed to keep capitalism intact and to expand the customer base of private health insurance companies. The self-righteous indignation frothing from the lips of commentators like Rush Limbaugh and Glenn Beck was hilariously misdirected, given that nothing remotely socialistic was on view. Second, it was bewildering to witness the fear and loathing that the word socialism invoked, particularly since the concept had been declared dead and buried with the collapse of the former Soviet Union. For an idea supposed to have been consigned to the graveyard of history, the twitching of the corpse appeared to have enough life to induce a frenetic fit of the vapors.

As the two of us began to talk about the book now in your hands, we realized that this temporary attention to the idea of socialism was in some ways fortuitous. Out of nowhere, socialism was now a part of the public discourse again in a way that it hadn't been since the start of the century. Even if the word was a sort of instigator of moral panic, it was still being used and was linked to the regulation of the banking, investment, and insurance industries, and to the provision of decent health care for the good of all. Both the bailouts and government takeovers of banks and insurance companies instigated by George W. Bush and the proposal for a publicly funded health care option were described as socialist. So from being unused and effectively outlawed, the word had suddenly jumped to the status of being a descriptor that the right wing was using to characterize the actions of both a highly conservative president and a self-described, bipartisan, democratic centrist president. All of a sudden, *socialism* was back as a shorthand term for the regulation of services and allocation of resources for the good of the majority. As you will see as you move through the book, we believe that figuring out what an authentic—and very democratic—socialism looks like is at the heart of what we understand as a radical approach. A radical approach breaks with an ethic of individualistic self-interest to ask "How should we act toward each other to promote the common good?" Answering that question leads to considering collective and cooperative ways of living and learning.

The two of us work at a university where fostering the common good is part of our mission statement. So we had often talked about what the common good represented and how it implicitly foregrounded collective compassion and responsibility. We had also been talking about the way that adult education discourse had seemed to veer to the right and the way that what had once seemed to be a mainstream idea in the field—that adult education's historic role was to help create and then defend democracy against the rise of unrepresentative elites—now appeared either daringly radical or dangerously passé. Our conversations moved toward what it meant to think, and more importantly, act as a radical adult educator. If radicalism represented a fundamental shift in the nature of the world, then the traditional project of adult education—creating and extending a genuinely participatory democracy—now seemed more radical than ever. And, since part of realizing democracy was (as Myles Horton was fond of arguing) creating economic democracy, it was impossible for us to explore radical adult education without considering democratic economic arrangements, particularly socialism. An economic democracy is one in which everyone is involved in deciding how the resources of society are to be distributed and allocated for the common good, which is as good a shorthand definition of socialism as you can get.

We think linking adult education to democratic socialism is radical for five reasons.

1. It challenges the dominance of capitalist ideology as representing the "natural" way of ordering economic life that ultimately rebounds to the interest of all. We grow up believing that capitalism guards liberty and guarantees individual freedom, so learning to question that belief requires some serious critical thinking.
2. It envisages a future that marks a qualitative break with the present. Democratic socialism requires a complete and deep-rooted reordering of society and the economy so that it is fundamentally different than it was before. Such a change deserves to be described as transformation.
3. It positions the practice of adult education in a way that stands in opposition to current ways of organizing programs and classes in that it emphasizes collective and collaborative work.
4. It requires a total rethinking of what the field stands for and how adult educators should assess their effectiveness. Adult education now becomes much more of an effort to illuminate, and then challenge, asymmetrical power relations.
5. It requires adult educators to undertake a serious political detoxification to free themselves (as much as that is possible) from a very successful program of ideological manipulation that has equated anything socialist with a form of totalitarian thought control that imposes top-down conformity and squashes creativity and difference.

ORGANIZATION OF THE BOOK

The book is intended to serve as an overview of the theory and practice of adult education interpreted from one particular perspective that we call radical. As such, it is designed to be a contemporary and comprehensive treatment of practices and ideas that comprise the understanding and facilitation of adult learning. We wanted to write a book that could stand as an introductory textbook to the field in that it included all the topics that adult education textbooks traditionally cover. These would be adult learning, adult development, program planning, training, teaching, and research. In each of the chapters on these topics we explore how these processes can be understood and practiced to help people learn what it means to participate fully in a genuine political and economic democracy. We begin by conceptualizing adult learning and development and then move to the analysis of training, program development, and teaching. The book then turns to exploring the impact of technology and globalization and forms of artistic expression. We end by analyzing how learning can be researched and how adult learning for participatory democracy works in a diverse society.

We call this book *Radicalizing Learning: Adult Education for a Just World* because we want our focus to be on the purposeful learning adults undertake in pursuit of political and economic democracy, whether or not that occurs within programs described as adult education. Much of our attention is on social movements and on organizing that takes place outside of formal institutions, and much of that is self-directed—guided by experimentation and trial and error without the benefit or guidance of an experienced teacher. For us, adult learning is inextricably tied to creating and extending political and economic democracy—to equalizing democratic control of and access to wealth, education, health care, and creative work, and to promoting collective and cooperative forms of decision making and labor. This is perhaps seen most clearly in community movements. Every act of adult learning in such a movement entails alternating and intersecting dimensions. When adults learn how to create a tenants' organization, build a grassroots coalition of environmental groups to stop a corporate-sponsored change in land use, organize a series of "take back the night" vigils, set up bar-room classes to teach literacy for voter registration, mobilize a citizen army to fight apartheid, establish a worker's cooperative in Turin, Clydeside, or Nova Scotia, they increase knowledge, skill, and insight. None of these activities is wholly technical, communicative, emancipatory, or emotional in terms of the learning that ensues; instead, each involves a complex web of actions, choices, and reasoning, with different forms and processes highlighted more strongly than others at different times. Our book begins by proposing this kind of learning as being particularly important and then works backward to explore how it is best encouraged, including the role of program planning, teaching and training in that endeavor.

OVERVIEW OF CHAPTERS

We open the book in Chapter One with an analysis of the term *radical* from two dimensions: getting down to the roots of a phenomenon to rediscover its essential nature or purpose and envisaging a qualitative transformation of society and the economy. We introduce the idea of democratic socialism and consider what it means to learn how to exercise common control and steward-ship of resources. In so doing, we argue that the values of fairness, creativity, inclusion, and difference are central, and we provide examples of radical adult learning, particularly that of Nelson Mandela. Chapter Two considers further the meaning of radical adult learning and how this involves recognizing and challenging dominant ideology, particularly as people build grassroots coalitions and collective economic forms. We then consider the intersection of these ideas with three prominent conceptualizations of adult learning in the field—transformative learning, critical reflection, and self-direction.

Adult development is the focus of Chapter Three. In this chapter we explain how we see normative and empirical elements as being always interwoven in understandings of development. We also argue that the concept of development can be reframed in a way that grounds it in the normative pursuit of true democracy—a democracy that is participatory and economic. Our interpretation of development from a radical perspective links it to collective identity development, to developing agency, and to the develop-ment of collective forms. The chapter ends with a discussion of how to teach for radical development.

Discussions of training are often excluded in texts on radical education because of its corporate connotations and its association with top-down, authoritarian approaches. Chapter Four challenges this conceptualization and argues that training has long occupied a central place in radical practice. We provide examples of this such as the citizenship schools in the U.S. Civil Rights Movement, the Nicaraguan literacy crusade, the landless workers movement of Brazil, and the Argentinian recovered factory movement. In Chapter Five we turn our attention to program planning and begin by establishing the central principles of radical program planning—critical self reflection, internationalism, love, discipline, flexibility, and sacrifice. These are terms very different from those usually contained in program planning texts, and they suggest specific practices. We then explore goals of program planning, such as promoting the political independence of working-class people, understanding the dynamics and trajectory of social and political change, understanding one's contributions to those dynamics and trajectory, and working with social movements. The chapter ends with an analysis of criteria for program evaluation including working with the demands of the dispossessed, establishing connections with wider struggles, building political independence, and developing leadership.

Teachers and the process of teaching are the foci of Chapter Six. We begin by outlining the functions of radical teaching and discuss what might comprise the elements of a radical curriculum. The chapter then turns to what radical teaching looks like. We try to establish its central practices and argue that it must not be confused with experimentation for experimentation's sake, or with students simply deciding what should be studied and how this should happen. Chapter Seven widens the context of the book to an analysis of the impact on globalization of adult learning. It includes a discussion of a political economy of globalization—an understanding of political process as shaped by economic forces—and argues that microchip technology represents a qualitative change in the nature of capitalism. The growing informal sector of the economy—those in temporary, fluctuating, independent, and seasonal work—is proposed as a new focus for adult educators.

The aesthetic dimension of adult learning is the focus of Chapter Eight. We begin by drawing on the work of Herbert Marcuse who argued that important radical transformation could be triggered by artistic encounters that lifted people out of the realm of everyday experience. We follow this with example of radical art drawn from music and the visual arts and then argue for several functions of radical aesthetics—sounding warnings, building solidarity, claiming empowerment, providing alternative

epistemologies, affirming pride, and teaching history. The chapter
ends by considering the work of the activist artist Paul Robeson.

What research for radical adult education looks like is explored
in Chapter Nine. We look at the ways participatory action research
was conducted by Ella Baker, Nelson Peery, Paulo Freire, and in the
labor movement. From our exploration we derive epistemological
and methodological principles for participatory research, and we
then propose key questions that should guide radical participatory
research. Chapter Ten is the last full-length chapter, and it considers
how diversity can sometimes be used to blunt radical progress even
as it appears to be revolutionary. We establish three projects for radical diversity—ideological detoxification, confronting difference, and
dismantling privilege—and consider in some detail W.E.B. DuBois'
work censored by the American Association for Adult Education in
the 1930s. The book concludes with an Epilogue that looks to the
future for adult education in creating a just world.

OUR AUDIENCE

Our audience is all those who are interested in understanding
better how people learn to challenge mainstream ideology and
how they then learn to build democratic, participatory, and collective social and economic forms. In more specific terms, we
think the book will be useful to graduate students new to the field
of adult education who are seeking to understand its historical
purpose. We think educators with an activist agenda—particularly
those in social movements, the media, community organizations,
and workplace learning programs will find something of interest
in here. We can see this book being used by staff, volunteers, and
activists in churches, in health care organizations, in labor unions,
in economic and housing cooperatives, in tenants' associations,
and in community development—in fact in any situation in which
people are learning to assert their rights against corporate capitalism, unresponsive bureaucracy, and mainstream media. Educators
who identify themselves as critical pedagogues will find this helpful
as will political and civic educators trying to encourage grassroots
conversation about what education or truly democratic citizenship
looks like. Environmental educators, queer activists, and cultural
and community arts workers should also find it instructive.

Acknowledgments

Stephen Brookfield offers his greatest acknowledgment to John Holst for collaborating with him on this book. Over numerous fish-and-chip lunches at Brits Pub in Minneapolis, John provided a constant stream of ideas and criticism that Stephen benefitted from enormously. John tightened up Stephen's thinking and introduced him to whole areas of practice and theory he had little or no awareness of. Stephen also thanks his bandmates in The 99ers—Molly Holley and Colin Selhurst—for understanding when rehearsals needed to be cut short and gigs refused because of deadlines imposed by the manuscript's completion. Finally, Stephen thanks Kim Miller for always being ready to remind him that the adulation of the crowd (or at least the scattered groups he is sometimes invited to address) means nothing next to the microreality of his daily actions and choices.

John Holst would like to first and foremost acknowledge his appreciation for Stephen's generous willingness to collaborate with him on this project. Stephen took the decisive steps in concretizing our long discussed plans for collaboration by coming up with the specific plan and outline of this book. Moreover, Stephen's expectations of clarity in the writing and in the presentation of ideas have been of enduring benefit. In terms of his own contributions, John would also like to acknowledge the significant debt he owes to Stephen and to all the exemplary educators referenced in these pages.

We thank the *Adult Education Quarterly* and the *International Journal of Lifelong Education* for allowing us to publish elements of this text that appeared in the form of articles in their pages.

We both know that thanks to editors often appear *pro forma*, but any readers who know our editor, David Brightman, will understand just how important his supportive critique was to this book. David was unfailingly helpful, full of useful ideas for the book's organization, and ready to ask provocative questions that helped us make the book what it is. In contrast to most acknowledgments that add a disclaimer to the effect that the people named had no responsibility for how the book finally appeared in print, we want to affirm that this is David's book as well as our own.

Stephen D. Brookfield and John D. Holst
Minneapolis-St. Paul, Minnesota

ABOUT THE AUTHORS

Stephen D. Brookfield The father of Molly and Colin, and the husband of Kim, Stephen D. Brookfield is currently Distinguished University Professor at the University of St. Thomas in Minneapolis-St. Paul, Minnesota, where he recently won the university's Diversity Leadership Teaching and Research Award and also the John Ireland Presidential Award for Outstanding Achievement as a Teacher/Scholar. He received his B.A. degree (1970) from Coventry University in modern studies, his M.A. degree (1974) from the University of Reading in sociology, and his Ph.D. degree (1980) from the University of Leicester in adult education. He also holds a postgraduate diploma (1971) from the University of London, Chelsea College, in modern social and cultural studies and a postgraduate diploma (1977) from the University of Nottingham in adult education. In 1991 he was awarded an honorary doctor of letters degree from the University System of New Hampshire for his contributions to understanding adult learning. In 2003 he was awarded an honorary doctorate of letters from Concordia University for his contributions to adult education.

Stephen began his teaching career in 1970 and has held appointments at colleges of further, technical, adult, and higher education in the United Kingdom, and at universities in Canada (University of British Columbia) and the United States (Columbia University, Teachers College and the University of St. Thomas). In 1989 he was visiting fellow at the Institute for Technical and Adult Teacher Education in what is now the University of Technology, Sydney, Australia. In 2002 he was visiting professor at Harvard University Graduate School of Education. In 2003–2004 he was the Helen Le Baron Hilton Chair at Iowa State University. He has run numerous workshops on teaching, adult learning, and critical thinking around the world and delivered many keynote addresses at regional, national, and international education conferences. In 2001 he received the Leadership Award from the Association for Continuing Higher Education (ACHE) for "extraordinary contributions to the general field of continuing education on a national and international level." In 2008 he was awarded the Morris T. Keeton Award of the Council for Adult and Experiential Learning for "significant contributions to the field of adult and experiential learning." In 2009 he was inducted into the International Adult Education Hall of Fame in a ceremony in Philadelphia.

Stephen is a four-time winner of the Cyril O. Houle World Award for Literature in Adult Education: in 1986 for his book *Understanding and Facilitating Adult Learning: A Comprehensive Analysis of Principles and Effective Practices* (1986), in 1989 for *Developing Critical Thinkers: Challenging Adults to Explore Alternative Ways of Thinking and Acting* (1987), in 1996 for *Becoming a Critically Reflective Teacher* (1995), and in 2005 for *The Power of Critical Theory: Liberating Adult Learning and Teaching* (2004). *Understanding and Facilitating Adult Learning* also won the 1986 Imogene E. Okes Award for Outstanding Research in Adult Education. These awards were all presented by the American Association for Adult and Continuing Education. The first edition of *Discussion as a Way of Teaching: Tools and Techniques for Democratic Classrooms* (2nd edition, 2005), which he coauthored with Stephen Preskill, was a 1999 Critics Choice of the Educational Studies Association. His other books are *Adult Learners, Adult Education and the Community* (1984); *Self-Directed Learning: From Theory to Practice* (1985); *Learning Democracy: Eduard Lindeman on Adult Education and Social Change* (1987); *Training Educators of Adults: The Theory and Practice of Graduate Adult Education* (1988); *The Skillful Teacher: On Technique, Trust, and Responsiveness in the Classroom* (2nd. edition, 2006); *Teaching Reflectively in Theological Contexts: Promises and Contradictions* (coedited with Mary Hess, 2008); *Learning as a Way of Leading: Lessons from the Struggle for Social Justice* (coauthored with Stephen Preskill, 2008); and *Handbook of Race and Adult Education* (coedited with Vanessa Sheared, Juanita Johnson-Bailey, Scipio A.J. Colin III, and Elizabeth Peterson, 2010).

John D. Holst John D. Holst is currently an associate professor in the Department of Leadership, Policy and Administration at the

University of St. Thomas, Minneapolis-St. Paul, Minnesota, where he teaches graduate courses in critical pedagogy, social theory, and educational research. He received his B.S. degree (1988) in U.S. history from the University of Wisconsin-Madison with an emphasis on labor and women's history, his M.S. degree (1994) in adult continuing education from Northern Illinois University, with an emphasis on urban adult education, and his Ed.D. degree (2000) from Northern Illinois University.

John Holst entered the informal field of adult education in 1984 as a social movement activist by working in the student, labor, anti-Apartheid, and Central American solidarity movements. He entered the formal field of adult education in 1988 as an instructor of English as a Second Language in community- and work-based adult education in Chicago. While teaching in factory lunchrooms, hotels, church basements, and government and nongovernmental organizations, John became actively involved in the labor union of adult educators at the City Colleges of Chicago.

He is the author of the book *Social Movements, Civil Society, and Radical Adult Education* (2002). In addition, he is the author of several book chapters and articles which have appeared in the *Adult Education Quarterly*, the *International Journal of Lifelong Learning, Educational Philosophy and Theory,* and the *Harvard Educational Review.* His work has been translated into Spanish, German, and Italian. He is a Houle Scholar Fellow (2001–2003) and, as such, he is currently working on the forthcoming text *Globalization and the Future of Radical Adult Education.*

RADICALIZING LEARNING

CHAPTER ONE

CONCEPTUALIZING ADULT LEARNING AND EDUCATION

We live in interesting times. The election of the nation's first biracial president, the apparent collapse of capitalism (apparent, not actual, owing to the massive government bailout of financial institutions that "are so big they can't be allowed to fail"), immersion in wars in Iraq and Afghanistan, and regular accusations from cable news commentators that we are on the verge of socialism in the U.S.—a claim viewed with much bemusement by European socialists. In a sense, these times begat this book. It has its genesis in the reactions of the two of us to the 2003 invasion of Iraq by the U.S. and Britain. One of us was born in the United States, the other born in England, and, as CNN beamed footage of the troops entering Baghdad, we asked ourselves how it had come to pass that these two countries had acted in direct defiance of the world and, in the case of Britain, in defiance of the clear majority of its citizens. As adult educators, both of us were concerned to explore the kinds of learning people undertook in order to organize mass protests against the war and the way they learned to fight back against the Bush and Blair administrations' ideological push.

As it happened, the Australian Mike Newman beat us to the punch publishing his magnificent *Teaching Defiance* (2006). But 2003 was the spur for the two of us to do a great deal of thinking about the way adult education seems to have lost its moorings and become uncoupled from its traditional, mainstream view of itself as a movement to create and build democracy. It also prompted us to think a lot about adult education's traditional concern to develop critical thinkers and the responsibility this necessarily entails of countering any process of brainwashing or ideological manipulation. This book is our attempt to remind ourselves, and the field, of how adult learning and the practice of adult education have traditionally been concerned with the health of participatory democracy. Indeed, for many adult educators across the world the most important project for the field, and the most significant contribution of adult learning, has been learning how to extend participatory democracy into the economic sphere, that is, with the creation of democratic and cooperative socialism.

These days, to talk of adult learning and education in the same breath as democracy or socialism can seem either hopelessly out of date (after all, many would say adult education should be focused on "skilling" or "retooling" America's workforce to compete in the global economy) or completely utopian (especially when viewed in the light of where federal and state funds overwhelmingly go for adult education—that is, to workforce training or basic skills). That this has not always been the case can be seen by studying what in previous decades were the writings of "mainstream" adult educators such as Lyman Bryson. Bryson, a well-published professor at Teachers College, Columbia University, was very active in the chief professional organization of his day, the American Association for Adult Education (AAAE).

In 1936 Lyman Bryson published his landmark text simply titled *Adult Education* in which he urged teachers of adults to inculcate principles of rational skepticism in adult learners that would help them "to stand firmly against the winds of doctrine" (p. 64). The mark of a good teacher for Bryson was the degree to which she helped adult students "to acquire a more alert attitude toward their already accepted and verbalized beliefs, and toward all new things offered them" (p. 65). The ability to do this was "the hallmark of a fit teacher for grown men and women" (p. 65). In other words, adult education was about teaching people to resist dominant ideology—such as that capitalism was a natural way of ordering the economic affairs of society and ultimately worked to the benefit of all, that the massive amount of material wealth possessed by the United States permitted it to act as an imperial invader, and that we live in a society distinguished by vigorous freedom of the press. In pursuing these aims, however, Bryson warned that teachers of adults would earn the dislike, criticism, and ridicule of society and its leaders. Bryson was as mainstream as it is possible to get in the field in the 1930s, a fact illustrated by his pressuring Alain Locke to prohibit the publication of a manuscript by W.E.B. DuBois in the African Negro Folk Associates Series of the American Association for Adult Education (a manuscript we view as crucial to the conceptualization of the field and that we examine in this book) because of its Marxism and Pan-Africanism (see Guy, 1993; Guy and Brookfield, 2009). Yet 70 years after Bryson wrote *Adult Education*, he now sounds daringly radical. That is a damning indictment of how conservative and fearful the field has become.

THE MEANING OF RADICAL

Most discussions of the term *radical* begin by saying it means getting down to the roots of something to discover its essence. In this sense, radical adult education would mean returning to the roots of adult education to rediscovering its essential purpose and mission. But what comprises the roots of the field depends very much on whose history is being consulted. For every historical example of mechanics institutes or worker cooperatives, one could cite counterexamples of adult education for cultural genocide or for the education of an officer class of an occupying army. The question is whose roots we are getting back to and whose purposes and practices we seek to rediscover. So, clearly, we need establish at the start of this book what we mean by radical.

Lens begins his book *Radicalism in America* (1969) declaring that "the role of the radical throughout the ages has been as an antidote to privilege" (p. 1) and that "where the byword for the reactionary is self-interest, for the radical it is equality—either full equality in which all things are held in common, or, short of that, equality of opportunity. To level the material differences between men *(sic)*, to replace hate with love, division with unity, war with peace—these have been the goals of the radical" (p. 1). Like Lens, we link radicalism to the abolition of privilege and creation of full material equality and, like him, we believe this entails two intertwined ideas: democracy and socialism. In his analysis Lens states "until early in the nineteenth century the radical fought in the main for a subversive concept called democracy; subsequently it was a subversive concept called socialism" (pp. 2–3). For us the radical purpose and practice of adult education is concerned with organizing education for and encouraging learning about the creation of democracy in political, cultural, and economic spheres. Political and cultural democracy entails learning how to recognize and abolish privilege around race, gender, status, and identity; economic democracy entails learning how to abolish material inequality and privilege around class. Both, in turn, entail the collective determination of how societal resources are to be used for the common good—in shorthand terms, socialism.

In one sense, this commitment to participatory political democracy and collective economic democracy (socialism) can't really be regarded as radical if by that term we mean returning to the roots of the field in the U.S. Quite simply, the U.S. has never had the creation of economic democracy—whether that be called participatory economics or *parecon* (Albert, 2003), cooperative economics or democratic socialism—as the chief project of adult education. Political democracy has been valorized and relatively uncontested, but not economic democracy. To argue for that has been seen as too radical in a country in which, apart from "blips" such as the Great Depression of the 1930s, capitalism has been unquestioningly celebrated as the most liberating and free of all economic forms. There have always been those in the field who saw adult education as education for economic democracy, or socialism, of course, but we would argue that they have never represented the field's mainstream.

In contrast, Stephen Brookfield grew up in England where the legacy of Mansbridge, Tawney, and Williams *was* the predominant tradition. Even though many see the hugely influential Workers' Education Association (WEA) as liberal rather than progressive, for him the connection of adult education to democratic socialism was quite clear and not very daring or remarkable. Socialism and patriotism were never seen as opposed, and the idea that citizens have basic survival needs met was viewed as blindingly obvious. Even Tony Blair, as he campaigned for his first term of office as British prime minister, felt compelled to speak about the kind of socialism he wanted (market-driven socialism that rewarded entrepreneurship).

ADULT EDUCATION AND DEMOCRATIC SOCIALISM

Of course our thinking of adult education as a force for political detoxification, or as an element in any significant oppositional movement, represents our own agenda as adult educators. Many in the field would profoundly disagree with this agenda and advance completely different views concerning the proper purposes for adult education. They might claim that adult educators should be neutral and should stay out of or be above politics. They might argue that the most useful purpose of adult education is to equip adult workers with the skills they need to flourish in the global economy of the 21st century. For some of the most influential, adult education's location is within the workplace, particularly corporate training, rather than in oppositional, grassroots movements.

Adult education is, like all sectors of organized education, a contested sphere. Different actors within this sphere have contrasting and sometimes contradictory agendas. However, no matter what the setting—an auto-repair class, a basic skills literacy program, a community meeting held to decide how to oppose the building of a Wal-Mart, an executive development seminar, an extension agent teaching crop rotation techniques, an antiracist agit-prop theater piece, a union organizer explaining procedures to unionize—the adult education tradition insists that these things happen democratically. The core purpose of adult education for the two of us is to build participatory democracy, and to that degree we are well in the historical mainstream. The break from that mainstream comes from our contention that democracy can only be realized if it is economic as well as political, which is where socialism comes in.

For us socialism and democracy are inseparable, and this is why to talk about adult education for democracy is, in our view, to talk about adult education for socialism. We are not alone in this, of course. For example, Myles Horton recognized the inseparability of socialism and democracy when he constantly stressed that political democracy is meaningless without its economic counterpart. But it is hard to focus on exactly what comprises a socialist perspective. As reviewers of socialism in the U.S. (for example Howe, 1986) point out, it is more accurate to talk of "socialisms" in the plural, given the different strands of theorizing and the different models of practice proposed that bear that descriptor. For example, Michael Newman's (2005) (not the Australian adult educator) recent short introduction to the idea examines how it is interpreted in Cuban communism, Swedish social democracy, materialist feminism, and ecological socialism, among other movements. These multiple interpretations sometimes mean that a depressingly predictable feature of debate among left-leaning movements is acrimony regarding which particular group, organization, or tendency is the true guardian and correct interpreter of the flame. Monty Python's Flying Circus hilariously parodied this in their comedy *Life of Brian.*

For us democratic socialism is a political and economic arrangement designed to answer one fundamental question: How best can we arrange society to foster compassion and enhance creativity? In our opinion such a society would be one in which, as much as it was humanly possible, fundamental survival needs (food, shelter, water, medical care) were met so that people's energies could be directed away from basic survival toward the realization of creativity in the widest possible forms. This would require that the available physical and human resources be commonly owned and controlled—stewarded, used, and distributed for the good of all. A crucial feature is that this stewardship is "subjected to democratic control from below by the people and their communities" (Harrington, 1992, p. 9).

The point to common ownership, control, and stewardship would be to create the optimal conditions for different people to pursue their individual passions and widely varying enthusiasms with as much creativity as they could exercise. Work—productive labor—would be conceived primarily as an opportunity for people to exercise their creative powers. The purpose of work would be to ensure that commonly agreed upon basic needs were met and then to help people to realize their potential. In such a society no one would claim for themselves a right or privilege that was not available to all, and neither would it be possible to inherit power and privilege through the accident of one's birth. It would therefore be impossible for a small minority to amass a disproportionate amount of wealth.

To bring about this kind of society—one that best fosters creativity and compassion—four conditions have to be in place. First, *basic survival needs* must be met. This means that construction, agriculture, public utilities, and health care will need to be commonly owned and controlled so that they can be coordinated to produce the goods and services sufficient to meet fundamental survival needs. Socialism is a social, political, and economic arrangement in which the resources available to all are shared equally, rather than being the property of sectional interests. Resources here include all the natural, physical, industrial, and cultural resources, and human properties, talents, and abilities available within a group. For us the exploitation and enjoyment of these resources is a matter for collective democratic deliberation, for a conversation that focuses on how these can best be stewarded for the common good. So socialism establishes some kind of common control over the economic system, so that whatever goods and services are produced are somehow controlled by the whole community or society. This requires some sort of coordinating agency or system of decision making—partly governmental, partly decentralized—to ensure this happens efficiently. Here is the link to participatory democracy through workers' councils, town meetings, cyberspace communication, and so on.

Second, if people are to decide how best to meet their material needs, what kinds of work will produce what kinds of goods and services, or how to apportion the performance of necessary and unpleasant tasks so that one group or person is not unreasonably burdened with these, decision making mechanisms will need to be in place that everybody perceives as fair. *Fairness* is central to the socialist ideal. This does not mean, by the way, that the same mechanisms will be employed every time we make a decision. The principle underlying fairness in decision making is that those who are most directly affected by a decision should play the major part in making that decision. In these ways socialism is both the ultimate form of participatory democracy—such a long-lionized ideal within adult education—and a movement from an individualist, competitive ethic to a collective ethic that prevents any individual or group from claiming a disproportionate influence in social, economic, cultural, and political spheres of life. It is hard to imagine a better context for the use of the much-invoked concepts of "transformative learning" and "transformative practice" in adult education than in exploring how people learn to manage the transformation of an

individualistic culture into the cooperative and collective ethic of
socialism.

Fairness also does not mean that wages are equalized, that all
small businesses are eliminated, or that creative entrepreneurship
is discouraged. Wages will differ according to the kind of labor
involved, its difficulty, the effort it requires, and its social necessity.
So, workers whose labor guarantees basic needs—builders, sewage
workers, health care providers, garbage collectors, farmers, and so
on—will earn more than those who work to produce goods that
make life pleasant, even if they are unnecessary to basic survival.
Workers willing to undertake tasks that are necessary but unpleasant, and thus avoided by those with the means to do so, would
receive higher remuneration. Small businesses that are owned and
run cooperatively by individuals, and not large corporations run
for the benefit of stockholders, would be actively encouraged.

Once survival needs are met, a third condition comes into
play, *creativity*, the chief criterion we employ to decide how our
time is best spent, how to organize education, and how work is to
be remunerated. The more diverse are our work and educational
practices, the more that social arrangements reflect the widest
possible range of preferences, and the more that the people's
different passions and individual interests are encouraged, then
the healthier a society will be. The point of common control of
resources to meet basic survival needs is to free people to develop
themselves to the fullest in whatever way they see fit, with the
proviso that this must not diminish the development of others. So,
unlike the stereotypical notion of socialism as bland conformity, a
properly socialist system celebrates difference.

And, finally, a democratic socialist society is one in which difference, creativity, and diversity are matched by *inclusion*. Such a
society recognizes that people differ firstly in talents, skills, interests, commitments, and physical capability. It further recognizes
the importance of identity politics, that people differ by racial
group membership, gender, ethnic affiliation, sexual orientation,
and cultural tradition. But these differences are not matched by
exclusion. A socialist democracy has no place for the "isms" and pho-
bias that diminish us all—racism, classism, ableism, and homophobia.
It honors difference and protects the rights of minorities from the
potential tyranny of the majority. The minorities that are constrained

are those that seek to accumulate a disproportionate amount of resources for their own exclusive use.

Each of these conditions of democratic socialism suggests any number of practices, and these practices in turn suggest various learning tasks. So the radical practice of adult learning comprises quite simply the learning required to enact these conditions of democratic socialism. Some of this learning will be self-directed, some collective; some will be formally structured, some more serendipitously accomplished; and some will be organized and run by credentialed teachers, some directed by peers, colleagues, and neighbors. In the next sections we explore in a more detailed way how the four conditions of socialism—meeting survival needs, fairness, creativity, and inclusion—each mandate a wide range of learning tasks.

MEETING SURVIVAL NEEDS

Survival needs are notoriously contextual. What one group or person in one place at one time considers necessary for survival differs enormously from how these needs are defined by other groups and individuals in other places and at other times. Given that the resources available to us are not infinite, there will have to be some kind of mechanism in place to judge (a) what comprises basic human needs, and (b) how these needs, once decided, can best be met given the resources available. This immediately suggests a number of learning tasks. People will have to learn about the range of judgments that exist in the society regarding how survival needs are defined, they will have to learn something about the resources available to all to address these needs, and they will have to learn to conceive and enact decision making mechanisms to meet those needs that are perceived as fair. At a very basic level, they will need to learn procedures to decide what needs should be met that allow everyone to feel their viewpoint has been represented in any decision made. We shall have more to say on this question of fairness in a few paragraphs.

For basic survival needs to be met there must be a way for societal resources to be stewarded and deployed in the interests of the majority. This aspect of democratic socialism—exerting common control over the stewardship and deployment of society's resources—is probably the feature of socialism most commonly expressed in different versions of the idea. The principle of common ownership of the means of production and distribution; the idea that governments should nationalize all major industries and public utilities (health care, transportation, power supplies, telecommunications, education, and so on); the vision of a society based on locally controlled worker cooperatives or agrarian collectives; and the notion of a planned economy with a central agency directing what goods need to be produced and how these should be allocated across the community—all these are variations of the idea of common stewardship of resources for the benefit of all.

Effective majority stewardship mandates many learning tasks. First, we have to learn about different forms of needs assessment, so that decisions about production and deployment can be made that meet people's real needs. Then we need to learn how to create mechanisms of communication—town meetings, factory councils, electronic voting—that allow full and free flow of information throughout society. This is a prerequisite for preventing ossification. Because people's needs and interests constantly change, we must learn how to accommodate and respond to these changes of direction. Learning how to manage resources, how to set up systems of production, and how to match job requirements to the different interests and abilities of individuals are all required for the value of fairness to be realized.

Meeting survival needs also requires that people learn how to organize and administer mechanisms to produce and distribute the goods and services that are necessary to meet these needs. This is a massive educational project. It necessitates studying how communities and societies across history have tried to do this. It means studying how well the fledgling systems people establish to produce goods and services actually perform their task. On the basis of that study, people have to learn how to improve these systems of production and distribution. That, in turn, obviously requires preservice and in-service training to prepare people to run and work within these systems. On a more detailed level, it means a continuous program of research must be put in place that will allow these needs to be met more fully. A guiding principle of this research will be that discovering new resources and new ways to use them will be done with the intention of addressing the widest possible range of needs.

The success of any attempt to discover people's basic survival needs, and then to organize production and distribution systems to meet these, will depend not so much on the internal logic of these systems but on whether or not they are perceived as fair. Any system that is perceived as disproportionately benefiting one group or individual will be actively sabotaged, or at best passively endured, by any groups that feel ignored. If a decision is to be perceived as fair, it will need to be trusted as having been reached only after the widest possible consultation and representation, and on the condition that in making that decision the fullest possible information has been taken into account. This is the essence of Habermas' (1996) discourse theory of democracy, and it is why we regard socialism and democracy as intertwined.

As mentioned earlier, we don't regard democracy as only one particular social arrangement; indeed, we believe democracy takes different forms in different situations and to accomplish different ends. The democratic value is one that holds that those affected by decisions are proportionally responsible for making those decisions. The more a practice or policy affects us, the greater should be our say in how that decision plays out. This is why a simple majority vote can be fundamentally unfair. After all, the votes of people far removed from my own problem or situation can always outvote me, even when the decision has no impact on their lives but a major one on mine. This means that decentralized forms of decision making are central to democratic socialism, which, in turn, means people need to be familiar with different kinds of decision-making mechanisms. So a central adult learning task becomes learning different decision-making mechanisms and learning how to judge which kinds of decision making are best suited to particular situations. From very local building, block, and neighborhood decisions to regional matters such as transportation or the location of health care facilities, to society-wide issues regarding educational provision or calculating what amounts of which products are necessary to meet people's basic needs—all these decisions require that people be educated to have full information about the issues they have to decide on and that they learn how to participate fully in decision making.

As already stated, fairness for us means ensuring that no individual or group has greater power or influence over others in a way that is arbitrary. In line with our argument above, we acknowledge that in some situations it is only right that some have more influence over certain situations that others. Knowing about the connection between secondhand smoke inhalation and lung cancer, heart disease and emphysema, I should have a disproportionate amount of influence in requiring you not to smoke in my presence. What we want to avoid is the situation where an arbitrary indicator such as our skin color, social class membership, place of birth, gender, and so on unalterably determines what material benefits we will enjoy in life and gives us the chance to order others around.

Fairness also means that the resources of the planet—both natural and humanly created—be shared equally among its inhabitants. The present situation where certain countries and a small minority of individuals within those countries disproportionately enjoy massive amounts of wealth, and also direct how the majority of resources are to be deployed, is patently unfair. So for fairness to be an organizing value for society, we must institute the collective stewardship of resources already discussed.

DIFFERENCE AND CREATIVITY

From fairness comes our insistence on the recognition of difference. One of the most common and fundamental misunderstandings of fairness is that it imposes uniformity, disallowing individual identities and agendas. The opposite is the truth. Basic fairness recognizes that people are different; they have different talents, different personalities, different interests, and different enthusiasms. They also belong to different groups, and those groups constitute a major part of their identity. Some self-identify by racial group membership, others by sexual preference. Still more self-identify by ethnicity, by culture, by tribe, by commitment to a spiritual creed, or by their being raised in a distinctive town, region, or terrain. A principle of fairness is that one group cannot unduly influence another group to be remade in the first group's image. Basic fairness insists that we recognize that people are different, both as individuals and as distinctive groups. And, recognizing this difference, fairness requires that ways be found to allow people to claim their identity in ways that are very distinct.

This commitment to recognizing difference in the interests of fairness mandates any number of learning tasks. Indeed, the contemporary emphasis on learning how to recognize and celebrate diversity of all kinds, how to communicate across racial and cultural difference, and on developing forms of antiracist practice can easily be understood as socialist forms of learning necessary to realize the principle of fairness. Fairness requires a good faith commitment of people of very different racial group memberships, ethnic affiliation, and cultural identity to learn to appreciate the different ways members of each group view the world and consider what counts as appropriate action. Fairness also entails learning to live with profound difference, so that the different needs and perceptions of groups can coexist in creative tension. Part of this is learning to be alert to the dangers of the tyranny of the majority. Finally, fairness means, at times, standing up to the agenda and power of a particular group that is attempting to undermine the development of a sense of collective identity or to promote hatred and bigotry. Fairness does not extend to groups who try to exercise their difference and creativity by diminishing the rights of others.

It is important to emphasize that acknowledging difference is not the same as a bland relativism that acknowledges every group's agenda and every person's viewpoint as being equally deserving of acknowledgment and as containing merit on its own terms. That kind of mushy refusal to take a stand plays into the interests of those in power, as Baptiste (2000) so cogently points out. In a society in which democratic socialism has been pilloried as conformist thought control that kills creativity, and in which even discussing a socialist alternative is portrayed as unpatriotic and un-American, anyone who attempts to get people to consider what a socialist economy and democracy looks like will have to fight against some very powerful interests. A skillful ideological manipulation has ensured that socialism is believed to be unworthy of serious attention and believed to be unworkable in the U.S. Allowing that view to go unchallenged—as representing the truth simply because it is expressed by a majority—means a socialist viewpoint will never stand a chance. Therefore, in the interests of fairness, it will be necessary to force people to pay attention to a socialist agenda. This is what Marcuse (1965) described as liberating tolerance.

We put difference and creativity together because for us the two are inseparable. The reason difference is so celebrated is because of its connection to creativity. The greater the difference we confront, the greater are the possibilities for creativity. Difference makes departures from the norm possible. It helps us envision alternative futures and confronts us with new forms of thinking and living. Difference helps us realize that what we thought was an unchangeable norm is always open to reinvention and re creation in new ways. Difference encourages new approaches to artistic creation, but it also leads to unique syntheses being made and new connections being drawn. The point of meeting survival needs in a fair way is to create the conditions under which we can live the most unconstrained, free lives possible. Freed from the need to meet basic survival needs, people are able to develop their creative natures in whichever way they see fit.

INCLUSION

At the same time as socialism recognizes difference and celebrates people's infinite creative possibilities, it also privileges inclusion. Indeed, the whole premise of socialist thought is based on the notion that those who labor should control the forms and fruits of that labor, whether it is waged or unwaged. Earlier socialist analyses such as those of the Frankfurt School (Brookfield, 2004) focused on the exclusion of the working-class and women from decision-making processes and from the possibility of creative endeavor at work. Capitalism's systematic exploitation was analyzed as producing alienated labor in which the products of people's work were owned and controlled by stockholders and the bourgeoisie. This analysis argued that labor was experienced as degrading and dehumanizing. As societies have become more racially and culturally diverse, as sexual liberation has broken down the silence over sexual identity, and as medical taboos regarding mental illness and physical conditions have receded (though hardly disappeared), contemporary theorizing has broadened its analysis to include other forms of exclusion. Now, it would be highly unusual to read any exploration of socialism that did not include any condemnation of racism, sexism, homophobia, or ableism.

The socialist argument for inclusion is moral, aesthetic, and utilitarian. Morally, it rests on the democratic principle that those who produce the goods and services that make life better for all should have the chief say in how those goods and services are used and distributed. Morally, too, it places the decisions about what goods and services are to be produced in the hands of labor. Aesthetically, it rests on the notion (also expressed in U.S. pragmatism) that the purpose of life is the experimental pursuit of beautiful consequences. In political terms, this means the pursuit of the fairest possible system for producing and enjoying social goods and services. Additionally, aesthetics mandates the widest possible scope of expressive forms; in social terms, this means creating a system that encompasses the widest possible scope for creative expression. Since creativity is enhanced by contact with multiple traditions, cultural forms, and conceptions of the good life, socialism requires that people be exposed to the widest possible range of influences.

Finally, socialism's justification for inclusion is that exclusion creates differences in power and status that just simply do not work. As one class, race, or gender claims a disproportionate amount of control and enjoys a disproportionate amount of resources, their position of privilege has to be maintained by a complex intersection of ideological manipulation and coercive force (the military, police, penal system, and so on). This is expensive to create and maintain and always destined eventually to fail. It may not fail to the extent of the system collapsing, but it will never ensure smooth, seamless cooperation. Sooner or later, in even the most rigid societies and communities, rebellion, creativity, and dissatisfaction combine to create challenges to and sabotage of the system. The more genuinely socialist the economy, the less a group will feel the resentment that costs so much time and energy for the dominant group to suppress. The more people feel included as partners in decision making and the more they enjoy full and equal access to available resources and services, the more productive and creative they will be. The existence of profit-sharing schemes and worker cooperatives in the most advanced capitalist economies, often in industries where capitalism has failed, recognizes this reality.

For readers who are by now saying "enough of the polemics, get on with it," we offer the next section. In it we are going to do our best to define, as precisely as we can, what we mean by the radical practice of adult learning.

WHAT MAKES ADULT LEARNING RADICAL?

We use *learning* as both a noun and verb. As a noun it refers to an identifiable change that has occurred in the learner, as a verb to the process that contributes to that change. Let's take the noun first. From our perspective, radical adult learning is an observable shift in knowledge and skill regarding the creation and maintenance of democratic socialism. From our perspective a single instance of such learning can cross the three learning domains famously identified by Habermas (1979) that have been so influential in adult education—technical, communicative, and emancipatory. For example, learning how to stand up to racist speech and racist acts—including one's own—involves technical aspects (becoming alert to how certain racist metaphors are used uncritically and instinctively in everyday speech), communicative dimensions (learning how to bring the reality of racism to another's consciousness so that it is considered seriously and not rejected dismissively), emancipatory processes (integrating an alertness to racism into one's daily reasoning and practice), and also emotional intelligence (learning to acknowledge yet not be derailed by the frustration, self-doubt, self-disgust, and embarrassment anti-racist work involves, especially for Whites).

But these intrapersonal and interpersonal learning activities are only the beginning. The democratic tradition in the field also requires such individual acts to be tied to political action—to creating structures, systems, parties, and institutions that equalize access to common resources to democratize access to education and health, and to organize around common interests. Learning to recognize and oppose racism—to take the example already mentioned—involves people organizing to enact legislation, create educational programs, establish alternate media networks, set up housing and other cooperatives, and launch neighborhood businesses. This project is pursued on different terrains and using different strategies and tactics. One person might be concerned to develop an Africentrically grounded adult school in which teaching and learning are in harmony with African-centered values, practices, and conceptual referents. Another might be concerned to set up a "media-watch" to monitor the presence of racist stereotypes in local news reporting. Still another might organize rallies to lobby for the civil rights of undocumented immigrants, for the establishment of neighborhood health centers staffed by native speakers of the language predominantly spoken by community members, or for stronger legal sanctions for clearly racist behavior. Such learning is not just concerned with changing individuals' perceptions and promoting individual changes of attitude. It is just as much focused on political projects all of which entail adult educational dimensions—people teaching people skills, knowledge, and understanding in collective settings—and all of which are tied together by an interest in extending participatory democracy.

So our understanding of adult learning is not that it is any effort by people over 21 to increase knowledge, enhance understanding, develop insight, or develop skill. For us, adult learning is inextricably tied to creating and extending political and economic democracy—to equalizing control of and access to wealth, education, health care, and creative work, and to promoting collective and cooperative forms of decision making and labor. This is perhaps seen most clearly in community movements. Every act of adult learning in such a movement will entail alternating and intersecting dimensions. None of these activities is wholly technical, communicative, emancipatory, or emotional in terms of the learning that ensues; instead, each involves a complex web of actions, choices, and reasoning, with different forms and processes highlighted more strongly than others at different times.

To create democracy, adults also need to learn about a range of alternative social and economic arrangements: socialist economics, participatory budgeting, worker cooperatives, collective decision making, negotiation strategies, conflict management, and so on. They also need to learn a structural world view, that is, one that sees supposedly individual crises and dilemmas as produced by the intersection of larger structural and systemic forces—particularly the intersection of monopoly capitalism and White supremacy—and one that analyzes the global dimensions that inform the seemingly most mundane local decisions and practices.

Workplace learning is currently one of the most frequently touted projects within adult education. We are also interested in such learning; the workplace is, after all, an important setting in which we exercise creativity and draw aspects of our identity. The stigmatization of unemployment and the shame and self-laceration it produces in those laid off pays eloquent testimony to how meaningful the concept of productive work is for people. But workplace learning does not happen just in waged situations. The unwaged doing motherwork and providing health care for family members, or those doing grassroots organizing or eking out existence while being artistically creative, are also engaged in workplace learning. The workplace, however it is defined, is where many of us develop networks, meet spouses and partners, locate friends, and realize our contribution to society.

From our perspective, then, workplace learning is tied not to enhancing U.S. competitiveness within the global marketplace, but to the creation of more meaningful work—work in which learners feel they are exercising creativity and control, which is regarded as fulfilling as possible and which is undertaken for ends that are seen as inherently important and socially necessary. Establishing the conditions for this kind of meaningful work necessitates a major learning project, that is, learning to recognize and then combat the alienation induced by capitalism. This understanding of adult workplace learning takes us directly to critical social theory's illumination of how the workplace impedes adult learning for creative fulfillment and enhances learning to become efficient consumers of the goods we produce.

For us, Marx's essay on alienated labor (published as one of his *Economic and Philosophical Manuscripts*, 1961) is a classic text of adult education. We see it as classic because it illuminates two prominent and disturbing learning tasks of adulthood: first, learning how to accept as normal a life spent working in profoundly alienating conditions, and second, learning how to rationalize away one's disquiet at this. As such, it should be required reading in adult education foundations and introductory or survey classes concerned with examining learning at the workplace.

In "Alienated Labor" Marx describes the way in which work in capitalist society has become objectified, that is, experienced by workers as separated from the exercise of creativity. Identity development under capitalism is understood by Marx as a process in which "the individual worker sinks to the level of a commodity, and to a most miserable commodity" (Marx, 1961, p. 93). Under monopoly capitalism, the owners of capital can command labor to produce goods that increase the return on the owner's investment. This produces a hierarchy in which "amassed things, that which is dead, are of superior value to labor, to human powers, to that which is alive" (p. 93). Work under such a system is physically exhausting, mentally debasing, and creatively moribund. Most damningly, it is also spiritually demeaning. Since people work for someone else, their labor becomes converted into someone else's property. The artifacts produced by people's labor have nothing of their own creativity or identity contained within them. In Marx's words "the object produced by labor, its product, now stands opposed to it as an *alien being*, as a *power independent of* the producer. The product of labor is labor which has been embodied in an object and turned into a physical thing; this product is an *objectification* of labor. The performance of work is at the same time its objectification" (Marx, 1961, p. 95, italics in original).

When labor is objectified, something peculiar happens to the worker's emotions. Workers feel more and more disconnected from their work which itself starts to be thought of as something separate from themselves, something outside their sphere of influence. In a famous quote from the "Alienated Labor" manuscript, Marx writes that "the more the worker expends himself in work, the more powerful becomes the world of objects which he creates in face of himself, the poorer he becomes in his inner life, and the less he belongs to himself" (Marx, 1961, p. 96). In devoting themselves to the production of objects, workers somehow find that their own identity has diminished as the power of the objects they produce has increased. Like the demented ventriloquist who sees his doll gain life and start to control him, so "the worker puts his life into the object, and his life then belongs no longer to himself but to the object (which) sets itself against him as an alien and hostile force" (p. 96). The tragedy of contemporary life is not just that workers are exploited and dominated by the owners of production, but also that they are overwhelmed by the world of objects itself which now becomes experienced "as an alien and hostile world" (p. 99).

It is the recognition that learning can become objectified and experienced by adults as irrelevant to their real needs and inner yearnings that has inspired so many adult educators to insist on the voluntary underpinnings of genuine adult education. From Lindeman (1926) to Horton (1990), a stream of adult educational thought has contended that adult education only happens when adults opt voluntarily for a program of learning that they have helped design. This tradition regards mandatory adult education as an oxymoron, a position often associated in adult education with the work of John Ohliger (Grace and Rocco, 2009). It focuses instead on how adult education can help learners develop skills and knowledge that will help them understand and change the communities in which they live. This learning happens through a collaborative analysis of adults' experiences during which roles of teacher and learner interchange among participants. Adult educators who attempt to follow this tradition do their best to replicate the features of participatory democracy, with all participants actively involved in deciding aspects of what and how to learn.

AN EXAMPLE OF THE RADICAL PRACTICE OF ADULT LEARNING: NELSON MANDELA

One well-chronicled example that illustrates the approach to understanding adult learning we are talking about is the learning project Nelson Mandela undertook to raise an army and conduct a program of sabotage against the military installations of the South African apartheid regime. In his autobiography *Long Walk to Freedom* (1994), Mandela describes his life in terms that constantly require learning, in particular, learning to question and change assumptions that had guided his life up to that point. For example, the lack of political progress made in response to the campaign of nonviolence initiated by the African National Congress (ANC) led Mandela to the gradual realization such tactics were increasingly impotent against the government's armed suppression of any dissent exercised by its opponents. In this situation Mandela had to learn to reframe his assumption regarding the tactical effectiveness of nonviolence. This episode of critical reflection led to the formation of the military *Umkhonto we Sizwe* group (Spear of the Nation), whose intent was to attack military installations and transportation links.

Once the campaign of sabotage had been decided upon, Mandela was faced with an enormous adult learning task. From scratch, he had to learn what it took to start an army to carry out this sabotage campaign. He had to learn this, moreover, without ever having been a soldier, fought in a battle, or even fired a gun at an enemy. Since obviously no formal accreditation or training was available to him (unlike the case of the South African military and paramilitary forces), he initiated a massive self-directed learning program to learn "the fundamental principles for starting a revolution . . . what circumstances were appropriate for a guerilla war; how one created, trained, and maintained a guerilla force; how it should be armed; where it gets its supplies—all basic and fundamental questions" (Mandela, 1994, pp. 274–275). The most prominent resource in this self-directed learning project was that of literature. Mandela describes reading the reports issued by Blas Roca (general secretary of the Communist Party in Cuba) about the years the party existed as an illegal organization in Batista Cuba; *Commando* by Deneys Reitz (on the guerilla tactics of Boer generals in the South African Boer War); works on and by Che Guevara, Mao Tse Tung, and Castro; *Red Star Over China* by Edgar Snow on Mao's campaign; *The Revolt* by Menachem Begin on how to lead an Israeli guerilla force in terrain without mountains or forests (very similar to the landscape of South Africa); books on the struggles of Ethiopia against Mussolini; books on the guerilla armies of Kenya, Algeria, and the Cameroons; and histories of South Africa. He also made a survey of the country's chief industrial areas and major transportation systems.

As well as the technical kinds of learning outlined above, Mandela had to engage in communicative learning as he sought to persuade his ANC executive committee colleagues and also its rank and file members of the accuracy of his analysis of the situation and his prescription for its alleviation (the movement to armed struggle). He also had to learn to live with the troubling stirrings of his own conscience regarding the neglect of his families of origin and marriage. Mandela writes of grappling with the question "Is politics merely a pretext for shirking one's responsibilities, an excuse for not being able to provide in the way one wanted?" (p. 181) and facing his constant awareness that neglecting his family is "my greatest regret, and the most painful aspect of the choice I made" (p. 600). What makes this a particularly appropriate example of adult learning for us is that these learning activities were all framed with the purpose of establishing a genuine social and economic democracy in South Africa. In the tradition of adult education that we are claiming as central to the field, Mandela's development of tactical skills, political insight, communicative competence, and technical knowledge—all geared towards the realization of democracy—is a quintessential example of adult learning.

Chapter Two

Understanding Adult Learning

How academics define adult learning and what adults themselves consider learning is as bewilderingly complex and diverse as the human condition itself. Some academics view learning through the lens of developmental theory, seeing adulthood as a time when the complexities of existence force themselves onto our consciousness and require that somehow we engage these (Tennant and Pogson, 2002; Taylor, 2000). Others focus on more specific models of cognition—of the ways adults interpret experience, process information, and reason their way through dilemmas—and how these differ in adults compared to children. Such models of cognition are often grouped together under the concept of post-formal operations (Sinnott, 1998). Still others focus on the specific adult learning projects adults undertake (Tough, 1971) and the self-directed ways they conduct these. In the English-speaking world at least, journals such as *Adult Education Quarterly, Studies in the Education of Adults, Convergence,* the *International Journal of Lifelong Education,* or *Studies in Continuing Education,* document the holy trinity of contemporary adult learning—transformative learning, self-directed learning, and critical reflection. Indeed, the first two of these now have annual conferences devoted solely to them, and the third is probably not far behind.

Adult education has traditionally viewed learning in an all-encompassing, expansive way as the deliberate attempts by adults to develop their skill, extend their knowledge, or cultivate certain dispositions in a particular direction. The logic of this expansive paradigm is a technical one. It tends to disconnect learning from any particular moral, social, or political purpose and to focus instead on its mechanics—on how some methods are favored over others, on how learners and teachers decide which resources are found to be most useful, on how people gauge the effectiveness of their learning, or on how to institute an optimal alternation between self-direction and teacher direction. When adult learning is seen as chiefly a technical affair, anything and everything is grist for the theoretical or research mill.

We start this chapter by trying to narrow down this expansive approach and to focus on the influences that frame our understanding of radical adult learning. As we think about examples of adult learning that we view as radical, we begin with our personal experiences. We both began our careers as adult educators in community development and community action, and John in particular has a history working with the labor movement, immigrants' rights groups, and social movement organizations. Those experiences undoubtedly influence how we think about learning. We also draw on how we have learned to confront problematic situations in our own lives; for example, learning to uncover the White supremacist and patriarchal ideology inscribed in these two White male authors, or (in the case of Stephen Brookfield) learning to challenge the shame of clinical depression in a patriarchal culture in which being masculine is equated with displaying no personal weakness.

These experiences mean that we choose radical examples of learning that are in some way socially committed. Angela Davis learning the mechanics of setting up free breakfast programs in Los Angeles and of developing school curricula for inner city children would be one example of this. Another could be the way the Zapatista Army of National Liberation in Chiapas, Mexico, learned to use the Internet to obtain support for their opposition to NAFTA, or the way the organizers of the London "Day Against Capitalism" learned to use it to mobilize protest. From the Civil Rights Movement we could choose Malcolm X's learning how to set up local chapters of the Nation of Islam and then Organization of Afro-American Unity, or Ella Baker's learning how to develop effective leadership by supporting the growth of others through judicious questioning and gentle encouragement.

Staying with charismatic figures, we could have chosen Paul Robeson's learning how to subvert the Hollywood film studio system and his learning to acknowledge his failure in that regard, Mary Macleod Bethune's learning how to set up the Daytona Educational and Industrial Training School for Negro Girls (now Bethune-Cookman University), or Nelson Mandela's learning how to work with the Communist Party of South Africa to bring down apartheid after initially dismissing any alliance.

Less famously, but just as dramatically, we could choose as examples of radical adult learning any of the numerous published accounts of how working-class learners of all races and colors confounded official assessments of their ability by producing work of great power, or the ways women immigrants to the United States who come from countries ravaged by civil war learn to deal with the trauma they have endured and to negotiate the new cultural pathways—including systemic racism—they are now confronting (Merriam, Courtney, Cervero, and McClure, 2006). One of us (Holst 2002, 2004, 2006) has studied the learning undertaken by members of two revolutionary organizations in the United States: the Freedom Road Socialist Organization and the League of Revolutionaries for a New America. In monthly district meetings, in campaigns to politicize consciousness around immigrants' rights, health care, or a minimum wage, in public forums, and in conversations with individuals in the community during leafleting campaigns, a significant amount of adult learning is occurring around raising consciousness and mobilizing citizenry.

While we don't place ourselves in any particular school of learning theory, we do believe that the way we understand learning is grounded in a particular project: that of learning to recognize and challenge the all-enveloping ethic of capitalism (and its associated ideologies and political-economic arrangements), and concurrently learning to replace this with cooperative, participatory, and collective arrangements such as parecon (Albert, 2003) or democratic socialism. In many ways we understand learning in the way it was summarized by Jane Thompson in a powerful book she authored over 25 years ago, *Learning Liberation* (Thompson, 1983). If, like us, you conceive adult education as part of a movement to realize genuine democracy—economic and cultural as well as political— then learning liberation is the cornerstone of the study of the field.

The liberation we are interested in learning is liberation from an uncritical commitment to the ideology and practice of capitalism; from its associated ideologies such as White supremacy, patriarchy, and homophobia; and from its reliance on social and economic structures that are organized to preserve capital's interests and that stand against the majority of working people.

LEARNING LIBERATION

In the popular consciousness, capitalism is seen as the guarantor of freedom and liberty and as the quintessentially democratic economic system guaranteeing that all have the opportunity to taste the fruits of life. Learning liberation from this ideology and these structures involves an imaginative leap to envision a form of humanistic socialism in which the valuing of human dignity and creativity is viewed as inseparable from the common steward-ship of social resources. It also entails the sorts of technical and interpersonal learning required when families, neighborhoods, workplaces, communities, and societies learn to conduct them-selves to serve the interests of all their members rather than the narrow, sectional interests of a privileged minority. This kind of learning requires a qualitative change in the way people think, not just a change in external political and economic arrangements. It involves learning to define one's interests as the interests of the group as a whole rather than as the pursuit of individual advan-tage, learning to view identity as collectively created and main-tained rather than individually crafted, and learning to view the personal alienation one feels in one's life, work, relationships, and recreational pursuits as inextricably linked to the way one's labor is defined and controlled by the interests of capital via large corpora-tions. Finally, it requires a kind of ethical learning of the maxim that we cannot seek any individual advantage unless that same benefit is sought for all.

One form of this learning we are particularly interested in is the way in which adults learn to recognize how dominant ideol-ogy is inscribed within them and the way they come to understand how this ideology shapes or, more accurately, circumscribes their individual choices, decisions, and actions. A major element in this learning is coming to realize the collective formation of personal identity—understanding that personal identity is developed not in a series of purely self-contained, individual choices, but that it is shaped by collectively generated and maintained roles, assumptions, images, and expectations associated with one's race, class, or gender. Even something as seemingly individualistic as what one buys is, of course, a culturally and economically framed choice reflecting aspirations and needs that are felt as individual but in reality are socially induced. Getting adults to realize this is the focus of the kind of adult consumer education proposed by Sandlin (2005) and others (Ozanne, Adkins and Sandlin, 2005). Learning to counter dominant ideology also involves realizing that what people see as purely individual changes (for example, getting better—or any—employment, getting better—or any—access to health care or decent education, stopping spousal abuse, or escaping slum housing) are only made possible when structures and systems change, and that such change only happens as a result of collective pressure. To paraphrase Frederick Douglass, power never gives up its position of preeminence unless it is forced to, and this usually only happens as a reaction to the power of numbers.

Individual acts, quixotic solo gestures, and going down in a martyr's blaze of glory are challenges to power that are much more easily deflected than an organized and determined mass movement. Ideologically, if the power of numbers is depicted in popular imagination as potentially dangerous and uncontrollable (large numbers of people are portrayed as always transforming into mobs waiting for a spark of unrest to ignite them into spontaneous and destructive violence) or as overly controlling (large numbers of people will soon ossify into structures that restrict individual liberty and freedom), then the impulse to organize collective action is successfully stopped in its tracks. Anyone seeking to organize a grass-roots organization, union, or social movement quickly becomes ideologically defined either as a loose cannon primed to lead people into violent confrontation or as a Stalinist waiting to impose his views on everyone and brooking no deviation. It seems to us that this kind of ideological manipulation is one part of the reason why socialist ideals have become less influential in recent years.

A particularly subtle form of learning we are interested in is how people learn to recognize when they are victims of what Herbert Marcuse (1965) called repressive tolerance. Repressive tolerance is what happens when individuals or a whole system realize a threat is emerging against the entrenched power of that system and head it off by appearing to concede to the demands being made while in reality making no real changes. It is what people sometimes describe as being coopted by the system. By allowing a limited amount of protest that is carefully managed, a societal pressure valve is created to release into thin air the stream of energy that would otherwise cause the system to make real change. Diversity days, Black History Month, people of color having positions as newscasters on local TV stations, colleges and universities featuring photos of Black, Brown, or Asian students on their publicity materials (when such students comprise only a small minority of actual students), profiling what are touted as quintessentially U.S. success stories of wealthy Black entertainers or athletes—all these can be seen as examples of repressive tolerance. How do people learn that such measures are band-aids covering much deeper cultural, political, and economic wounds? How do they learn a measure of vigilance so they are alert when repressive tolerance springs into action? How do they learn to communicate its presence to skeptical friends and colleagues who believe that racial problems have been solved, fundamental inequalities abolished? And how do they learn to carry on fighting against such tolerance when they are the only ones who notice what's happening? What learning do they need to undertake to avoid radical pessimism?

Another form of learning that captures our attention is learning within and about building communities and movements that challenge existing relations of power and advantage. How do people learn to build grassroots coalitions? How did local organizers of a march protesting the 2003 American invasion of Iraq get 10,000 people to the center of Minneapolis to express their opposition to the Bush administration? The march's organizers had to learn how to publicize its existence, how to coordinate a mass protest with law enforcement agencies, how to alert media to this march without the march's logic being distorted, and how to direct the march as it occurred. Participants in the march had to learn how to make their voices heard and how to explain their participation to those who were uninformed about the war (such as very young children) and to those who were active supporters of the war. Clearly, the day of protest involved a massive amount of learning.

On a different scale, what skills and knowledge does one need to acquire to establish a local food cooperative or to organize a local chapter of a union in a nonunionized workplace? And what learning must be accomplished for workers to set up their own independent local chapter when they feel their national union has betrayed them? When worker-employees take over a business, what do they have to know and how do they ensure they locate and then assimilate all necessary information? When tenants organize a rent strike, or citizens take on city hall to demand action on environmental pollution or to advocate for better housing, education, or health facilities, what do people who never completed high school have to learn to do? What learning was involved when workers set up factory councils in Turin or took control of the Scottish Clydeside shipbuilding plants? When mothers who had family members kidnapped by Argentinian security forces during the military dictatorship of the 1970s formed the Mothers of the Plaza de Mayo, how did they learn to face their fear, establish networks of communication, publicize their cause, and bring international attention to the government's "dirty war," as it came to be known, waged by the dictatorship against dissidents amongst its own citizenry? How did members of the previously all-powerful South African security forces learn to acknowledge they had detained and tortured Black South Africans, and how did the citizenry learn to face their torturers at the Truth and Reconciliation Commission hearings?

We view these kinds of learning as subsets of a much larger democratic project—learning to organize the economy, the political system, civil society, and cultural production for the benefit of all. This kind of learning is truly transformative, requiring that many existing structures be transformed in the public interest so that they work for the benefit of the mass of "ordinary" working people, rather than to increase profits enjoyed by a small minority. This is why we emphasize the inseparability of democracy and socialism. In the United States, dominant ideology (in particular the discourse of democracy) has very effectively and brutally severed this link so that socialism is seen as a form of state tyranny, with a small band of grey demagogues ensuring that everybody think and act alike and possessing a determination to rid the world of individual liberty and creativity. It is an interesting exercise to ask students—even those in critical theory courses—who they think wrote that the organizing principle of society should be "securing for every member of society . . . an existence not only fully sufficient materially, and becoming day by day fuller, but an existence guaranteeing to all the free development and exercise of their physical and mental faculties." Liberty and justice (not to mention creative fulfillment) for all, indeed. Washington? Lincoln? Jefferson? The answer, of course, is Friedrich Engels in his essay on socialism (Engels, 1950).

Let us take an example of ideological learning that touches the life of every reader—health care. Few people would argue against the notion that part of a decent life and a humane society is the knowledge that when you or those close to you fall ill, you will receive decent treatment. And few would contradict the idea that it is fundamentally unfair if a system over which you have little control determines that, because of limited economic opportunities, you will receive no or blatantly inferior medical attention. Again, we believe that if you ask the question of the majority of people "Should the health care system be organized primarily to increase the profits of multinational pharmaceutical corporations, or should it be organized to ensure no one is denied medical attention?" the answer would be obvious. Yet, in the United States, dominant ideology has successfully torpedoed all attempts at wresting control of the health care system away from pharmaceutical and health insurance companies in the interests of the majority of citizens by characterizing this as "socialized" medicine, meaning, in dominant ideological terms, something that restricts individual choice. As we write these words, the right is equating the Obama administration's proposal for a publicly funded insurance option with socialism, defined as a dystopian system in which death panels will decide by committee who is to live and who is to die.

The huge ideological irony of this, of course, is that it is the interests of pharmaceutical companies and for-profit health companies that are restricting, even completely removing, any individual choice. There is no kind of choice when you can't afford a health plan or even a doctor's visit because you're unemployed, employed illegally, working for minimum wage, or keeping down two or three part-time jobs with groceries and rent taking all your income. Barbara Ehrenreich's hugely popular *Nickel and Dimed* (2008) and *Bait and Switch* (2006) effectively show the personal impact of this ideological con trick on the working- and middle-class alike.

We view this kind of ideological manipulation as a fantastically successful confidence trick because it completely contradicts what socialism really is—the organization of society and the economy so that people protect and share the abundant resources that could be at the disposal of all. There is no way that this will happen if any one group has permanent control or disproportionate influence over this process. There is also no way this will happen according to market principles, since the market is not an organically evolving "natural" phenomenon free of power or human intervention. It is, rather, a way of organizing the economy that ensures that ever-greater wealth accrues to those that already have. To say the market is an entity somehow free of human intervention and undistorted by power is as fallacious as saying a free press exists (when it exists only for those individuals and corporations with enough wealth to create a mass medium of communication such as a TV network, newspaper, or monopolistic software program).

Socialism is the freedom for people to realize their own creativity without being forced to devote their lives working for institutions that have the maximization of profit as their overarching purpose. When socialism is defined as creating systems whereby those who are most affected by social and economic decisions have the chief responsibility for making those decisions, its democratic core is apparent. What is democracy other than trusting people enough to give them control over the decisions that affect their lives? If socialism is regarded as a project to develop structures in which labor is an enjoyable source of personal fulfillment, its connection to individual creativity is clear. But as long as rampant "marxophobia" (McLaren, 1997) causes socialism to be equated with totalitarian thought control and the denial of creativity, democratic adult educators face a massive challenge in transformative adult learning.

In the following section, we look at what we referred to previously as the holy trinity of contemporary adult learning—transformative learning, critical reflection, and self-directed learning—and the way these intersect with learning to challenge ideological manipulation. Each of these has been claimed as a distinctively adult form of learning, at least in the United States, and each is a familiar focus of doctoral dissertations, research papers, and even rubrics for practice. All three are strongly modernist in their assumption that through diligent self-examination people can come to self-knowledge and can learn to recognize and execute decisions that are in their best interests. Yet, all three have all too often been captured by and framed within the ideology of capitalism. In the rest of this chapter we want to propose ways of conceptualizing these core concepts in ways that are framed by an ideology of socialism rather than capitalism. Let us turn first to transformative learning, a concept that has captured the imagination of adult educators concerned with freedom, social change, environmental stewardship, personal growth, and spiritual exploration.

Transformative Adult Learning

Transformative learning is associated chiefly with the groundbreaking theoretical work of Jack Mezirow. Single-handedly, and alone among adult education scholars of his time, Mezirow developed a theoretical position that has had enormous and far-reaching influence. This was originally termed *perspective transformation* but has more recently become known as *transformative learning* (Mezirow, 1990, 2000). In no less an august authority than the *International Encyclopedia of Adult Education* (English, 2005), transformative learning is defined as "a process by which previously uncritically assimilated assumptions, beliefs, values, and perspectives are questioned and thereby become more open, permeable, and better validated" (Cranton, 2005, p. 630). The developmental imperative of adulthood according to Mezirow is to transform one's meaning schemes (sets of assumptions governing particular situations) and meaning perspectives (broader worldviews) so that they explain the disorienting dilemmas (situations that take us by surprise and cause us to question assumptions) we inevitably encounter as we journey through adulthood. In the process, we alter how we see ourselves, our purpose in the world, and the way that purpose can be realized.

For Mezirow, then, "development in adulthood may be understood as a learning process—a phased and often transformative process of meaning becoming clarified through expanded awareness, critical reflection, validating discourse, and reflective action as one moves toward a fuller realization of agency" (2000, p. 25). Mezirow sees this kind of transformation as happening both as a result of intentional critical reflection and as something we are catapulted into by events. Mezirow's describes the arc of transformative learning as a ten-stage process in which a disorienting dilemma causes one to question assumptions, seek others also going through this experience, contemplate new roles, develop new skills and knowledge to match these, and then integrate these into a reordered life.

For us transformative learning is a rich hermeneutic since moving toward more cooperative, collective, democratic, and socialist ways of thinking and living requires a transformation in the ways we think, the ways we act toward each other, the ways we organize society and politics, the ways we distribute the resources available to us, and the ways we understand the purpose of life. On a broad social stage, it usually takes a societal disorienting dilemma—the collapse of the stock market, a declaration of war, a military coup, a major economic depression—to trigger a critical mass of transformations in individual circumstances that coalesce into a massive act of transformational change. Our position—similar to that of situated cognition theorists (Lave and Wenger, 1991)— is that cognition is fundamentally a function of social organization and location. This is also Mezirow's view. For him "identity is formed in webs of affiliation within a shared life world," and "it is within the context of these relationships, governed by existing and changing cultural paradigms, that we become the persons we are" (Mezirow, 2000, p. 27). How and what one thinks is shaped by one's class, race, and gender (one's social location or positionality), by the cultural streams within which one swims (and which, like a fish in water, one is unaware one is swimming in), and by dominant ideology (the set of beliefs and practices, reflected in the structures and systems of a society, that are accepted as natural, common sense, and working for the good of all).

If cognition is situated in these phenomena, as theorists of situated cognition (Lave, 2003) hold, then changing cognition, by implication, depends on changing culture and ideology. In Mezirow's terms, "transformative learning involves liberating ourselves from reified forms of thought that are no longer dependable" (2000, p. 27). Reified forms of thought is as good a shorthand definition of ideology as one could have, but it implies that dominant ideas and practices have an existence somehow independent of the environment that produced them. In reality, reified forms of thought and their associated practices (decisions, actions, and behaviors) are produced, buttressed, and nourished by sociopolitical and economic structures and systems. By implication then, changing reified forms of thought and practice can only happen if the structures producing and sustaining those phenomena are changed. And, if capitalist structures produce and sustain individualized, competitive practices, with people acting on the basis of self-advancement and assuming that others' poverty or oppression is the result of "natural" forces working to favor the most capable (the survival of the fittest), then only a move to cooperative, democratic, socialist structures will serve to instigate a truly transformative change of consciousness.

From our perspective, then, transformative adult learning theory is a useful way to explain first how adults learn to recognize the way in which the exchange dynamic of capitalism (I give you this labor and you give me that wage in return) has permeated their life worlds, to use Habermas's (1987) term. It also constitutes a theoretical starting point for understanding how people learn a whole new way of being—a way of thinking, acting, feeling, and creating—that moves from acquisition to creative fulfillment in association with others. This is what Erich Fromm described as the movement from having to being (Fromm 1968). The logic of both situated cognition and transformative learning is that such a developmental project can happen only through people creating new collective forms of social, political, cultural, and economic association. Such forms would embed ways of ordering common affairs that have as their chief rationale the attainment of liberty and justice for all. In other words, learning new forms of being can only happen when a socialist ethic informs how we live together, regulates our common affairs, and decides how necessary tasks are to be fairly distributed and how the products of our collective labors are fairly enjoyed. It is hard to imagine a more profound example of transformative learning. This is why we say studying how the processes and conditions under which people learn the transformation to socialism is one of the most important transformative learning research agendas.

CRITICAL REFLECTION

In the history of American adult education scholarship, the year 2000 marked a mini-watershed. This was the first time that one of the decennial handbooks of adult education published by the American Association for Adult and Continuing Education was organized around a concept and form of practice deemed to be universal enough to merit its anchoring the book's contributions; that concept and practice was critical reflection (Wilson and Hayes, 2000). In that handbook one of us was charged with writing a framing chapter that articulated the constituent elements of critical reflection (Brookfield, 2000a), and that is where we start this analysis.

Critical reflection is an equivocal concept, a contested idea, whose use reflects the ideology of the user. For some, it is a deeper, more probing form of reflection on the assumptions—epistemic, systemic, individual—that are foundational to one's being. This is roughly how Mezirow (2000) uses the term. For him "becoming critically reflective of assumptions underlying content, process, or premise (of problem-solving) is common in both instrumental and communicative learning" (p. 21). In transformative learning, Mezirow sees critical reflection as integral to "focused and mindful" transformations (as against those involving "mindless assimilation"). It is primarily a process that can be applied in a range of different situations: *objective reframing* "involves critical reflection on the assumptions of others encountered in a narrative or in task-oriented problem-solving" (p. 23), while *subjective reframing* "involves critical self-reflection of one's own assumptions" (p. 23) about one's own narratives of experience, economic and political systems, the workplace, feelings (emotional intelligence), interpersonal relations (psychotherapy), and the way one learns (epistemic cognition).

We share Mezirow's emphasis on critical reflection as a learning process in which people learn to probe their experiences, actions, and patterns of reasoning to discover the assumptions that inform these. For us, however, this can be described as reflection, pure and simple, or maybe deep reflection. It is something we learn to do in many different domains of our lives for many different purposes. What makes something an example of *critical* reflection, for us, is its connection to uncovering ideological manipulation and learning new forms of thought and practice that fit a socialist rather than capitalist ethic. We call this form of reflective learning "critical" because the presence of critical theory informs our use of the word *critical*. Let us take a specific context to explain what we mean—the context of workplace learning.

The work of Argyris (2000) on critical learning, thinking, and reflection can be represented by executives' use of lateral, divergent thinking strategies and double loop learning methods. Argyris skillfully identifies the undiscussable elements in organizational practices that torpedo efforts at organizational change. Here adult workers learn critically when they examine the assumptions that govern team building, organizational interventions, and business decisions by checking whether or not these assumptions are grounded in an accurately assessed view of market realities. Inferential ladders are scrutinized for the false rungs that lead business teams into, for example, a disastrous choice regarding the way in which a brand image upsets an important group of potential customers. The consequence of this exercise in critical thought is an increase in profits and productivity, and a decrease in industrial sabotage and worker dissatisfaction. People feel a greater sense of fulfillment and creative satisfaction in their work that rebounds to the good of the organization, its employees, and the shareholders. However, as critical reflection helps us discover more creative or humanistic ways to organize production or sell services, capitalism is left unchallenged. The free market is infused with a social-democratic warmth that curtails its worst excesses. The ideological and structural premises of the capitalist workplace remain intact.

For us, critical reflection in the workplace cannot occur without an explicit critique of capitalism (Collins, 1991; Simon, Dippo, and Schenke 1991). Here workplace critical reflection questions the morality of relocating plants to countries where pollution controls are much looser and labor is much cheaper. It challenges the demonizing of union members as corrupt Stalinist obstructionists engaged in a consistent misuse of power. It investigates who owns the means of production and the different forms of capital; the ways in which profits are produced, measured, and distributed; and the conditions under which work is organized. It points out and queries the legitimation of capitalist ideology through changes in language; for example, the creeping and ever more widespread use of phrases such as "buying into" or "creating ownership" of an idea, the description of students as "customers," or the use of euphemisms such as "downsizing" or worse "rightsizing" (with its implication that firing people restores some sort of natural balance to the market) to soften and make palatable the reality of people losing their livelihoods, homes, families, relationships, self-respect, and hope.

Finally, critically reflective learning at the workplace would happen when workers learned to conceive and experiment with forms of socialist practice, such as the creation of worker cooperatives. In terms of transformative learning, the workplace is transformed when cooperative democracy and worker control become the de facto models for organizing production, when the objects of productive work are goods and services intended to enhance the well-being of the majority of "ordinary" people, and when the need for creative and fulfilling work replaces the distribution of profits among shareholders as the chief rationale for production. The factory councils in Turin, the Clydeside shipbuilding sit-in (Scotland), the 1968 occupation of the Renault factory outside Paris—these would be well-known examples of critically reflective learning at the workplace in this perspective.

SELF-DIRECTED LEARNING

Ever since the groundbreaking work of Allen Tough in the 1960s and 1970s (Tough, 1971), self-directed learning (SDL, first known as self-teaching) has exercised a powerful hold on the imaginations of adult educators. It was taken up by Malcolm Knowles (1988) who tied it to his notion of andragogy, and one of us did his doctoral work in this area (Brookfield, 1980). Most adult educators who stand behind the concept of self-direction do so because they sense that there is something about this form of learning that dignifies people and respects their experiences. For them, self-direction represents a break with authoritarianism and educational totalitarianism. It means that control over the definitions, processes, and evaluations of learning rests with those who are struggling to learn, not with external authorities or formal institutions. The belief that through self-direction adults can gain increasing control over their lives (however naïve this belief might subsequently turn out to be) is an emancipatory belief. When asked to justify their commitment to SDL, most practitioners invoke concepts of empowerment and transformation. Although these words have been robbed of their political import, they can be reconstituted and rearticulated in a counterhegemonic way to emphasize standing against oppressive interests. That this is possible is represented in Gelpi's (1979) view that "self-directed learning by individuals and of groups is a danger for every repressive force, and it is upon this self-direction that we must insist . . . radical change in social, moral, aesthetic and political affairs is often the outcome of a process of self-directed learning in opposition to the educational message imposed from without" (p. 2).

We believe that self-directed learning can be reinterpreted with a political edge to fit squarely into the tradition of emancipatory education. The case for reframing self-direction as an inherently political practice rests on two arguments. First, at the heart of self-direction is the issue of control, particularly control over what are conceived as acceptable and appropriate learning activities and processes, and that control is always a political issue involving questions of power. Second, exercising self-direction requires that certain conditions be in place regarding access to resources, and these are conditions that are essentially political in nature.

One of the most consistent elements in the majority of definitions of self-direction is the importance of the learner's exercising control over all educational decisions. What should be the goals of a learning effort, what resources should be used, what methods will work best for the learner, and by what criteria the success of any learning effort should be judged are all decisions that are said to rest in the learner's hands. This emphasis on control—on who decides what is right and good and how these things should be pursued—is also central to notions of emancipatory education. For example, when talking about his work at the Highlander Folk School, the radical educator Myles Horton (1990) stressed that "if you want to have the students control the whole process, as far as you can get them to control it, then you can never, at any point, take it out of their hands" (p. 152). Who controls the decisions concerning the ways and directions in which people learn is a political issue highlighting the distribution of educational and political power. Who has the final say in framing the range and type of decisions that are to be taken and in establishing the pace and mechanisms for decision making indicates where control really resides.

Self-direction as an organizing concept for education therefore calls to mind some powerful political associations. It implies a democratic commitment to shifting to learners as much control as possible for conceptualizing, designing, conducting, and evaluating their learning and for deciding how resources are to be used to further these processes. Thought of politically, self-direction can be seen as part of a populist democratic tradition which holds that people's definitions of what is important to them should frame and instruct governments' actions and not the other way round. This is why the idea of self-direction is such anathema to advocates of a core or national curriculum, and why it is opposed so vehemently by those who see education as a process of induction into cultural literacy. Self-directed learning is institutionally and politically inconvenient to those who promote educational blueprints, devise intelligence measures, and administer psychological tests and profiles that attempt to control the learning of others. Emphasizing people's right to self-direction also invests a certain trust in their wisdom, in their capacity to make wise choices and take wise actions. Advocating that people should be in control of their own learning is based on the belief that if people had a chance to give voice to what most moves and hurts them, they would soon show that they were only too well aware of the real nature of their problems and of ways to deal with these.

If we place the self-conscious, self-aware exertion of control over learning at the heart of what it means to be self-directed, we raise a host of questions about how control can be exercised authentically in a culture which is itself highly controlling. Self-direction is an inauthentic confidence trick if it involves people making key decisions about their learning all the while being unaware that this is happening within a framework that excludes certain ideas or activities as subversive, unpatriotic, or immoral. Controlled self-direction is, from a political perspective, a contradiction in terms, a self-negating concept as oxymoronic as the concept of limited empowerment. On the surface, we may be said to be controlling our learning when we make decisions about pacing, resources, and evaluative criteria. But if the range of acceptable content has been preordained so that we deliberately or unwittingly steer clear of things that we sense are deviant or controversial, then we are controlled rather than in control. We are victims, in effect, of self-censorship, willing partners in hegemony.

From our perspective, important projects for self-directed adult learning focus on learning how best to undertake collective action, how to establish alternative socialist economic models, how to form a progressive, revolutionary political party to spearhead change, and how to maintain hope in the face of struggle. Learning socialism involves a number of tasks—learning about various forms of socialist philosophy, learning how to analyze the workings of capitalism and its intersection with White supremacy, the degradation of women, the marginalizing of LGBT people, the destruction of the environment, and learning the mechanics of devolved decision making in social, cultural, economic, and educational spheres.

A major element in socialist learning is learning the skills and information to establish socialist alternatives to capitalism—establishing worker cooperatives and collectives being a major part of this project—and learning to do this in a culture that views such initiatives as alien, even unpatriotic. Part of this learning also involves challenging an internalized capitalist ideology in which individuals are seen as self-contained units making judgments in their own self-interest (which is defined as maximizing one's economic advantage)—the ideology on which so much economic planning is currently based. Part of this also entails dismantling in the popular imagination the connection of socialism and state-sponsored totalitarianism and reestablishing its connection with democracy. In American terms, this means claiming Marx as the original democrat, committed to a society where major decisions are made by the mass of the people—the working class in other words—rather than by the bourgeoisie or capitalist class. These are self-directed learning projects not usually covered in the official curriculum of adult education, unless we expand our understanding of adult education way beyond the usual notions of workplace learning or liberal education. But we place these projects within the rubric of self-directed learning because the learning they require is often self-organized, conducted without the benefit of institutional sponsorship, in opposition to dominant cultural values, and evaluated with no reference to formal "official" assessments.

Typically, socialist organizations such as the International Socialist Organization, Democratic Socialists of America, and the Freedom Road Socialist Organization differ strongly with each other in the most effective strategy for establishing socialism. Integral to them all, however, is a simple democratic idea: that those affected by decisions should be the ones that make those decisions. This principle is often described as self-determination. To us, self-direction and self-determination are one and the same, and both are grounded in the ultimate U.S. value, democracy. Hence, to argue for self-directed learning is to argue that a prime adult educational project is helping people to understand the whole range of options open to them for organizing their social, cultural, and economic affairs—including socialist ones—and then, after a full and informed consideration of all these options, to learn how to create systems that represent the preferences of the mass of people based on their definition of what they most need. As Paul Robeson was fond of saying, "The large question as to which society is better for humanity is never settled by argument. The proof of the pudding is in the eating. Let the various social systems compete with each other under conditions of peaceful coexistence, and the people can decide for themselves. I do not insist that anyone else must agree with my judgment, and so I feel that no one is justified in insisting that I must conform to his beliefs. Isn't that fair?" (Robeson, 1958, p. 40).

CONCLUSION

Adult learning can be viewed operationally and extrinsically as any attempt by adults to learn new skills or knowledge. Conceived this way, adult learning is chiefly a technical matter concerned with how information is processed, how learning activities are sequenced, how learning is evaluated, and so on. The operational approach is broad enough to encompass everything from learning parenting, how to rewire a basement, or how to speak a foreign language (to use benign examples) to learning how to disseminate the ideology of White supremacy, how to convince the recently unemployed that their situation is as unpredictable and uncontrollable as a hurricane, how to justify political deception, or how to ensure that people view cooperative economic arrangements as fundamentally unpatriotic (to use inflammatory examples). Clearly, we reject this operational, technical approach as too narrow. While we acknowledge that matters of technique are important and valid (we have both suffered in the past from being students in programs where our teachers could have done with more technique), we regard adult learning as irreducibly value-based. For us, adult learning as an overarching process is concerned with learning how to live a more authentic and creative life. Central to such a project is learning to create a society in which people are concerned to protect and share resources for the benefit of all and learning to create systems in which those affected by decisions are the same people who make them. We regard this as learning a democratic socialist ethic and practicing a democratic socialist politics.

CHAPTER THREE

UNDERSTANDING ADULT DEVELOPMENT

Development, like so many other words in the discourse surrounding adult learning, sounds on the surface unobjectionable, even benign. Education, learning, training, change, development—these can only be good, only improving, can't they? Our position is that these terms are always problematic; that is, that although they seem on the surface to be empirically neutral, when they are employed in speech and used to justify action, they are always normatively based, always representing a set of interests deemed to be inherently desirable by those holding them. In this chapter we examine the concept of development from two perspectives. First, we want to explain more fully how we see normative and empirical elements as being always interwoven in understandings of development. Second, we want to argue that the concept of development can be reframed in a way that grounds it in the normative pursuit of true democracy—a democracy that is participatory and economic. As part of this reframing we need to examine the developmental tasks facing adults that this entails—the development of a worldview in which individual and collective well-being are seen as fundamentally interwoven, the development of agency, and the development of collective forms of association, communication, and production. This reframing of the concept of development connects it directly to the discourse of transformative learning and critical thinking that, as we saw in the last chapter, is so powerful in the field of adult learning.

ADULT DEVELOPMENT: AN EMPIRICAL OR NORMATIVE CONCEPT?

Both of us have worked enthusiastically in agencies and movements that declared themselves explicitly to be engaged in development. Stephen's first full-time job as an adult educator was as a "Lecturer/Organizer" (yes, that was the official job title) for a Department of Community, Social, and Environmental Development. Implicit in the job descriptor was the assumption that the things Stephen was working to develop in the community would somehow benefit the lives of those involved and that the way development was understood enjoyed broad support from the community at large. This neatly sidestepped the conflicts of interest based on race, class, gender, sexuality, and ideology that represent different groups' notions of what should be developed and what that process should look like.

In their review of adult development and cognitive development, Merriam, Caffarrella, and Baumgartner (2007) outline the dominance of psychological models of development in adult education though they also acknowledge that sociocultural models are becoming more prominent. In both these approaches, development is defined as the ability to engage in increasingly complex forms of thinking about an ever more differentiated array of ideas, situations, and actions. As the canvas of adult life is drawn ever more widely, adults need not only to create meaning out of anticipated events but also to learn how to resolve unexpected crises. They not only learn from experiences that confirm existing intuitions but also from confronting multiple contradictions, and from trying to reconcile discrepancies between what actually happens to them and what they believe should be happening to them.

As adults negotiate the events of their lives, they are often said to be involved in what a cluster of cognitive and developmental psychologists have called postformal operations—ways of reasoning that are more complex than the formal operations stage identified by Piaget as typically reached in late adolescence. From the postformal perspective, an adult who exhibits cognitive development is able to move easily between universal forms of reasoning ("one should always tell the truth") and particularistic, context-based forms ("in this situation I need to conceal my intentions or those more powerful than me will defeat me"). This is what Basseches (1984) calls dialectical thinking. Such an adult also has a self-conscious awareness of how she reasons, what evidence is most convincing to her, why she judges certain evidence to be most reliable, accurate, and valid, and what errors she is most prone to. This cluster of characteristics has been described as epistemic cognition (King and Kitchener, 1994). Postformal adults can view a problem from multiple perspectives and gain some sense of how someone who lives very differently than they do thinks about a specific situation. This is what Habermas calls intersubjective understanding and Mezirow calls perspective-taking. The way postformal adults apply logic is dependent as much on the context of a situation as on classic forms of deductive reasoning. This is described as practical logic (Sinnott, 1998) or embedded logic (Labouvie-Vief, 1980). So, for example, a postformal adult in an Off-Track Betting shop will apply logic to conclude that a certain horse is most likely to win a race if that horse is ridden by a particular jockey against particular competitors and if certain conditions pertain that particular day at the race track.

So far, so good. Up to now, our discussion seems to suggest that adult development is, by definition, desirable. It enables us to account for the bewildering fragmentation of life in a diverse, rapidly changing world. However, the notion of development begs the massive questions of direction, interest, and purpose. It is quite possible to extrapolate the logic described above and apply it to purposes that many would consider harmful and immoral. And, by extension, objectors would probably argue that that kind of development should be stopped, killed before it gets totally out of hand. Development is not neutral—it is always in a certain direction, always serving some interests rather than others. Like self-directed learning (which is often spoken of as similarly desirable and disconnected from questions of direction or interest), development is always for a purpose. We learn and develop (or others desire us to learn and develop) in certain ways to accomplish certain objectives or to bring about a particular state of affairs. And sometimes the development of one person or group in a particular direction can only be achieved by the suppression of others.

Take the example of White supremacy or other doctrines of racial purity involving ethnic cleansing. Those who subscribe to the idea of Aryan superiority as embedded in particular bloodlines have developed ever more sophisticated arguments as to why their ideology is empirically correct. They have developed a capacity to quote evidence selectively and to choose methods of communication that use symbolism, imagery, and pageantry to persuade others of their case. The use of the term *cleansing*, with its connotations of removing the dirty, staining elements, is one such trick. Calling a unilateral, imperialist invasion a "war of liberation" is another. Advocates of racial purity deliberately develop the ability to propose arguments that counter the most frequently voiced objections to their ideology. They also wish to implement curricula and organize education that develop others in this direction. Those devoted to White supremacy can meet the empirical conditions of development identified earlier (of reasoning in more complex ways about an increasingly wide range of issues and problems) while being passionate advocates of their cause.

The same argument could be made of those who develop a capacity for other forms of ideological manipulation. Political leaders develop the ability to ignore contrary evidence and to argue in the strongest possible ways for a cause that others consider reprehensible. The commitment of the Bush and Blair administrations to the invasion of Iraq is one such example. Such leaders see part of their political leadership as using the bully pulpit of office, along with various forms of nepotism, to persuade opinion leaders, and through them the broader citizenry, to develop public opinion in a certain direction. A developmental imperative in such a situation becomes creating the widespread perception that expressing opposition to an invasion is an unpatriotic act that only gives succor to democracy's enemies. Along similar lines, corporations, governments, sports teams, and other entities seek to develop a brand to identify what they stand for, communicate a particular message, and build support for their activities. Any countermessage to this branding stands no chance of being heard in the mainstream media who themselves are corporations dependent on other corporations and governments for licenses, funding, and advertising dollars.

Of course, as one group seeks to develop its capacities in one direction, other groups seek development in contrary directions. The oil industry wishes to develop the tax system and environmental policy in one direction, Greenpeace in another. The World Bank wishes to develop the economy in one direction, the Democratic Socialists of America in another. In families, communities, and organizations, individuals and groups have strong commitments to developing themselves and their surroundings in ways that conflict directly with each other. And we must remember that the playing field on which these developmental wars are waged is not level. The dominant ideologies of capitalism, White supremacy, and the tyranny of the democratic majority ensure that socialist ethics and organizations are defined as undemocratic and/or irrelevant and that racism is seen as having been addressed by desegregation legislation and affirmative action. White supremacy defines racism as a matter of individual choice rather than as systematic form of control in which media images and legal frameworks intersect to convince people that affirmative action has ensured all now start life equal. So there is nothing inherently humanistic or benign about development; it all depends on the ways people frame its purpose and direction.

A much more normative approach to conceptualizing development that parallels our argument is adopted by a group of researchers inspired by Sternberg's 20-year span of work on wisdom, intelligence, and creativity (1997, 2003, 2004; Sternberg and Jordan, 2005). The choice of wisdom as a developmental outcome is itself bound up with notions of maturity, intelligence, and wise action that are, of course, highly normative. But, as Sternberg points out, intelligence can be applied to any number of immoral acts whereas wisdom has endemic to it notions of compassion and working for the common good. Intelligence can exist independent of wisdom normatively defined. After all, Joseph Goebbels was highly intelligent in his development of an effective propaganda machine to advance notions of blood purity and Aryan supremacy. But few outside the Nazi movement would claim he exhibited wisdom. In commenting on Sternberg's work, particularly his more recent explication of foolishness, Merriam, Caffarrella, and Baumgartner (2007) observe how the foolishness of people with incredible wealth and power "has led us into wars, polarizations among those who could make a positive difference, and inconceivable hardships for people worldwide . . . being bright does not necessarily equate with being wise" (p. 353).

In 1968 Hardin's influential article "The Tragedy of the Commons" outlined how people acting in solitary and apparently rational self-interest ensure their own diminution. Since then, the idea of democratic stewardship of common resources has become relatively uncontroversial. When wisdom is explicitly tied to knowledge of and action for the common good, its connections to democratic socialism become much more discernible. At the center of this idea of the common good is an explicit criticism of sectarianism and privilege, of one group or association of groups exercising disproportionate wealth, power, and influence over the majority. In contemporary humanist circles, books such as *Habits of the Heart* (Bellah, Madsen, Sullivan, Swidler, and Tipton, 1996), *The Good Society* (Bellah, Madsen, Sullivan, Swidler, and Tipton, 1992), *Bowling Alone* (Putnam, 2001), and *Democracies in Flux* (Putnam, 2004) have charted the collapse of the public sphere, the decline of civil society, and the growth of radical privatism. All of these developments have eroded the notion of the commons— the idea that there are resources, services, and practices that need to be held in common for the good of all to enjoy. Much discussion of the commons has focused on nonrenewable planetary resources, but books such as *Common Fire* (Parks Daloz, Keen, Keen, and Daloz Parks, 1996) explore the "lives of commitment in a complex world" (to use the book's subtitle) that seek to build common interests across racial and class divides through a deliberate engagement with otherness.

For us the development of wisdom described by Sternberg as balancing the common good with individual interests and the development of social capital as outlined by Putnam are liberal humanist ideas that open a link to the discussion of democratic socialism. At the heart of the socialist idea, from Saint-Simon to Proudhon and Marx, is that resources, goods, and services must be under common ownership and control as a means of ensuring equity and fairness. A socialist economy is focused on the satisfaction of authentic human needs, not on the accumulation of profit, and places the stewardship of the commons as the highest form of social practice. If wisdom and development have as their purpose to prepare people for responsible stewardship, and if this stewardship is to involve the majority of the populace controlling the commons for the good of all, then the purpose of adult development is easily conceptualized as preparing people for cooperative, collective, and democratic forms of association such as socialism.

A RADICAL APPROACH TO DEVELOPMENT

A radical approach to conceptualizing development sees it as a process of collective movement in a certain direction, that of democratic socialism. Constructivist approaches to development place individual development in a cultural context and acknowledge that development happens in community as individuals interact with peers, colleagues, family members, and authority figures. Class, race, culture, ideology, gender—all these factors intersect to develop people in a certain direction. We share this constructivist orientation but add to it a normative commitment to understanding development as the process by which individuals come to realize and enact their common class, gender, and racial interests. In this conception, adult development entails people resisting dominant ideology and confronting structures that systematically diminish them. In Marxist terms, adult development is the process by which members of the working class come to see their common interests and become members of a class for itself (rather than a class in itself) united in opposition to the bourgeoisie and owners of capital. In Africentric terms, adult development is the process by which members of the African diaspora come to see their common identity and interests and then intentionally develop self-ethnic reflectors in the cause of race pride. Self-ethnic reflectors are images, practices, and ideas that are grounded in African, rather than Eurocentric, cultural values. They are developed in opposition to White supremacist ideology and emphasize the communitarian nature of tribal life, including cooperative economics or *Ujamaa*, what Nyrere called African socialism (Nyrere, 1968).

A radical understanding of development entails three distinctive developmental tasks. First, as outlined above, is the development of a perspective in which the majority of people recognize how their individual well-being and their identity development is inextricably linked to the interests of the wider group. Second is the development of agency, defined here as the inclination and capacity to act on and in the world in a way that furthers socialist values and practices. Third is developing collective forms, movements, and organizations.

TASK 1: COLLECTIVE IDENTITY DEVELOPMENT

Here adult development describes the process by which adults start to question the privatized perspectives and practices into which they have been socialized by dominant ideology, and then to develop a sense of personal identity that is tied to the collective. Privatization here is defined as a way of living that places self and family at the center of the universe and interprets behaving responsibly as striving to gain the greatest advantages and greatest measure of protection for self and family. It sees competition for advantage (rather than competition linked to creative inspiration, as when one musician competes with another to crank out the rawest power or most beautiful melodic inspiration) as the natural condition of humankind. It also regards any form of state control—no matter how participatory or accountable—as inherently totalitarian and diminishing of humankind.

Countering a privatized worldview is a massive and daunting developmental project, involving as it does confronting the full weight of history and socialization. It also entails great risks. One need only think of the history of the trade union movement in which all and every form of intimidation up to and including murder have been employed to "persuade" workers that unions will lose them jobs and livelihoods and therefore stand against their interests. Of course, in naked political repression or union busting the lines of combat are clearly defined. In the hegemony of everyday socialization, things are murkier as ideological manipulation persuades people that it is in their best interests not to contemplate any form of collective ownership or control. Thus, workers at Wal-Mart are persuaded that introducing unions will impose strict limits on employment, restrict individual advancement, and reduce profitability in a way that will lead to layoffs. Parents of children in state schools see draconian budget cuts and the resulting increase in class sizes and conclude that their best educational option as caring parents is to gain a place at a private academy for their child. Uninsured citizens see the run-down state of inner city hospitals, long waiting lines for treatment in emergency rooms, and the inferior care provided by Medicaid, and decide that state-provided universal health care is inherently inferior to private insurance. This causes them to oppose any extension of government care as restricting choice and the thin end of the wedge of totalitarian repression.

TASK 2: DEVELOPING AGENCY

The second radical developmental task is to develop the inclination and capacity to act on and in the world in a way that furthers socialist values and practices. Because capacity is as important as inclination this means that development has to be understood as working with others to create collective movements and institutions. Hence, agency is exerted in such initiatives as the effort to unionize, to mobilize protests against illegal invasions, to create worker or economic cooperatives, to institute universal health care, to abolish private education, and to create and nurture a revolutionary party. Several strategic and tactical dimensions to the development of agency are discernible. There is the creation of clear agendas and goals, so that whatever energy is available is not wasted on fruitless endeavors. The history of the left is awash with examples of massive expenditures of energy on the pursuit of ideological purity and the castigation of the betrayals of fellow travelers, rather than on the creation of organizations with a common purpose. Developing agency involves learning to keep the broad social goal of long-term transformation in mind, while working on short- and medium-term goals that are achievable. Achieving short-term goals is itself inherently empowering, giving people the sense that their agency is real and waiting to be galvanized.

Developing agency also means creating support among groups of like-minded peers that cross lines of race, class, gender, and sexuality, in mainstream political terms the creation of "rainbow" coalitions. The literature on self-help groups (White and Madara, 2002) has established beyond doubt the crucial role such groups play in keeping members focused on their goals for change and feeling that their efforts are valued by others. Strategically, support groups are vital for all kinds of survival—psychological, physical, professional, and so on. As Paulo Freire would often remark, acting alone is the best way to commit suicide. Anyone who has lived underground, subscribed to an ideology outlawed by the state, come to new sexual identity in the face of rampant homophobia, or developed race pride in a White supremacist world knows how irreplaceable is the support offered by groups of peers. In McGary's (1997) view, the ability of African Americans "to form their own supportive communities in the midst of a hostile environment"—even in the worst of slavery—allowed them "to maintain healthy self-concepts through acts of resistance and communal nourishment" (p. 292). The considerable literature on transformative learning pays strong empirical testimony to the importance of groups for the development of radically new perspectives, meaning schemes, and habits of mind (Mezirow, 2000; Taylor, 2000). Adults in the throes of transformative change usually depend on such groups to provide arenas in which new identities can be tested out and confirmed. We shall say more on this in our discussion of holding environments.

Finally, developing agency also entails the capacity to stand fast and deepen commitment in the face of strengthening opposition, even in the face of failure. For those with an interest in democratic socialism, such a capacity has always been crucial given the power of monopoly and global capitalism. However, since the fall of the Berlin Wall many who previously were potential allies now see socialism as a totally discredited idea. It does not seem to matter that many socialists were as critical of what they considered to be the state capitalism, rigid ideological control, and suppression of dissent (both internally and among members of the Warsaw Pact) exercised by the Soviet Union, as were the most right-wing, free-market thinkers. Additionally, the surge in postmodernist ideas has meant that "grand" ideas such as justice, fairness, and equity are now seen as suspect and that neo-Marxism and critical theory are viewed by many as irrelevant analyses because they were produced by dead, White, European males. Standing fast and deepening commitment are well nigh impossible tasks unless the support groups mentioned previously are present.

Task 3: Developing Collective Forms, Movements, and Organizations

The third developmental task is developing collective forms, movements, and organizations. Working-class culture has long been lionized for its mutuality and collective nature—seen most famously perhaps in the trade union movement—but these values are also present in other settings. To take two brief examples, scholarship on gender has explored "the tradition that has no name" to use Belenky and others' formulation (Belenky, Bond, and Weinstock, 1999). Building on their notion of connected knowing as a female form of epistemology (one that looks for interconnectedness and empathy in others' ideas), Belenky and her coauthors elaborate a social and political tradition of interconnectedness that allows women to survive in the face of oppression and also to pursue interests held in common. This is the tradition of interdependence that holds that the well-being of the individual and of the collective can never be separated. In their study of groups of women in rural Vermont, Belenky and her coauthors note how the women studied view leadership as developed and exercised collectively and how the task of leadership is to raise up one's peers rather than to persuade them to one's will.

The same tradition is embodied in the motto of the National Association of Colored Women's Clubs (founded in 1896)—"to lift as we climb"—ensuring that "we must climb in such a way as to guarantee that all of our sisters, regardless of social class, and indeed all of our brothers, climb with us" (Davis, 1990, p. 5). In the face of sexism and patriarchy, women have provided emotional support and practical assistance to each other as the institutions of the state and civil society have proved unwilling to deal with their subjugation. The defining characteristic of the sisterhood of feminism is viewing the oppression of one as the diminution of all. This calls forth the need to organize across lines of race and class around "a revolutionary, multi-racial women's movement that seriously addresses the main issues affecting poor and working class women" (Davis, 1990, p. 7).

The Africentric paradigm, as articulated by writers such as Asante (1998a,b) and explored in adult education by Colin (1988, 1994, 2002) similarly views individual and collective identity as intertwined. In recent years, the African American Pre-Conference of the annual Adult Education Research Conference, along with activities of scholars such as Colin and Guy (1998), Guy and Colin (1998), and Sheared (1999), have generated a vigorous discourse around what constitutes an African-centered interpretation of adult educational practices and adult learning concepts. Instead of drawing on a Eurocentric body of work, Africentrism argues for the generation of an alternative discourse—including a discourse of criticality—that is grounded in the traditions and cultures of the African continent. It believes that work that draws on European traditions of thought, however well intentioned this work might be and however much these traditions might be reframed in terms of African American interests, always neglects the cultural traditions of Africa. Since such traditions are crucial constitutive elements of the identity of African Americans, the Africentric paradigm holds that it is these traditions that should dominate theorizing on behalf of African Americans.

Africentric thought is held to be epistemologically distinctive, to comprise ways of knowing, experiencing, perceiving, and meaning making that stand apart from the Eurocentric ideal of the monological self coming to truth through rational, self-directed reflection. To Colin and Guy, the Swahili concept of *Nguzo Saba* is emblematic of the Africentric paradigm. Its values—*Umoja* (unity), *Kujichagulia* (self-determination), *Ujima* (collective work and responsibility), *Ujamaa* (cooperative economics), *Nia* (purpose), *Kuumba* (creativity), and *Imani* (faith)—stress community, interdependence, and collective action. In Colin and Guy's view, "this differs significantly from traditional Eurocentric perspectives of individualism, competition, and hierarchical forms of authority and decision-making" (1998, p. 50). Africentric values focus on self-ethnic liberation and collective empowerment. Africentric adult education practices and understandings are thus framed collectively. The race moves forward as a race, not through a series of individual forays into the White world. Education happens collectively with other members of the race involved as students, teachers, and program designers. Race pride and race unity are central to educational practice and development and are fostered when those in roles of authority look, speak, think, and act like those they are serving, and when materials studied and methods employed are African-centered. Hence, the development of one's racial identity only happens as individuals combine with others of the African diaspora to advance the interests of the race.

The importance of the collective is acknowledged in developmental literature's stress on the necessity for adult development of a holding environment. As described by Kegan (1994), holding environments are places and groups of people that confirm a person's emerging identity by providing support and encouragement over a period of time. Such environments remain in place prior to and after any individual's membership of them, and they are always available should anyone wish to return. But a holding environment does more than nourish and support development in a particular direction. It also challenges people to develop in ways they had not anticipated. Hence, an individual who joins a union for the purpose of protecting their personal livelihood may move into advocacy for better working conditions for all and eventually into advocating the socialist transformation of society. A personal experience of discrimination leads to membership of an antiracist collective. An experience of illness results in community advocacy for better and universal health care. As surveys of life-long activists amply illustrate (Parks Daloz, Keen, Keen, and Daloz Parks, 1996; Colby and Damon, 1994), people grow into activism sometimes almost without realizing it.

Holding environments—collectives in which new identities are forged and confirmed by like-minded peers and mentors—are crucial to all kinds of transformative identity development. In the adult education doctoral program at National Louis University in Chicago (where Stephen teaches as an adjunct), students of the African diaspora (and White Africanists) meet peers and faculty— particularly Dr. Scipio A. J. Colin III—who provide an Africentric holding environment that assists students interested in developing an African-centered identity. Course modules, reading materials, curricula, assignments, and dissertations are reframed through an Africentric lens for those students who wish to affirm their African identity. A master's program in adult education at Mount Saint Vincent University in Halifax, Nova Scotia (like the National Louis program also using a cohort format), is a wholly Africentric program and thus a major holding environment in which a new identity and loyalty that challenges White supremacy is forged (Brigham, 2007). Holding environments in the lesbian, gay, bisexual and transgendered communities are crucial in providing support for those individuals otherwise unable to "come out" (Hill, 2006). In times of war, when jingoistic fervor fuelled by media enthusiasm tends to sweep the populace, holding environments allow for the emergence of antiwar movements. Interestingly, where adult learning is concerned, the cohort format, which holds the potential for forming holding environments, is now the preferred option for graduate study in many universities.

It is important to stress, however, that a cohort in and of itself is not by definition a holding environment. The phenomenon of automaton conformity—of the cohort exerting a kind of group-think pressure to toe the party line—is one that can clearly be seen in the kind of cohort style programs that are so popular with some advocates of accelerated learning. One of the dark sides of the cohort format is the unacknowledged possibility of automaton conformity. In accelerated cohort programs that involve a degree of participation, even of student-governance, there is a danger of a few strong voices defining the agenda early on in the cohort's history and of this agenda mimicking the dominant culture's ideology. Alternatively, when students meet as a group free from faculty interference to decide on which curricular demands or requests they wish to present to faculty, there is the risk that dissenting minority voices will be seen as obstructive, as getting in the way of a speedy resolution. Students' desire to come to consensus and thereby present a united front to faculty overrides the need to be alert to implicit pressures for ideological conformity. For interesting perspectives on how it feels to be participants in an accelerated learning cohort doctoral program in adult education in which students have a role in governance of the program, readers should consult the articles by Baptiste and Brookfield (1997), Avila et al. (2000), and Colin and Heaney (2001).

DEVELOPMENT, TRANSFORMATION, AND CRITICAL THINKING

Transformative learning and transformative education are, as we have already noted, dominant discourses in the field of adult learning and education. And, like development, transformation is used normatively as well as empirically to describe a generally desirable movement forward in a certain direction. Hence, transformative learning refers to a broadening of meaning schemes and perspectives—our habitual ways of creating meaning and interpreting experiences—so that they become more comprehensive, inclusive, and differentiated. The new habits of mind developed in transformative learning are thus capable of creating meaning out of experiences that are increasingly complex and contradictory. Part of this developmental dynamic entails the willingness to considering radical alternatives to one's habitual ways of thinking and acting.

However, where the development of expanded meaning schemes and perspectives to include socialistic forms of thought and practice are concerned, the openness necessary for transformative development is often not present because of the rampant "knee-jerk 'marxophobia'" (McLaren, 1997, p. 172) faced by those who draw, however critically or circumspectly, on socialist traditions. Marxophobia holds that even to mention Marx is to engage in un-American behavior. Despite repeated attempts by all the Frankfurt School theorists to disassociate Marxist analysis from notions of state totalitarianism, popular opinion equates Marx with repression, standardization, bureaucratization, and denial of creativity or liberty. One reason for this, as West (1982) points out, is the immediate association of Marxism with Stalinist centralization. West remarks, "It is no accident that in American lingo Marxism is synonymous with Sovietism. It is as if the only Christianity that Americans were ever exposed to was that of Jerry Falwell's Moral Majority" (p. 139).

TEACHING FOR RADICAL DEVELOPMENT

How might adults be brought to the point of taking seriously collective, cooperative, and socialist forms of social and economic arrangement? One approach to answering this question is to draw on critical theory's formulations. As a body of work, critical theory, particularly that associated with the Frankfurt School, draws on Marx to explore how capitalism and bureaucratic rationality can be challenged and transformed into socialism. From Marx's 11th thesis on Feuerbach (that the point of philosophy is to change the world) onward, it is clear that the theory is full of activist intent. Indeed, as Horkheimer (1995) argued in his essay defining critical theory (first published in 1936), critical theory can only be considered successful if it produces revolutionary change. Theorizing exists so that people can understand the dynamics of political, economic, racial, and cultural oppression. With that understanding they can then began to challenge these dynamics and learn to create new social forms, particularly new conditions of labor, that allow them to express their creativity. So to teach informed by critical theory is, by implication, to teach with a specific social and political intent. Critical theorists intend that their analyses and concepts will help people create social, cultural, and economic forms distinguished by a greater degree of democratic socialism.

Although teaching critically has a transformative impetus, there are noticeable differences in the ways different theorists pursue this. However, one theme—the inevitably directive nature of education—remains constant across all critical theory. Critical teaching begins with developing students' powers of critical thinking so that they can critique the interlocking systems of oppression embedded in contemporary society. Informed by a critical theory perspective, students learn to see that capitalism, bureaucratic rationality, disciplinary power, automaton conformity, one-dimensional thought, and repressive tolerance all combine to exert a powerful ideological sway aimed to ensure the current system stays intact. Critical thinking in this vein is the educational implementation of ideology critique, the deliberate attempt to penetrate the ideological obfuscation that ensures that massive social inequality is accepted by the majority as the natural state of affairs. Adults who learn to conduct this kind of critique are exercising true reason, that is, reason applied to asking universal questions about how we should live. Some of these questions might be: What kind of social organization will help people treat each other fairly and compassionately? How can we redesign work so that it encourages the expression of human creativity? What is the best way to ensure that democratic, participatory control of the means of production and distribution does not ossify into an oligarchy imposing its will on the majority and enforcing it with terror? How will we ensure that no group disproportionately enjoys or controls the resources available to all?

This form of critical thinking is, however, only the beginning of critical theory's educational project. The point of getting people to think critically is to enable them to create true democracy—what Fromm, Marcuse, West, and others regard as the cornerstone of socialism—at both the micro and macro level. If adults think critically in this view they will be demanding worker cooperatives, the abolition of private education, the imposition of income caps, universal access to health care based on need not wealth, and public ownership of corporations and utilities. Critical thinking framed by critical theory is not just a cognitive process. It is a developmental project, inevitably bound up with helping people realize common interests, reject the privatized, competitive ethic of capitalism, and prevent the emergence of inherited privilege.

Development informed by critical theory is, therefore, inherently political. It is political because it is intended to help people learn how to replace the exchange economy of capitalism with truly democratic socialism. It is political because it makes no pretense of neutrality, though it embraces self-criticism. It is political because it is highly directive, practicing, in Baptiste's (2000) terms, a pedagogy of ethical coercion. This politicized emphasis is scattered throughout the history of critical theory. It is there in Marx's (1961) belief that the point of philosophy is to change the world. It is there in Gramsci's (1971) view of the adult educator as a revolutionary party organizer working to direct and persuade the masses to replace ruling-class hegemony with proletarian hegemony. It is there in Marcuse's urging the practice of liberating tolerance that entails exposure only to dissenting viewpoints and in his acknowledgment that clear differences exist between teachers and learners (Marcuse, 1965).

Teaching politically is evident too in West's (1999) conception of the adult educator as a critical organic catalyst galvanizing activists in grassroots oppositional movements. hooks' (1994) recognition of the need for teachers to confront students with the reality and injuries of dominant ideology embodies this directive spirit as does Davis' (1998) insistence that teaching about women's issues such as rape, abortion, access to health care, domestic violence, and sexual harassment cannot be separated from a broader analysis of the destructive effects of capitalism. Foucault's (1980) analysis of how specific intellectuals fight repressive power at specific sites, Fromm's (1956) belief that learners must be taught to realize how individual problems are really produced by structural forces, and Habermas' (1984) urging that educators illuminate how the life world has been invaded by capitalism and bureaucratic rationality—all these indicate the inescapably political nature of critical teaching.

Although critical theorists share a common recognition of the politically directive nature of educational development, they do not advance any kind of methodological orthodoxy to describe how such education should take place. However, four contrasting methodological clusters or emphases are discernible. One of these is the importance of teaching a structuralized worldview, something well conveyed in the title of C. Wright Mills' book *The Sociological Imagination* (1953). In the preface to *One-Dimensional Man* (1964), Marcuse wrote of "the vital importance of the work of C. Wright Mills" (p. xvii) that had successfully interpreted individual experience in terms of broader social and economic forces. A structuralized worldview always analyzes private experiences and personal dilemmas as structurally produced. At root, this idea is grounded in Marx's theory of consciousness with its argument that what seem like instinctive ways of understanding the world—our structures of feeling to use Williams' (1977) phrase—actually reflect the material base of society. This idea recurs throughout critical theory in concepts such as the colonization of the life world, one-dimensional thought, and disciplinary power.

Two theorists who strongly advocate teaching a structuralized worldview are Erich Fromm (1956) and Angela Davis (1998), though to a degree all in critical theory advocate this. Fromm's perspective as a therapist and social psychologist is that adults' intellectual development means they are much better equipped than children to realize that forces external to their own whims and inclinations shape their lives. He feels that adults' accumulated experience of life provides the curricular material that can be analyzed for evidence of the impact of wider social forces. Davis consistently urges that any teaching about women's issues must always illustrate how individual lives are shaped and injured by the workings of capitalism. For her this is crucial to the development of political consciousness and to women's psychological well-being. They learn that what they thought were problems visited on them by an arbitrary fate or the result of personal inadequacy are in fact the predictable outcome of the workings of capitalism and patriarchy. This is a life-saving realization.

A second pedagogical emphasis in critical theory explores the need for abstract, conceptual reasoning—reasoning that can be applied to considering broad questions such as how to organize society fairly or what it means to treat each other ethically. Critical theorists, particularly Marcuse (1964) and Habermas (1987), argue that critical thought is impossible if adults have learned only to focus on particulars, on the immediate features of their lives. For example, people need some basis for comparing the claims of various groups that they should be treated differently because of their history, race, culture, religion, and so on. As long as we live in association with others there has to be restrictions placed on the liberty of those who behave in ways likely to injure others. How we decide what these limits should be is based on some broad concepts of fairness or social well-being. Someone's "right" to smoke a cancer-inducing cigarette cannot be exercised in a small room containing asthma, lung cancer, or emphysema sufferers. So if living socially requires the development of rules of conduct that go beyond individual whims, then we need to be comfortable thinking in broad abstract terms. Deciding which rules should be followed and how these might be established in ways that ensure their general acceptance are matters that require a level of thought beyond that of saying "this is what I want because it works for me in my life." Freedom, fairness, equity, liberation, the ethical use of power—all these "big" ideas are central to the critical tradition and all contain a level of universality entailing the exercise of abstract, conceptual thought.

A third element stressed in some variants of critical theory is the need for adults to become "uncoupled from the stream of cultural givens" to use Habermas' phrase (1990, p. 162). This momentary separation from the demands and patterns of everyday life allows them to view society in a newly critical way. Both Gramsci (1971) and Marcuse (1964) argue that a temporary detachment from social life is a necessary spur to critical thought, with Marcuse conducting a sustained analysis of how separation, privacy, and isolation help people to escape one-dimensional thought. Stephen has argued that this strand of critical theory connects directly to adult educators' concern with self-directed learning and the practices that foster this (Brookfield, 2000b). This element in critical theory receives less contemporary attention probably because privacy is now, as Marcuse admits, a resource available chiefly to the rich. Also, Marcuse's emphasis on how a powerfully estranging, private engagement with a work of art leads to the development of rebellious subjectivity smacks to some of elitism. It also raises the specter of unrestrained individualism, an element of dominant ideology that prompts deep skepticism among many of a critical cast. Collins (1991), for example, has authored a well-framed critique of the individualist and technicist nature of much of what passes for the facilitation of self-directed learning. We depart somewhat from Collins in believing that self-directed learning still offers a valuable language and practice of critique and that it can be interpreted to fit squarely into the radical tradition of adult education.

Cohort groups are another setting for a fourth pedagogic emphasis in critical theory, that of dialogic discussion. Fromm (1956) and Habermas (1987) are the two theorists who emphasize this approach most strongly with both of them viewing a widespread facility with dialogic methods as the guarantee of democracy. Fromm's emphasis on the dance of dialogue in which speakers lose their ego in a selfless attempt to understand the positions advanced by others is very much a forerunner to Habermas' ideal speech situation. Both theorists believe that decisions arrived at through fully participatory, inclusive conversation are the cornerstone of democracy, and both believe education can play a role in teaching adults the dispositions necessary to conduct such conversations.

CONCLUSION

We have argued in this chapter that development is inherently normative and that a radical understanding of development necessarily entails knowing how people develop their own agency in creating the habits of mind, and social and economic forms, of democratic socialism. This is clearly a partisan perspective and one that many readers will take issue with. We have also argued (again) that socialism and democracy are necessarily intertwined and that political without economic democracy is meaningless. To think in these explicitly politicized ways is not usually the manner of developmental psychologists, but for us it is absolutely crucial. Development that is encouraged by educators is always in a certain direction. Even when we profess to be purely nondirective facilitators of self-directed learning who are guided by whatever developmental paths learners choose for themselves, this usually occurs within certain parameters. Who reading this book would unthinkingly work to support a learner who said they had the developmental project of learning to poison others so as to leave no trace of human intervention? Or one who said they wished to develop the skills of building a "dirty" bomb or to develop the technique of smuggling weapons past airport security? Or one who was attempting to develop an educational program to teach people the empirical accuracy of White supremacy? These may be extreme examples for some readers, but we use them to underscore the point that adult development is, at heart, a normative concept. Every educator who works to assist adults develop has a set of preferences, ideals, and desired directions informing their practice, even if these are beneath the surface of practice and even if the educator professes to be value-neutral and only student-centered. You may disagree with the particular normative basis we outline for development, but at least you know exactly what that is.

CHAPTER FOUR

LEARNING IN THE CONTEXT OF TRAINING

We begin this chapter on training by considering the example of Che Guevara. This may seem a strange starting place to begin an analysis of how adults learn in training contexts, but we choose it for two reasons. First, we want to challenge the easy distinction that adult educators often make between education as an inherently enriching process that is partly under learners' control and training as the narrow inculcation of predetermined skills by an authoritarian figure or agency. Second, we want to show that even in what might be considered some of the most rigid conditions for training (such as the military and political training of anticolonial combatants), co-learning principles of a democratic nature are at the heart of the endeavor. In Guevara's case, not even the harsh conditions of military combat justified giving up on a training regime he described as shared learning. The role of the trainer in Guevara's pedagogy is not one of merely inculcating narrow skills, although this is for certain a part of the process, but one that also includes being trained by the trainee in order to become a better trainer and to be exemplary in one's conduct.

By the summer of 1965 in Cuba and in circles that followed events in the island nation, it was clear that something was up with Comandante Ernesto Che Guevara. He had not been seen in public for an unusually long period for a major figure. By the time that wild rumors began to circulate about his whereabouts, he and a group of about 120 Cubans were a few months into the first of his two major international guerrilla training missions, this one in what was then called the Republic of the Congo (now called the

Democratic Republic of the Congo). This mission had come about as a result of Guevara's diplomatic trip to Africa in February and March of 1965 where African anticolonial liberation movement leaders reiterated their requests for military supplies and training from the revolutionary government of Cuba. Since one of the pedagogical principles of Che Guevara was that the most effective learning is learning in action (Guevara, 2000), he insisted that African liberation fighters be trained not in institutes or in the countryside of Cuba, but on the battlefields of their own colonized nations. As was characteristic of Guevara, since he suggested this idea, he decided that he should be the one to carry it out.

By August of 1965, four months into the training mission, it was becoming apparent that for a number of reasons, the training mission was not going well. Rumblings of frustration were growing among the ranks of the Cuban trainers. In response, Guevara (2000) drew from the experience of his training work of the previous eight years to write a lengthy memorandum to his fellow trainers. In part the memo read:

> Our experience must be transmitted in one form or another to the fighters; the urge to teach should be paramount—not in a haughtily pedantic manner, but with the human warmth that goes with shared learning. Revolutionary modesty should guide our political work and be one of our basic weapons, complemented by a spirit of sacrifice that is an example not only to the Congolese comrades but also to the weakest of our own men . . . . Finally, we should not forget that we know only a tiny part of what we ought to know. We have to learn about the Congo in order to attach ourselves to the Congolese comrades; but we also have to learn the things we lack in general culture and even the art of warfare, without thinking that we are know-alls or that it is all we are required to know . . . . Our primary function is to educate people for combat . . . . This is achieved when the teacher can be taken as a model for the students to follow. (pp. 73–74)

In the United States, by the time the Cuban revolution triumphed on January 1, 1959, Septima Clark and Bernice Robinson at the Highlander Folk School in Tennessee were already in their fifth year of training teachers to conduct what the first students and literacy worker in 1956 had named Citizenship Schools (Horton and

Freire, 1990). These schools, like the national literacy campaign in Cuba of 1961, were a part of a larger liberation struggle. Among African Americans in the U.S., this struggle would come to be called the Civil Rights Movement or the Freedom Movement. As the Freedom Movement developed, the Student Nonviolent Coordinating Committee (SNCC) created what it called Freedom Schools and Community Centers as a part of its 1964 Freedom Summer project in Mississippi.

For those schooled in the canonical texts of the field of adult education today, it might come as a surprise that those involved in the formation of the Citizenship Schools and the Freedom Schools saw no contradictions in describing their work in the development of teachers for these schools, as well as the education that went on in them, as training. Septima Clark (1962, 1964, 1996) clearly saw her work with teachers and the work those teachers did with students in the Citizenship Schools as a form of participatory and democratic training. Her hope was that this would develop local leadership that would advance the interests of communities along with the demands of the broader Freedom Movement. SNCC also saw and labeled its work with the Freedom Schools and Community Centers as training ("Mississippi Freedom School Curriculum," 1991). By today's adult education standards, the participatory and democratic pedagogy employed in the formation of teachers and in the actual work of schools for the Freedom Movement would hardly fit within the definitions that are now employed to describe training. One could even think that it would be insulting to describe as merely "training" the rich and exemplary pedagogical practice of the African American Freedom Movement; yet those who developed this practice seemed to have no qualms about using the terms *education* and *training* interchangeably to describe their work.

In recent decades, the term *training* has suffered a downgrading to the point that, as Edmée Ollagnier (2005) says in the *International Encyclopedia of Adult Education*, "many adult educators in North America . . . avoid using the word" (p. 619). We are not surprised by this statement when we consider the generally narrow and restricted notions of training that are reflected in the field's canonical texts. These notions do not, however, reflect the rich history of participatory and democratic training practices in the radical tradition.

DEFINING AND DEBATING TRAINING

In this section we turn first to a review of contemporary definitions of training and discuss the unfortunate narrowing of what is generally considered to be training today. We then turn to a number of historical and contemporary examples of training within the radical tradition. As we will see below, in the radical tradition, training is not conceived so narrowly, and in fact we can find numerous examples where training and education are synonyms for the democratic and participatory form of education we see at the core of the radical tradition. We conclude the chapter with a thematic summary of what we consider to be training within and for a democratic socialist adult education project.

A good place to start teasing out the prevailing definitions of training is with the most recently published handbook in the field, the *Handbook of Adult and Continuing Education* (Wilson and Hayes, 2000). Like the 1989 *Handbook*, yet unlike most previous *Handbooks*, there is no chapter with the word "training" in the title. Moreover, in the latest *Handbook*, training on its own is not given a separate listing in the index; if you want to find the word training in the index, you must look under "vocational training" or "workplace training." The field's notion of training has become so narrowed and undesirable that even human resource development professionals, at least those represented in the *Handbook* (Bierema, 2000; Fenwick, 2000), seem reluctant to use the term *training* in preference for "workplace learning" or "organizational learning." Two other major texts in the field similarly reflect narrow definitions of training. Merriam and Brockett's (2007) *The Profession and Practice of Adult Education*, outside of a brief mentioning that Highlander has "a long history of training community activists" (p. 21), confines its few uses of the term *training* to activities in the workplace. In the mere four-paragraph subsection ("Training and Development") specifically devoted to training—and only workplace-based training—we read "while some adult educators embrace the notion of training as a part of their identity, others have eschewed it" (p. 151). Similarly, Merriam, Caffarella, and Baumgartner's (2007) *Learning in Adulthood*, the field's major comprehensive text on learning, also confines its few uses of the term *training* to discussion of the workplace.

the *International Encyclopedia of Adult Education* mentioned above also tells us that

> Training is the procedure whereby knowledge is transmitted with an instrumental and operational vision of the learning process and of its expected results. Training is usually related to achieving precise objectives. . . . [T]raining has been mostly related to the world of work. . . . Many adult educators see training as the opposite of education. (Ollagnier, 2005, pp. 618–619)

A similar definition of training and its contrast to education is also present in Peter Jarvis' (2002) *International Dictionary of Adult and Continuing Education*: "A planned and systematic sequence of instruction under supervision, designed to impart skills, knowledge, information and attitudes. Frequently contrasted to education and used with reference to *vocational education*" (p. 187).

The strong connection between the workplace and training is not new in the field; the first *Handbook* from 1934 has a chapter titled "Training by Corporations." The restriction of the use of the term *training* almost exclusively to the workplace and the reluctance of being associated with the term are, however, a more recent development. Who would want to be associated with the term when in the second sentence of the *International Encyclopedia* entry on training a reference is made to its application to animals? If we go back a few decades within the major texts of the field, we begin to see a period in which the very definition of training was under discussion, a discussion that, as we see it, was carried through to its current-day conclusion by the heavy influence of the neoliberal political economy on the orientation of the field toward workplace learning driven by employer needs over employee needs. We will have more to say about this below, but first let us take a look for a moment at the debates over the definition of the term itself.

Darkenwald and Merriam's (1982) *Adult Education: Foundations of Practice*, the forerunner to Merriam and Brockett's *The Profession and Practice of Adult Education* mentioned above, like the other texts discussed thus far, confines the discussion of training to organizations, and by organizations, they generally mean places of employment. The text does, however, offer insight into the debates over the definition of training in the 1970s and 1980s by providing two conflicting perspectives on the nature of training. What we can call the narrow definition of training, the dominant definition today (and the one generally "eschewed" by adult educators) is associated with the ideas of Thomas Patten (1971) and Leonard Nadler (1970). Darkenwald and Merriam (1982) write, "Patten views education as socialization and 'thus outside the purview of organizations'" (p. 65) and that he regards training "as the 'formal procedure which is used to facilitate employee learning so that their resultant behavior contributes to the organization's objectives'" (p. 65). They summarize Nadler's ideas on training, education, and development by stating that training consists of activities designed to improve a worker's performance in the job they have. In contrast to training, Nadler argues that education prepares workers for different jobs than the ones they have now, and development consists of activities that allow for the workers to move at the pace, goals, and desires of the organization (p. 65). Darkenwald and Merriam (1982) then contrast these exclusionary definitions of training versus education with Charles Watson's (1979) insistence on using training and education synonymously, since "people act as integrated beings, whose knowledge, skills, and attitudes are interrelated and inseparable. To make a distinction between training and education is to ignore these interrelationships" (pp. 64–65). Michael Collins (1991) also comments on the need for a broader definition of training, comments with which we are in general agreement. For Collins, to argue that training and education are "antithetical is fallacious and unhelpful" (p. 87). Both "education and training are concerned with the systematic development of individuals and communities. Their purposes and processes overlap" (p. 87).

The debate over the distinctions between training and education was also evident in the 1970s. In *Philosophical Concepts and Values in Adult Education,* Ken Lawson (1979) makes the argument that learning widely generalized principles distinguishes education from training. In Lawson's example, an engineer who has learned the general principles of a machine or structure that can be applied to other machines or structures has been educated. A mechanic who has merely learned how to operate a specific machine for which the knowledge learned is limited to the operation of this specific machine has been trained. With this definition, it is not the subject matter in question that distinguishes education and training but whether or not general principles rather than operational steps are being learned. The other distinction Lawson makes concerns values. Education implies a set of humanistic social values embedded in the process. Hence, learning the general principles of torture so that one could apply methods of torture in multiple situations is not education, but training. For Lawson, the values that justify training are separate from the actual training process; this is not the case with education.

In a response to Lawson's text and other emerging distinctions being made between education and teaching and training, Jane Thompson (1976) published an article titled "The Concept of Training and its Current Distortion." Summarizing the problem with these distinctions she comments that

> We might thus caricature this model of the conceptual relationship between teaching and training as the broad avenue called Teaching, with its intrinsic interest, variety and underlying planning principles, gradually narrowing and becoming the repetitive, monotonous, featureless Training street. Somewhere along the way the traveler crosses over a boundary, leaving Education for some poorer realm. (p. 146)

Among adult educators at the time, however, she notes that "examples of the close juxtaposition of the terms training and education or training and teaching abound in common use without any hint of incompatibility or the superiority of one over the other" (p. 147). This, we should add, is generally what we find in examples from training and education in social movements. Thompson argues that the methods and content of teaching and training can be the same and that the only distinctions between training and teaching are in the fact that "the striving to bring about an understanding of principles so central to the teaching concept is incidental to training" (p. 151) where we cannot speak of a process of "discovery" but more in terms of working "toward a goal outlined in advance" (p. 151). Moreover, the idea of a predetermined goal has to do with the fact that "training is for mastery of a selection of pursuits, and selection is a limiting process" (p. 152). The process of limiting, however, is only in terms of the specific goals of training and does not refer to the possible range of methods or content for the training process. Simply put, Thompson argues that the only distinction between teaching and training is that "the central task of teaching is achieving the understanding of principles" while "the central task of training is achieving mastery of action" (p. 153).

So where do we stand on this debate? How do we define training? While we would agree with Thompson's rejection of training as somehow lesser and narrower than teaching and agree that method or content do not distinguish them, we question the distinctions based on principles. In our reflections on training in social movements, we find that an understanding of principles is central to and linked to the "mastery of action." We would agree with Thompson that training has to do with the mastery of action, but we would argue that radical training as we are outlining it in this chapter can be conceived as actually less narrow than most mainstream definitions of teaching, precisely *because* it is about mastery of action. This because radical training combines theory and practice or mastery of principles and mastery of action in a way that sees these two in dialectical relationship. Mainstream definitions of teaching can conceive of mastery of principles in a scholastic sense, without any necessary implementation or mastery in action. In the radical tradition this is nonsensical. It was not enough, for example, in the African American Freedom Movement to train people merely to master the action of voting. In the earliest efforts on Johns Island, South Carolina, that led to the first Citizenship School, Alice Wine memorized the laws and sections of the state constitution dealing with voting and successfully passed the examination designed to prevent African Americans from registering to vote (Clark, 1996, p. 46). This mastery of action, however, was not enough for those who envisioned the Citizenship Schools. The point was to master the actions necessary for voter registration, but at the same time to master the principles of citizenship.

EXAMPLES OF RADICAL TRAINING

The relationship between principle and action in radical training will become more evident as we turn to descriptions of examples of radical training.

We can begin this section with a more detailed description of training for and in the African American Freedom Movement's Citizenship Schools. For Septima Clark (1964), the purpose of the Citizenship Schools was "discovering and developing of local community leaders" (p. 118) who would be "trained to carry on an ever growing program of community development" (p. 118). Clark understood that local communities throughout the South had leadership, but this leadership generally needed training in order to build the emerging Freedom Movement from the local level outward. In 1961 the Southern Christian Leadership Conference (SCLC) agreed with Highlander Folk School to take over the training program for the Citizenship Schools. In a memo titled *Leadership Training Program and Citizenship Schools*, SCLC head, Martin Luther King, Jr. (n.d.) makes clear that literacy training for citizenship should go beyond the mastery of action of successfully learning to read and write for voter registration. For him, literacy training required a mastery of the various interrelated principles of a sociopolitical economic nature that determined the conditions of the African American citizenry of the South.

> In order that the Negro in all walks of life may achieve and enjoy the full benefits of citizenship it has been found necessary that full understanding through training be placed at his disposal. The use of the ballot effectively requires a systematic knowledge of politics. To safeguard civil rights necessitates understanding government and those who control it. To protect and improve jobs, wages, working conditions, business opportunities, the use of borrowed money demands an understanding of the economics of living. To protect civil, public and private rights, a knowledge of common and statutory law is required. To break down the barriers of segregation, to destroy the institutions of prejudice, to successfully apply mass direct action through picketing and boycotting a knowledge of these techniques is desirable. To affect the social change by protest necessary to achieve full citizenship a full understanding of nonviolence and its application must be learned. (p. 1)

Clearly, what Clark and others called training in Citizenship Schools went far beyond a narrow and restricted instrumental use of literacy skills for successful voter registration. This robust training was present both in the schools themselves and in the training of the teachers who trained within them.

In her book *Echo in My Soul,* Clark (1962) gives a description of the residential workshops developed at Highlander and later conducted for the SCLC at the Dorchester Center in McIntosh, Georgia. About 40 people would be invited for about one week. Workshops began by collectively defining a community problem at hand and gathering as many facts as possible on the topic from participants, particularly facts that related to the problem as it played out in each participant's local context. Once the problem was defined, the overall goal of the workshop was to develop locally based solutions to the problem. The idea was "to develop a plan of action that if put into operation would provide solutions, and to arouse the participants to the necessity of returning to their homes and initiating *immediately* the beginning phases of such a plan of action" (p. 183). Some local problems were fairly universal and local solutions could be applied elsewhere; the workshops could at times develop replicable strategies for solving a problem with similar manifestations in multiple localities.

The workshops were normally scheduled with general, large-group sessions in the mornings and smaller group meetings in the afternoon. The smaller sessions centered on specific problems and tended to be more informal. The general sessions often involved discussions of issues raised in the smaller meetings or carried over from the previous day's activities. The evenings usually consisted of a guest lecture, a film, or music and singing. All of these were intended to be relevant to the overall topic of the workshop. The vision of the workshops was one of mastery of action (technique) and of principles. As Clark (1962) said, "From our workshops, community leaders have returned to their home communities to find and train other leaders in techniques that bring success" (p. 188). Beyond technique, they also learned mastery of principles of voting rights and leadership development. "They come home knowing *how*. . . . Highlander has trained leaders who in turn go into their home communities and train their people" (p. 188).

In terms of literacy pedagogy, all the methods employed in the workshops (such as singing, role playing, speaking, and use of multimedia) were intended to model for teachers how they could use them in their own citizenship teaching (Clark, 1964). Dorothy

Cotton, who became the director of Citizenship School Teacher Training when it was moved to SCLC, provides an account of a particular pedagogical technique in a letter describing the program (Cotton, 1961). The letter describes how two types of teaching were practiced by the workshop. In the first example, the group was taught about habeas corpus by the teacher presenting a definition of it in lecture format. In the second example, the teacher wrote leadership on the board and elicited a discussion on what the participants thought was good leadership. Then the teacher presented a specific community issue of the need for a hospital and asked the group to develop a leadership plan for successfully bringing a hospital to the community.

> Because the class participated and determined through their own thinking, discussion and participation they had a greater perception of what leadership was all about. Afterwards, we pointed up the difference between our presentation of the term habeas corpus and leadership. The class was really excited about their new realization of the most effective way to teach. (p. 2)

After participating in a residential workshop, post-workshop training consisted of follow-up with the results of local work. Clark (1962) believed that the "follow-up programs . . . [were] of greatest importance and value, because they reach down to the grassroots" (p. 191).

The combination of theory (principles) and practice (action) was also evident in the actual Citizenship Schools. Literacy skills were taught by drawing on locally generated materials and on materials of a more universal interest that were developed by those who oversaw the teacher training at Highlander and later at SCLC. The classes generally ran for a three-month period meeting two evenings per week. According to a Highlander memo from 1960, the unity of theory and practice was built into the program through "classroom instruction, which is practiced continuously in the community" (p. 2). Charles Payne (1995) describes how the Citizenship Schools' evaluation form reflected the fact that the schools were as much about training leaders and activists as teaching literacy. The evaluation form asked such questions as: "Has the graduate been instrumental in getting others to vote? Engaged in demonstrations? Become more effective in community action? Worked for an unselfish cause? Rendered more help to his or her neighbors?" (p. 331). Well before the Brazilian pedagogue Paulo Freire coined the phrase "reading the word and the world" to describe this type of literacy training, the African American Freedom Movement had developed it and understood it in these terms. In an SCLC report on the Citizenship Schools, Dorothy Cotton (1963) underscores the unity of principles and actions in the training that went on in the Citizenship Schools.

> [A] reading lesson in a citizenship class is much more than learning words and sentences. Citizenship training seeks to prepare an adult to understand his community, what makes it function as it does and to help him [sic] share intelligently in his community life . . . . The adult student in the citizenship class is learning to read, but at the same time he is gaining a knowledge of his community and how he can participate in a way that seeks to deal with his own problems. (p. 1)

Clark (1996) reports that in just the period from 1962 to 1965, when SCLC joined forces with the Congress of Racial Equality (CORE), the National Association for the Advancement of Colored People (NAACP), the Urban League, and SNCC in the Voter Education Project, nearly 10,000 teachers were trained. The Citizenship Schools, according to Andrew Young, laid the foundation for the expansion and success of the whole Civil Rights Movement (as cited in Clark, 1996, p. 70).

Instrumental in encouraging SNCC to join forces with the other organizations that made up the Voter Education Project was lifelong organizer and activist Ella Baker (Ransby, 2003, p. 269). Baker understood and argued for the idea that voter registration did not necessarily derail SNCC from its commitment to direct action, but rather would help SNCC build local power through organizing around voter registration. As Payne (1995) puts it, to be successful at voter registration "Baker argued [that] . . . activists had to form relationships, build trust, and engage in a democratic process of decision-making together with community members. The goal was to politicize the community and empower ordinary people" (p. 270). This knowledge flowed from Baker's decades-long experience as an organizer and leader of several organizations dating back to her days in New York City in the 1930s. These organizations included, among others, the Harlem Adult Education Experiment, the Young Negroes Cooperative League, the Works Progress Administration's (WPA) Consumer Education Project, NAACP, and SCLC. Throughout her work in these various organizations, Baker developed and advocated a form of training based on what Ransby (2003) calls a "popular democratic pedagogy . . . [emphasizing] the importance of tapping oppressed communities knowledge, strength, and leadership in constructing models for social change" (p. 74).

A democratic and participatory form of training was at the heart of Ella Baker's work. What bothered Baker about many organizations was that they emphasized mobilizing over organizing. For Baker mobilizing involved putting people on the streets or getting people to a rally. This type of activity, while necessary in social movements, could be done through glitzy advertising-type work, demagogic populism, or the charisma of a messianic leader. Mobilizing lacked precisely the pedagogical and the participatory elements that defined organizing. Baker saw organizing as a developmental or pedagogical process whereby people themselves learned to critically understand their situations and to take increasing control over the relations and institutions that impacted their own lives (Payne, 1989). Organizing, however, did not take place spontaneously; it required a particular leadership that was also pedagogical. While Baker (1980) argued that "strong people don't need strong leaders" (p. 53), this did not mean that leadership was not important. Baker (1960) advocated for what she called "*group-centered leadership*, rather than . . . *a leader-centered group pattern of organization*" (p. 4, italics in original). A group-centered leader was a democratic and participatory trainer who put the development of the organization and the individuals in the organization at the center of their leadership. In other words, as Payne (1995) says, for Baker "leadership should be a form of teaching, where the leader's first responsibility is to develop the leadership potential in others" (p. 93).

Baker's ideas on leadership and training can perhaps best be seen in her work as director of branches of the NAACP in the 1940s. With the theme of "Give Light and the People Will Find the Way," Baker developed leadership training conferences for activists in the local branches of the organization (Grant, 1998). Baker's main strategy for training was to help local activists identify and build organizing campaigns around issues of local importance, provide local activists with organizing strategies, and help local activists understand how their local issues had connections to wider, regional, national, and even international issues (Payne, 1995). Payne states that Baker's leadership training conferences "were both skill-enhancing and consciousness-raising" (p. 89); or in the terms we are using here, they emphasized dialectical mastery of action and of principle. It was important for Baker (as cited in Grant, 1998, pp. 228–229) that through training, leaders grow closer to and gain a greater understanding of their communities while also coming to understanding that their primary role as leaders was to develop the capacities of others.

Baker's ideas on training and organizing were also evident during her work with SCLC even though she disagreed with the organization's leader-centered focus. In an October 1959 memo to the SCLC leadership, Baker outlined a plan for what she called a Crusade for Citizenship. The idea of the crusade had four main components. First, it could use SCLC's resources to seek out and support already existing local leaders in the South. Second, it could recruit ministers throughout the South for door-to-door voter registration canvassing. Baker estimated that 1,000 ministers working 8 hours per month for 10 months could reach 300,000 people. Third, the crusade could recruit women, church groups, and sororities for a literacy campaign that would provide local people with necessary literacy skills for social action. Fourth, the crusade could create teams to conduct training in nonviolent resistance techniques in local areas (Payne, 1995, pp. 94–95).

There are striking similarities between Baker's proposed crusade and that of the 1980 Sandinista National Literacy Crusade in Nicaragua. First, and most obviously, both used the term *crusade* to denote the mass nature of the endeavor. Second, both crusades were directed at using training and education for building capacities at the local level. Third, both crusades saw the training of local people and local leaders as a necessary form of decentralizing popular power and for creating and maintaining social change.

The Sandinista National Literacy Crusade came on the heels of the triumph of the Sandinista Revolution in July of 1979. The social transformations of the revolution opened up new opportunities and new challenges for poor and rural people. They were suddenly faced with a situation in which they could exert much greater control over the social relations and institutions that governed their reality. Land reform gave landless peasants an opportunity to gain control over the land they worked and the conditions of their work. These new rights, however, also required new skills. They needed to know, for example, the various financial, administrative, and agronomy skills of running an agricultural cooperative (Arnove, 1986). The literacy crusade was developed with precisely these challenges and opportunities in mind. As two of the planners put it, the crusade "was designed to help Nicaraguans acquire the skills, understanding, and empathy necessary for participation in a society undergoing rapid transformation" (Cardenal and Miller, 1981, p. 3). Skills and understanding or mastery of action and mastery of principles were at the heart of the literacy crusade. This was perhaps clearest in the training of literacy workers where the "primary purpose . . . was to have people master the materials and methods while developing skills necessary to solve social problems creatively and sensitively" (p. 21).

The planners also saw the literacy crusade as an example of the decentralization of power whereby the masses of people themselves would take increasing command of a major social institution or public service such as education. That is why, not unlike the Citizenship Schools, the then vice minister of education in Nicaragua saw the literacy crusade as a political project with pedagogical implications, not a pedagogical project with political implications (as cited in Hirshon, 1983, p. 7). This was evident in the fact that after the literacy crusade ended, classes continued with the most capable literacy students taking over the role of the *brigadista* (literacy worker), now named coordinator, and the classes were held under the new name of Collectives of Popular Sandinista Education (CEPS). In a particular region, a coordinator would be chosen to become a promoter among the region's coordinators. The promoter would act as a conduit between the region and the national organizational structure of education.

This was a way for the people themselves to begin to take control of their own education (Hirshon, 1983; Torres, 1983).

The Sandinista National Literacy Crusade was truly a historic phenomenon. According to the Centro de Investigaciones y Estudios de la Reforma Agraria (1984), between March 23 and August 23, 1980, 406,056 illiterate Nicaraguans learned how to read and write by working with 119,556 literacy workers who were trained in 4 months. In other words, in about 9 months over 100,000 literacy workers were trained and over 400,000 people were taught to read and write at a basic level. If we combine the literacy workers and students to come up with a figure of 500,000, we can say that this crusade directly involved just over 20 percent of the total Nicaraguan population of the time of about 2.4 million people. That would be the equivalent of mobilizing over 60 million people in the United States today.

In order to train over 100,000 literacy workers or brigadistas in 4 months, a very innovative, participatory co-training method was developed. Valerie Miller (1985) describes how 80 teachers and university students were trained by the 7 members of the National Training Team during a 2-week session followed by a one-month practicum and then one week of evaluation and planning. This group of 80 then trained 630 teachers and university students in a 2-week session. These 630 trained 11,000 teachers and 1,000 university students, and then these 12,000 trained 125,000 primary school, secondary school, and university students over 12 years of age to be brigadistas. This decentralized Training Multiplier Model allowed for rapid training of large numbers of literacy workers, allowed for those trained to gain practical experience through their role of trainers of the larger groups that followed them, allowed for a co-training model in which the trainee/trainer role was quickly reversed, and allowed for training to take place throughout the country in the various regions were literacy work would actually take place (p. 108).

The brigadista training employed participatory and democratic methods that the planners called a "pedagogy of shared responsibility" (Cardenal and Miller, 1981, p. 21). The "role of the workshop director was one of facilitator . . . that involved motivating, inspiring, challenging, and working with the participants who were encouraged to become active problem solvers"

(p. 21). The pedagogy of shared responsibility was designed to "enhance the initiative and imagination with which people acquire and apply knowledge" (p. 21). Common training strategies were "simulations, role playing, group discussions, debates, murals, poetry, drawing, songs, and some artistic forms of expression from Nicaraguan folklore" (p. 21). Like the training pedagogy of Septima Clark and Bernice Robinson, the literacy crusade planners used techniques that modeled participatory and democratic training practices that the brigidistas would use once they began their own literacy work. Given the time constraints of trying to eliminate or at least drastically reduce the 50 percent illiteracy rate in one year, the crusade planners might have thought a narrow and trainer-centered methodology would have been most efficient, but they did the opposite and were able to reduce illiteracy to about 12 percent in less than one year winning the UNESCO Krupskaya Prize for Literacy in 1980.

We can find more recent examples of democratic and participatory training in Latin America in the region's largest social movement, the *Movimento dos Trabalhadores Rurais Sem Terra* (MST) or Brazil's Landless Workers Movement. The MST began in 1984 and centers on peasants and rural workers (who are homeless, landless, or poor) occupying and cultivating unused or underutilized land in Brazil. Under the banner of "occupy, produce, resist" the MST establishes encampments on land and begins the process of establishing all the necessary social, political, and economic institutions for a sustainable rural cooperative settlement. According to the organization's English-version website (www .mstbrazil.org), the movement currently involves approximately 1.5 million members in over 2,000 settlements. These settlements are complex alternative social institutions with democratic political structures, schools, health clinics and other social services, cooperative housing arrangements, and cooperative agricultural production and distribution. The settlements stand as functioning alternatives to capitalist sociopolitical economic arrangements.

Since landless and poor rural Brazilians involved in MST settlements are solely responsible for the success of the settlements, education and training are an integral part of the movement. People who have never built housing or run an agricultural cooperative or a school must learn the necessary skills to do so.

Moreover, cooperative forms of living and governance reign in the settlements, and people must also become trained in the theory and practice of cooperative forms of organization. As Marta Harnecker (2002) makes clear, a significant part of MST training is informal: embedded in the actual practice or actions of the movement itself. Through cultivating occupied land and building and organizing settlements, people learn and grow. The mere act of cutting down a fence that encloses long-fallow land and arguing one's rights to the land, for example, trains people in principles that challenge the grossly unjust distribution of rural land in Brazil. The basic unit of the land occupations is groups of families. These groups must collectively form commissions and work teams that are responsible for the settlement's social infrastructure (Harnecker, 2002, p. 45). These family groups form larger coordinating bodies made up of leaders of each family group. General assemblies are the maximum decision-making body of the settlements. The principles that govern the settlements are democracy, participation by everyone in decision making, division of labor, and collective leadership (p. 46). By taking over the land and organizing themselves to maintain and build their settlement, the MST are trained not only in agricultural vocational skills but also in the science and business of agriculture and the principles of collective decision making and participatory democracy.

The MST also engages in extensive training of teachers for the numerous schools in the MST settlements. As Roseli Salete Caldart says, training is "a process through which educators develop the social, political and technical skills necessary for their creative participation in transformatory action" (as cited in Kane, 2001, p. 100). Liam Kane (2001, p. 100) provides a description of the MST's two-and-a-half-year teacher training program. The training is highly participatory and democratic while still being rigorous and demanding. From the very start, participants form a cooperative. The cooperative, in coordination with the trainers, takes responsibility for housing and domestic tasks, the curriculum, the timetable for the training, assessment, and organizing commercial ventures, generally through MST-produced agricultural products that will help fund the training. The last stage of the training consists in an individually conducted research project that must provide the MST with useful knowledge to advance the movement in some way, while giving the students practice in research, writing, and presentation skills (p. 100). Teachers are trained democratically in the mastery of teaching skills and the mastery of democratic and participatory pedagogical and social organization principles.

The MST slogan of "occupy, produce, resist" has been recently taken up by laid-off factory workers in Argentina. These workers have occupied and restarted their workplaces shut down and abandoned by their former employers. This movement of cooperatively run recovered workplaces in Argentina was the subject of the 2004 documentary *The Take* produced and directed by Avi Lewis and Naomi Klein. In the recovered factory movement in Argentina, we find forms and conceptualizations of workplace training qualitatively broader than the narrowly defined workplace training that currently prevails in the field of North American adult education. As we mentioned above, the concept of training was gradually taken over in the 1980s by what is now commonly called neoliberal ideology. The premise of neoliberalism is that market relations should govern all aspects of human interaction, including all social services. Education, health care, social security, the post office, disaster relief and recovery, roads, parks, and all other government services should be run privately for profit. For workplaces, the watchword of neoliberalism is flexibility. Workers should be prepared (trained) for a work world in which the only stability is instability. Workers need to be flexible in their outlook, expectations, and skill set so that they can meet the ever-changing needs and demands of employers (Mojab, 2001). Training in this paradigm is of, by, and for management.

The Argentine recovered factory movement has turned all of this upside-down. Argentina, like other Latin American countries, was an early testing ground for neoliberal economic policies through the U.S.-backed dictatorships that welcomed U.S. neoliberal economic advisors and their ideas in the 1970s and 1980s (Harvey, 2005). These policies, now increasingly under scrutiny in the region, led to what can only be described as an economic meltdown in Argentina in 2001. The economy and government ground to a halt, and millions of workers found themselves with workplaces shut down and abandoned by their employers. In response to this crisis, a number of workers began to organize to reoccupy their workplaces and run them themselves. The movement currently includes about 170 recovered workplaces, ranging from factories to hotels to newspapers, involving about 10,000 workers (Lewis and Klein, 2007).

Like the MST, a significant portion of training that takes place among the recovered factory movement is of an informal nature and stems from the activities of the movement itself. Modifying Griff Foley's (1999) term of "learning in action" to describe learning in social movements, we can call this "training in action." As Lewis and Klein (2007) argue, "workers in this movement are politicized *by* the struggle, which begins with the most basic imperative: workers want to work, to feed their families" (p. 11). Occupying a factory, like occupying land, challenges the principle of private property and poses the alternative principle that factories belong to those who work in them. Mastering this political principle requires rigorous and sustained learning. So, beyond the specific skills that are needed in cooperative management, marketing, and product distribution, the recovered factory workers need training in this political principle. By embarking on takeovers of their abandoned workplaces, these workers are rewriting the principle of private ownership for one of collective ownership (The Lavaca Collective, 2007, p. 35). They are providing an alternative system of economic production and distribution as the recovered workplaces begin to form their own supply and distribution networks. Moreover, they are being trained in the principle that they can run the workplaces themselves. At one factory, for example, "one worker remembers the hardest thing he had to face . . . . was convincing his co-workers that they were perfectly capable of running the factory themselves . . . . Being their own bosses gave the workers a new image of themselves" (p. 43).

A further principle that is being rewritten by these workers is that bosses are not only unnecessary, but they are, in their opinion, a cost burden to production. In the Lavaca Collective's view, "through the experience of worker management, the workers have discovered the real reason behind their companies' bankruptcies . . . . : what bankrupts them are employer costs" (The Lavaca Collective, 2007, p. 40). When the workers run factories successfully with greater productivity and higher wages, all the employer costs prove to be unnecessary (p. 41). The almost unthinkable question that this raises for contemporary adult education is whether we can imagine workplace training without bosses? The Argentineans in the recovered workplaces can, and they implement it. Here we have training of, by, and for employees. This is no longer a question of if and when management's ideas for human resource development coincide with employees' needs (Schied, Carter, and Howell, 2001). It is the workers who, after debating "strategy and business deals, account balances, and legal tactics" (a form of informal worker self-training), determine if it is necessary to "bring in advisors . . . to explain technical issues" (The Lavaca Collective, 2007, p. 39). But the final decision to do this or not is in the hands of the workers themselves (p. 39). In one of the factories, the workers have gone so far as to establish an accredited school in metalworking training, and in many other recovered workplaces, the workplace becomes a center of community life (p. 42).

Worker-oriented training as briefly described here in the Argentinean case is not unheard of in the field of adult education in the U.S.; it is in fact a part of the radical tradition that we see as the historical legacy of the field itself. And while it has been pushed to the margins, contemporary examples in the U.S. can be found in, among other places, workers centers (Fine, 2006) and progressive trade unions (Peres and Raab, 2007). Historically, we can see examples in labor colleges (Altenbaugh, 1990) and the Highlander Folk School (Horton and Freire, 1990). Interestingly, the hegemony of employer interests in workplace training is even beginning to come under scrutiny from within the subfield of human resource development with the emergence of critical perspectives within HRD (Fenwick, 2005).

CONCLUSION

In the early 1990s, when John Holst was active in the then newly formed union of adult basic educators at City Colleges of Chicago (CCC), one of the first contract demands of the union was to change our job title from training specialist to adult educator. We collectively felt that training specialist was insulting and lessened the value of our work; we thought of ourselves as educators not trainers. We had internalized the narrow and restricted notions of "trainer" and "training" then and now prevalent in the field.

Training does not, however, have to be a narrow, restricted, and "poorer realm" that educators eschew or avoid like the 1,600 training specialists did at CCC. As we have tried to show here, the field is abundant with training work in its history and contemporary practice far richer than much of the mainstream practice that passes as education or teaching today. When we consider these radical training practices we find the following themes:

- Training is the mastery of action (practice) and the mastery of principle (theory) conceived dialectically.
- A central element is affective and relational—building the skills, understanding, and confidence of people.
- A significant amount of training takes place in the actual activities of social movements; it is training in action.
- Training is a mutual relationship where both the trainer and the trainee are trained.
- Training is participatory and democratic in its methodology.
- Training is not neutral.
  - It is oriented to serving the needs of specific sectors of society.
  - It attempts to advance social change activism toward a more participatory and democratic society.
  - It is, therefore, as much a political act as it is a pedagogical act.

CHAPTER FIVE

PLANNING EDUCATIONAL PROGRAMS
Principles, Goals, and Evaluation

When asked what makes for a radical education, Myles Horton, cofounder of the Highlander Folk School, responded with the following:

> If I had to put a finger on what I consider . . . a good *radical* education, it wouldn't be anything about methods or techniques. It would be loving people first. If you don't do that, Che Guevara says, there's no point in being a revolutionary . . . . And then next is respect for people's abilities to learn and to act and to shape their own lives . . . . The third thing grows out of caring for people and having respect for people's ability to do things, and that is that you value their experiences." (Horton and Freire, 1990, p. 177)

These ideas by Horton are important to us for two reasons. First, it is noteworthy that Horton puts the principle of love before methods or techniques. We agree with him and believe that principles such as love not only come before technique, but, as is implied in Horton's response, frame subsequent methods and techniques. As we argue throughout this book, certain dispositional, political, and ideological principles are central to the actual practice of adult education, if not to the formalized theories of adult education. Generally, formalized theory and writing in adult education tends to shy away from these principles so as not to seem partisan. This stance, as should be clear by now, for us is itself partisan and tends toward the maintenance of whatever taken-for-granted notions prevail in any given social setting. In this chapter on program planning we will be openly partisan.

The existing literature on program planning in adult education is quite extensive and provides models of planning (see for example, Caffarella, 2002; Gboku and Lekoko, 2007; Houle, 1996; Knox, 1986; Langenbach, 1988; Waldron and Moore, 1991); thorough analyses of the power dynamics at play in program planning (see for example, Cervero and Wilson, 1994, 2006); and case studies (see for example, Cervero, Wilson, and Associates, 2001; Neufeldt and McGee, 1990). We are in general agreement with the literature that unveils the nature of power in program planning, so we do not have much to add in this area. In this chapter we will focus on what we consider the essential principles, goals, and evaluation criteria that should inform program planning and development in the movement for a democratic socialism.

The second reason we find Horton's ideas important is that he invokes the Argentine-born Cuban revolutionary Che Guevara when discussing program planning. This got us thinking about and investigating the work of Che Guevara (Holst, 2009). When one analyzes the work of Che Guevara from a planning perspective, one finds a comprehensive set of principles he developed for his own program planning and development. This may come as a surprise until you consider that, while Che Guevara's most famous activities were planning and engaging in armed struggle, the majority of his time in Cuba was actually spent in leadership positions involving economic planning and workplace-based training and development oriented at building a democratic socialist society. There is in fact, in Cuba, a whole body of literature and practice of human resource development for democratic socialism based on the ideas and practice of Che Guevara. Moreover, he was very conscious of the fact that much of his planning work involved informal, nonformal, and formal education. Recognizing that most of us do not live in revolutionary societies, we will ground the program planning principles we derive from Guevara in contemporary and historical social justice-oriented education and activism in the United States. The principles we identify in Che Guevara's work are present, for example, in the history of the African American freedom struggle and contemporary popular

education programs in the U.S. What Che Guevara provides us
with is a comprehensive set of principles for program planning
for democratic socialism, which we believe are applicable to many
different contexts and settings.

After outlining the principles we find essential for guiding
program planning, we will turn to a discussion of the goals of program planning. By goals we refer to the idea of what we believe
should be the outcomes of educational program planning for a
democratic socialism. For this section of the chapter, we will draw
upon the work of Antonio Gramsci. Gramsci's work is prevalent
in adult education literature which address hegemony, or the
commonsensical notions that prevail in a given society. Here,
however, we want to use Gramsci's work to help us formulate
goals of program planning appropriate for democratic socialism.
In the last section of the chapter, we will present a list of criteria
for evaluating programs aligned with the principles and goals we
outline.

PRINCIPLES OF PROGRAM PLANNING

The idea of principles for program planning is not alien to the field
of adult education. When discussed, it is generally in the contexts
of the social purpose of adult education (Cunningham, 1989;
Heaney, 2000; Merriam and Brockett, 2007); professionalization of
the field (Collins, 1991; Johnson-Bailey, Tisdell, & Cervero, 1994);
standards for graduate programs (Commission of Professors
of Adult Education, 1986); codes of ethics for adult educators
(Cunningham, 1992; Sork and Welock, 1992); and civic education
and participation (Gastil, 2004). Whether implicit in our practice
or explicitly defined, principles are the "values of those who are
responsible for the program (that) determine what is actually
taught" (Cervero and Wilson, 1994, p. 163). It could be argued
that principles derived from the praxis of Ernesto Che Guevara
and social justice movements in the U.S. limit the relevancy of
these principles to those in what Merriam and Brockett (2007)
call the "unacknowledged side of practice." Nevertheless, with
careful consideration of the different historical and social contexts of our own and that of the movement leaders and activists we
drawn upon, these principles can be seen as a framework to guide

any adult education planning focused on maintaining the historic affinity between our field and the goal of social justice.

By way of introduction, we find the following principles as essential for democratic socialist program planning: internationalism, anti-imperialism, intrinsic motivation of love and empathy, discipline, honesty, truth, self-criticism, flexibility in thinking, audacity, an orientation toward service, a willingness to sacrifice, and a rejection of privilege. In what follows, we will detail the presence of these principles in social justice–oriented education and activism in the U.S. and relate them to program planning.

INTERNATIONALISM AND ANTI-IMPERIALISM

Despite the United States' historical emergence as an imperialist power, there is a long-standing anti-imperialist and internationalist tradition within the U.S. Nineteenth-century literary figures Henry David Thoreau and Mark Twain, for example, opposed imperialist wars against México and the Philippines respectively. From an organizational perspective, the Women's International League for Peace and Freedom (WILPF), founded in 1915 in opposition to World War I with Jane Addams as its first president, is an example of an organization whose U.S. branches have educated and organized for nearly a century in opposition to U.S. imperialism and in favor of internationalist principles of social justice and peace.

In the history of the African American Freedom Movement, prominent leaders, often to their personal detriment, have linked the struggle of African Americans to the international struggle against colonial and imperial subjugation. W.E.B. DuBois, for example, understood that his Pan-Africanist efforts on behalf of ending colonialism in Africa were part and parcel of the struggle of African Americans in the U.S. For DuBois (2001), "[t]o help bear the burden of Africa does not mean any lessening of effort in our own problem at home. Rather it means increased interest" (p. 104). DuBois, along with Paul Robeson, were signatories to the Civil Rights Congress' 1951 petition to the United Nations calling for relief of genocide against African Americans by the U.S. government. This famous "We Charge Genocide" petition was an effort to internationalize the African American freedom struggle while highlighting the importance of the struggle in the U.S. for the peoples of the world. As fellow signatory, William Patterson (1970) stated, "a policy of discrimination at home must inevitably create racist commodities for export abroad—must inevitably tend toward war" (p. xv).

In the decade after the genocide petition, Malcolm X (1989) would insist that the African American struggle must be elevated from a domestically based civil rights issue to an internationally based human rights issue. Malcolm X's travels to Africa in the early 1960s developed into a co-learning relationship between him and several African liberation movement leaders. He returned from these travels convinced that "African problems are our problems and our problems are African problems" (p. 73). From this, he insisted that the problems facing the African American minority in the U.S. should be taken to the United Nations as a human rights issue where it could be taken up by the African, Asian, and Latin American world majority. Here the struggle of African Americans in the U.S. would take its rightful place as one example of the then unfolding "global rebellion of the oppressed against the oppressor" (p. 217).

INTRINSIC MOTIVATION OF LOVE AND EMPATHY

Motivation is a topic of great interest to educators. Its absence is at the heart of many educators' laments of student disinterest, and building motivation is seen as a precursor to learning. For Ernesto Che Guevara, motivation for social justice must come from within. This is not, however, for Guevara an innate characteristic. Programs must be organized in such a way that they instill people with a disposition for social justice that intrinsically motivates them to act.

The principles of love and empathy as motivating factors are evident throughout social justice movements in the U.S. Involvement in such movements, itself, often sparks a humanistic, intrinsic motivation and propels a deeper commitment. In the Civil Rights Movement, for example, love and empathy were at the heart of what caused people to involve themselves in what were often very dangerous activities given the harsh repression faced by activists. As one Freedom School trainee wrote after participating in the training sessions before heading south in 1964, "now that I've felt what it is to be involved and committed, it seems hard to believe that I could be content with any other kind of life" (as quoted in Sutherland, 1965, p. 24). In adult education this would probably be called an example of transformative learning. When people organize, the experience of collectivity often motivates individuals and collectives to push forward on demands as victories build upon one another or as people see others making gains in similar contexts. Intrinsic motivation for social justice takes root when people no longer see engagement in movement activity as a choice; it becomes something they have to do. The activist and artist Paul Robeson (1958) expressed this succinctly when he explained his support of the Spanish Republic in the 1930s. "The artist must elect to fight for Freedom or for Slavery. I have made my choice. I had no alternative" (p. 52). Robeson spoke of this motivation as the "power of spirit" at "the very soul" of African American people.

DISCIPLINE

Along with internal motivation stemming from ideals, Guevara (1985) also believed that an internal discipline "spring[ing] from a carefully reasoned internal conviction" (p. 153) was essential. More generally, we can say that when one learns to be internally driven by humanistic love and empathy, one also gains an orienting framework to guide and propel one's action. External motivators and orienting mechanisms are decreasingly necessary if program planning gives people the personal and social space and institutional support in order to pursue actions and further learning guided by deeply held ideals.

Strict discipline of a military nature found in the guerrilla units led by Che Guevara can be found in the history of armed struggle–oriented U.S. social movements. John Brown's Kansas free-state militia, for example, adhered to a strict code of military discipline, yet this was codified in a highly democratic set of by-laws to which members voluntarily adhered (DuBois, 1972). The Black Panther Party (Foner, 1970) also developed a strict set of rules for its membership.

Beyond examples of a more military nature, training in social movements that we saw in Chapter Four instills people with a discipline, confidence, and conviction that only through their own efforts things can change. Ella Baker, for instance, always worked to instill in local people the idea that they were both responsible for and capable of solving their own problems if they engaged in collective action. Honesty, hard work, and organizational and individual discipline were central principles in her training work (Baker, 1972, 1980; Grant, 1998; Ransby, 2003).

HONESTY, TRUTH, AND SELF-CRITICISM

Self-criticism is a pedagogical tool for learning and teaching that should be a principle of program planning. In order to be effective, however, it requires honesty and an environment in which people can express their assessments of their strengths and weaknesses in a collective spirit of improvement. To engage in honest and open self-criticism is to teach others through example the exercise of self-assessment, self-awareness, and the desire for self-improvement. While self-criticism is essential for the individual, this is also essential at the level of groups, communities, and institutions to avoid bureaucratic stagnation.

Honesty and truth are constant themes throughout the work of DuBois. In the founding document of the Niagara Movement ratified on the 100th anniversary of John Brown's birthday, we find the following statement: "We . . . believe in John Brown, in that incarnate spirit of justice, that hatred of a lie, that willingness to sacrifice money, reputation, and life itself on the altar of right" (DuBois, 2001, p. 33). In DuBois' journalist work with the NAACP newspaper *The Crisis*, he made the truth of the African American situation a weapon in the struggle for freedom arguing "the greatest gift a scholar can bring to Learning is Reverence of Truth" (p. 23).

A self-critical stance, both toward oneself and one's people is evident in the work of Malcolm X (1989). His disapproval of the strict nonviolence of the Civil Rights Movement was a critical stance toward the movement. He argued that it made no sense for African Americans to act violently as U.S. soldiers in imperial wars overseas, only to return and ignore racist violence at home. He made a point of exposing this contradiction in his educational oratory. Like Guevara, as critical as he was of others, he was equally self-critical and openly discussed this self-criticality as a way of instilling it in others. This can be seen in his open break with the ideas of the Nation of Islam as well as in his personal and political transformation after his visits to Mecca and Africa. In a public statement on his changing views as a result of these travels, he says that he has "always been a man who tries to face facts, and to accept reality of life as new experiences and knowledge unfold it" (p. 60).

CREATIVE, FLEXIBLE, NONDOGMATIC THINKING AND AUDACITY

Given the growing national and global economic inequalities, an adult education program should develop students disposed to a critical, nondogmatic understanding of the political economy of exploitation, along with the analytical flexibility to understand how this plays out in different ways in today's globalized society. We can see this being done in contemporary popular education-oriented organizations such as Project South based in Atlanta, Georgia, and the School of Unity and Liberation (SOUL) based in Oakland, California. Both of these organizations provide participatory popular education training on, among other issues, the nature of globalization both internationally and in local communities in the U.S. Their purpose is to put education at the service of movements orienting them toward the idea that unity among poor and oppressed people locally and internationally is necessary to build a socially just order. While some may argue that these organizations are on the margins of the field, even within the area of human resource development (HRD), leading authors (Bierma, 2000; Fenwick, 2000) are calling for an orientation that puts human values, social justice, and a critical understanding of globalization at the heart of our programs and practice of adult education.

The historical levels of migration and immigration today are part and parcel of neoliberal globalization (Guskin and Wilson, 2007; Sassen, 1998). The recent waves of immigration to the U.S. have been accompanied by innovative social movement activism among immigrant workers. These workers are some of the most vulnerable and oppressed sectors of U.S. society, and yet they have exhibited an audacity that has put them at the forefront of community, citizen rights, and labor activism. The principle of audacity is embodied in the popular slogan "*Sí, se puede* [Yes, we can]" of the immigrant rights movement in the U.S. This slogan originated with the farm workers' movement of the 1960s and later reemerged among the mainly Latino immigrant janitors in their successful unionization struggle against major U.S. corporations in Los Angeles. It was only through the audacity of these "marginalized" workers that they were victorious. Without daring to struggle, they would never have won. Fundamentally this is a pedagogical stance—to show through your own audacious example that people are capable of things well beyond their sometimes limited self-image.

SERVICE, SACRIFICE, AND OPPOSING PRIVILEGES

Sacrifice imbued with love and empathy transformed into service was a central part of the hegemony that Guevara believed ought to permeate the new Cuban society. The permeation of a society with hegemony as Gramsci (2000) teaches us is not a natural process but an educational process; "every relationship of 'hegemony' is necessarily an educational relationship" (p. 348). Guevara understood this very well and argued forcefully for the power of what he called direct and indirect education in the formation of the new man and woman guided by the principles we are outlining. In the new society, sacrifices would not seem as such, but would be the "natural" way of being and acting in a society oriented toward social justice. The principle of service was of particular import for professionals with whom Guevara frequently spoke during his time in Cuba. Professionals were products of the hard work and advances of the society to which they should be committed. Echoing the ideas of Freire (Shor and Freire, 1987) that the educational professional cannot be neutral, Guevara (1969) extended this argument to all professionals.

   Program planning should develop service-oriented people willing to make sacrifices for others. Aptheker (in DuBois, 2001) comments that central to DuBois' educational philosophy was "the demand for sacrifice, for a life of service, and an insistence that while such a life will bring hardships and temptations it also will bring fulfillment" (p. xiii). The best of social activists have always embodied this principle. Activists rarely attain personal benefit from the risk taking involved in organizing and educating for change, which, more often than not, results in personal sacrifice.

This orientation is already latent in U.S. society and becomes evident in disaster situations. When natural disasters hit communities, it is common that hundreds and at times thousands of people from around the country respond by immediately dropping everything and showing up on the scene to volunteer their efforts to save people and restore communities. Garcia (2005) reports on individual efforts and those of Veterans for Peace in the Gulf Coast region after Hurricane Katrina. These grassroots efforts grew out of and posed a direct challenge to the failed neoliberal response effort of the various governmental agencies. This pedagogical aspect of service was a central principle behind the service programs of the Black Panther Party. They provided free services such as schooling, health care, and before-school breakfasts, as an example of serving the people, as a way to expose government neglect, as a way to exemplify democratic socialism, and as a way to instill an orientation to service in those who participated in these programs.

GOALS OF PROGRAM PLANNING

In the previous section, we outlined a set of principles for program planning, and we showed how these principles are present in the history of the movement for democratic socialism in the United States. In this section we will present what we consider to be the most important goals of program planning for a democratic socialism.

POLITICAL INDEPENDENCE OF WORKING-CLASS PEOPLE

To begin, we should clarify that by working class, we are not referring to an early 20th century, industrial-based definition of the working class. In defining the working class, we draw on the work of Zweig (2000) in considering the contemporary make-up of the working class in the United States. Following Zweig, working-class people are those who, when they are employed, work for someone else and have a minimum amount of control over the conditions of their work, regardless of the color of the collar they wear on the job. By this definition, the working class constitutes about 63 percent of the U.S. population. For a democratic socialism to be successful, program planning should work to achieve political independence for the working class. In the U.S., this will need to be manifested in the formation of a multiracial, multiregional working-class political organization. This organization will need to clearly identify a working class in the U.S. as the majority class with distinct interests from the class in power. For the working class to become, in Gramsci's (2000) words, "distinct and individuated" (p. 38), it will need to proceed from a break with existing mainstream political organizations, that do not work from nor for the interests of working-class people. In addition, an organization of this nature will need to articulate the demands of the so-called new social movements (issues of race, gender, sexuality, identity, and the environment) from a working-class perspective. In other words, it will need to reflect the interests and demands of the working class as it actually is: majority female, disproportionately formed by people of color, and disproportionately affected by environmental disasters and degradation.

UNDERSTANDING THE DYNAMICS AND TRAJECTORY OF CHANGE

It is essential that program planning help working-class people understand and anticipate the dynamics and trajectory of sociopolitical economic change; Marx and Engels (1948) called this the "line of march" and Williams "the long revolution" (Williams, 1965). As Gramsci (2000) explained, "political genius can be recognized precisely by this capacity to master the greatest possible number of concrete conditions necessary and sufficient to determine a process of development" (p. 86). This is a fundamental aspect of leadership at the individual and organizational level, and without it a person or organization follows events rather than shapes political action. People must be able to understand the complexities of their sociopolitical economic context in order to consciously work to change it in the direction of a democratic socialism. Educational planning, then, should have as a goal helping people come to a robust understanding of their reality and to help them be able to anticipate the trajectory of change. This goal is a part of the popular education organizations of SOUL and Project South mentioned above.

UNDERSTANDING SOCIAL CHANGE AS A HISTORICAL PROCESS

Gramsci (1994) understood that social change emerges as an interrelated process of economic, social, and political transformation. We tend to only consider political upheavals as indicators of social change, and in this way, we fail to understand the interconnectedness of economic, social, and political transformations. Europe of Gramsci's time was going through a qualitative economic transformation from a largely rural-based society to an industrial-based society. The revolutionary change taking place, the social and political upheaval, was mainly a struggle to determine whether this economic transformation would take place in the interests of the working class or in the interests of the dominant classes of the time. In other words, would industrialization take place in a society in which the economic output would be distributed in a socially just way or in a manner that mainly benefited the owners of industry?

Closer to home, take the example of the Civil Rights Movement in the U.S. We generally think of this as involving marches, sit-ins, and judicial and political demands to end segregation laws. This, of course, is a major part of the story, but as the social and political aspects, they are only the most visible. A fundamental aspect of the Civil Rights Movement was the economic transformation, through mechanization, of the southern agricultural sector that drove thousands of African Americans and Whites off the plantations and into southern and northern cities. Without this economic aspect, African Americans, isolated and severely oppressed on southern plantations, were not able to qualitatively transform their social and political struggle for freedom in the way they were able to from southern cities after the mechanization of southern agriculture.

To see social change as an interrelated process involving economic, social, and political transformation allows people to understand how these objective transformations (like the mechanization of agriculture over which working-class people have little say) transform the playing field upon which people fight for their demands. These objective changes make social and political change more or less likely. If one is to be successful, educational planning for a democratic socialism should have as a goal helping people understand social change as a process in which objective changes can enable or disable their quest for a more just society. In Chapter Seven we will raise the question of whether today's economic transformations through microchip-based technology are creating more, or less, favorable conditions for a democratic socialism.

UNDERSTANDING ONE'S PLACE IN HISTORY

Today we are witnessing national and global economic polarization of rich and poor that is transforming the nature of social classes. Any program planning endeavor for democratic socialism should have as a goal an understanding of the nature of the particular epoch one is working in, the prospects for change, the nature of that change, and the likely agents of that change. In today's climate, we believe it is essential that educators confront the fact that the traditional organizations of social change such as trade unions are in serious crisis. Is this an indicator of epochal change? In the United States, as the labor movement is increasingly moribund and working people are seeking new forms of organization outside of the trade unions in workers' centers, poor people's movements, and noncollective bargain-based organizations such as the Coalition of Immokalee Workers. In Latin America, the landless, the homeless and the unemployed are organizing outside the traditional left organizations as well. Are the new forms of organization emerging among the working-class and dispossessed sectors of society today potentially invigorating a movement for democratic socialism? Raising, addressing, and seeking answers to these types of questions should be goals of educational planning.

The goal of understanding social change as a historic process is present in the popular education programming on globalization developed by Project South (2002). As a part of their workshops, Project South uses a timeline in order to "help participants understand the roots of an issue, and how that issue has developed over time" (p. 16). This three-layered timeline incorporates economics, government policy, and popular movement history, helping people understand the multiple forces that shape an issue over time. When people are asked to place themselves and the relationship of their own community to the issue on the timeline, they begin to place themselves in history. They also can begin to see how popular movements have changed the direction of history and can continue to change society today.

WORKING WITH AND FROM THE MOVEMENTS OF WORKING-CLASS PEOPLE

We need theory to understand the sociopolitical economic epoch through which we are moving and the prospects for change in this period. But as much as we need theory, however, education must also be based in the spontaneous struggles of working-class people around their real needs and interests. The best indicator of the line of march, as Gramsci (1977) argued, are people themselves. In his view, "by the spontaneous and uncontrollable movements which spread throughout their ranks and by relative shifts in the position of strata . . . , the masses indicate the precise direction of historical development" (p. 173). For Gramsci, radical praxis of an authentically educational nature does not consist of preaching a dogma, but rather working in a dialogical, pedagogical, and directive way with the real needs of those most negatively impacted by unfolding sociopolitical economic changes. This means working chiefly with those for whom a new social order is a vital necessity. Education planning should therefore have as a goal working with and for those most severally impacted by sociopolitical economic transformations. The Coalition of Immokalee Workers (n.d.) uses the slogan "from the people, for the people" to explain the nature of their organization. Educational work that they call "reflection and analysis" is at the heart of their program planning to build the community power of farm workers in Immokalee, Florida.

CRITERIA FOR EVALUATING PROGRAMS

Given the principles and goals that we have outlined thus far, how do we know if programs are helping build a movement for democratic socialism? In order to address this point, we will present eight criteria with which we can assess our program planning. While these criteria are framed in terms of yes or no questions, the answers to these questions will be on a continuum. Given their specific contexts, individual planners and planning collectives or groups need to consider if they can move further in an affirmative direction for each criterion. Moreover, as Youngman (1986) insists, program evaluation should be the responsibility of all those involved in the educational process, a process through which everyone takes responsibility for their own role in achieving the aims of the educational program.

DOES OUR WORK BEGIN WITH THE PRESSING DEMANDS OF THE DISPOSSESSED?

This is important for two main reasons. First, in any given situation, the most dispossessed have the least at stake in the prevailing relations of power that maintain a given society. Moreover, the dispossessed can often represent the future for sectors of the society not yet on the losing end of prevailing relations. In today's society, for example, where technological advances are making stable and permanent work a luxury for a shrinking sector of society, the economically dispossessed represent the future for more and more people. The Poor People's Economic Human Rights Campaign's University of the Poor (Baptist and Theoharis, 2008) has this criterion at the center of their program planning and their definition of the poor. Since they define the poor in a similar way that we are defining the working class, as about 60 percent of the population, they see a movement of the poor as increasingly representing the interests of a growing sector of society.

DOES OUR WORK HELP THE DISPOSSESSED UNDERSTAND THE HISTORIC NATURE OF THEIR EXISTENCE, AND DOES IT EXPOSE THE GROWING CONTRADICTIONS WITHIN EXISTING SOCIOPOLITICAL ECONOMIC RELATIONS?

These interrelated criteria are particularly important today, given our assumption (detailed in Chapter Seven) that we are in a period of fundamental transformation characterized by a growing polarization of wealth and poverty on a global scale. In other words, as Baptist and Theoharis (2008) argue, contemporary poverty is an expression of the growing inability of prevailing relations to satisfy the basic needs of life of the poor (food, clothing, housing, etc.) in the midst of surpluses. The human species produces more food than we can eat, yet millions go hungry. In the U.S., there are enough housing units for everyone, yet we have growing homelessness. As more and more work is done by microchip-based technology, human workers become superfluous to the production process, and, therefore, to a society based on profit derived from human labor. The dispossessed today are on the cutting edge of a long-term process of growing productivity with less and less need for human labor. The resolution of their needs becomes the lynchpin for the fight for a democratic socialism where distribution of the basics of life is based on need, not on the ability to pay for them. This is why organizations such as the Poor People's Economic and Human Rights Campaign plan their programs on the basis of human rights. In today's world, the demands of the poor, who are marginalized from the labor market, cannot be resolved along the old socialist demands of workers' rights. These demands must be framed on the basis of human, inalienable rights.

Identifying contradictions is at the heart of the Chicago office of the American Friends Service Committee's (AFSC) Coyuntural Analysis (American Friends Service Committee, 1997). Derived from the work of Antonio Gramsci, Paulo Freire, and Latin American and Canadian popular education, *coyuntural* (Spanish for conjuncture) analysis is a "type of critical analysis that examines the dynamic relationship of forces that affect our lives at one point in time" (p. 44). A contradiction for AFSC is "a situation in which forces in opposition share a common element" (p. 44). The contradictions of housing and food mentioned above are examples of contradictions according to AFSC. For AFSC, the goal of program planning based on coyuntural analysis is to understand the nature of contradictions and the relations of forces involved in order to find opportunities for change.

Finding opportunities for change is also the focus of Newman's (2006) problem-solving program planning training model. His model is based on three questions: What's wrong? What will we do? What can we do? By systematically and critically applying these three questions in specific contexts, people can come to an understanding of the objective conditions at play and the balance of forces that make certain tactics more likely than others.

DOES OUR WORK ALLOW PEOPLE TO UNDERSTAND THE INTERCONNECTEDNESS OF THEIR LOCAL SITUATION AND THE BROADER CONTEXT?

Moses Coady (1939), the progressive Catholic priest who was central to the establishment of the Antigonish movement of adult education and cooperatives in Nova Scotia, Canada, in the 1930s, said that "one of the greatest impediments to the possibility of ushering in . . . [a] new society is the inability of the people to see the big picture" (p. 163). Isolated, people rarely see their problems as emblematic of broader social problems. When people come together, however, they are much more likely to see how their own situations are not individual aberrations but social problems rooted in prevailing asymmetrical power relations. Radical program planning should ensure that people come to an understanding of the interconnectedness of themselves, their social reality, and the wider society. Auerbach and Wallerstein's *ESL for Action* (1987) textbook has an example of precisely this type of program planning. It presents a typical popular education practice of helping ESL students distinguish which of the problems or issues they face are individual problems and which are social problems. When people such as immigrant workers begin to discuss their "individual" problems, it generally does not take long for them to realize that they all share a set of problems in common. Problems held in common across a social sector or class, by definition, are not individual problems but social problems in need of social solutions.

The work of the Highlander Research and Education Center on runaway factories is also an excellent example of this type of program planning. The movie they produced in conjunction with the Tennessee Industrial Renewal Network (1993) *From the Mountains to the Maquiladoras* documents educational planning in which workers in factories that closed in Appalachia visit the factories in Mexico where the factories reopened with Mexican workers. Any anger the Appalachian workers may have felt toward Mexican workers disintegrated when the workers actually saw the working and living conditions of their Mexican counterparts. Through the process of visiting and meeting with the Mexican workers, they all began to see how they are facing the common enemy of corporate greed and power that takes jobs from U.S. workers, only to keep Mexican workers in impoverished conditions.

DOES OUR WORK BUILD AN ACTIVE AND ENGAGED POLITICAL INDEPENDENCE OF THE GROWING DISPOSSESSED SECTORS OF SOCIETY? DOES OUR WORK BUILD UNITY AMONG THE DISPOSSESSED?

Radical program planning must be based on the centuries-old adage that the working class (as broadly defined above) must be in charge of and responsible for its own emancipation and education. While this is a tenet of socialist movements, it also resonates in many other contexts. The long history of Black nationalism in the U.S. has as a central principle that Black people must be in charge of their own liberation. When SNCC adopted the concept of Black Power in 1966, it declared that "if we are to proceed to true liberation. . . . we must form our own institutions, credit unions, co-ops, political parties, write our own histories" (Bloom and Breines, 1995, p. 155). One of the main architects of the idea of Black Power, Stokely Carmichael, at the time of this declaration had been organizing for African American political power and independence in Lowndes County, Alabama, where he and fellow SNCC activists used the symbol of a black panther for African American candidates running for local offices under the Lowndes County Freedom Party. This is the symbol that Huey P. Newton and Bobby Seale adopted for the Black Panther Party (BPP) they organized in 1966. SNCC, once it adopted the concept of Black Power, and the BPP operated as African American organizations. They believed this operational independence was necessary for African American people. Both organizations, however, believed in working in alliances or coalitions with progressive and revolutionary non-African American organizations. The BPP inspired the formation of and worked with a number of similar organizations among youth: Chicanos (Mexican Americans) formed the Brown Berets; Puerto Ricans formed the Young Lords; Chinese

Americans formed the Red Guards; and White Americans formed the Young Patriots. The women's movement has also had a long-standing tenet that insists that women must organize independently of men; that only in women-run and controlled organizations, will women gain the knowledge and skills necessary to successfully fight for their own liberation.

Many of the organizations mentioned above, whether they are racially or ethnically based or gender-based, see a dialectical relationship between their own organizational independence and the need for broader unity to ensure the liberation of all oppressed people. As Ella Baker (1972) argued, organizational independence is necessary for people to "understand that they had something within their power that they could use, and it could only be used if they understood what was happening" (p. 347). Independently, oppressed groups must develop themselves, and then, and only then, can they join in with other sectors on an equal footing in order to take on the organizational power that holds all oppressed groups back. We can look at the program planning of the Poor People's Economic Human Rights Campaign (PPEHRC) as a contemporary example of organizing within a specific sector but with a long-term vision of broader unity. The PPEHRC's University of the Poor organizes leadership schools for poor people specifically designed to develop their knowledge and practical skills in order to be able to take leadership positions within the poor people's movement. Their formal vision statement calls for the unity of the poor across color lines, and they see the poor as "the leadership base for a broad movement to abolish poverty" (PPEHRC, n.d.). Given their analysis of a qualitatively new form of poverty today that we saw above, the resolution of the human needs of the poor requires a qualitative transformation of our society into a cooperative or socialist society. Therefore, unity around the issues of the poor can be the basis for a broad-based movement that speaks to the demands of the working-class majority.

DOES OUR WORK BUILD ORGANIZATION THROUGH WHICH THE DISPOSSESSED CAN EXERCISE POWER?

Program planning for power is a long-term project, yet short- and medium-range planning should also keep this criterion front and center. Social change runs along the lines of reform because movements for fundamental social transformation work for demands raised by people who call for those reforms. Reform-oriented work, however, becomes more revolutionary when it helps expose the contradictions of society and when it helps people exercise power in extracting victories (reforms) from the existing power structure (Luxemburg, 1973). So, for example, the program planning of the Coalition of Immokalee Workers is exemplary of this type of work. As they have organized for better wages and working conditions (reforms) as farm workers, they have come to realize the interconnectedness of various corporate powers at play in the agricultural and fast food industry. Eventually, they decided to launch boycotts of big fast food chains such as Taco Bell in order to force these companies to put pressure on the growers in order to pay them one penny more per pound for the tomatoes they pick. Through creative tactics, they have won a number of reform victories. These victories have allowed them to exert increasing power in determining the conditions of their work and standards of living, while also raising their consciousness of the political economy of agriculture and the food industry.

DOES OUR WORK DEVELOP THE SKILLS AND KNOWLEDGE THAT ALLOW PEOPLE TO LEAD?

A radical approach to program planning for democratic socialism must be more than political education aimed at raising people's understanding of the interconnectedness of social reality. If we are serious about people exercising power and decision-making capability over the social, political, and economic forces impacting their lives, then people need knowledge and skills in order to make informed decisions and to be able to lead. Youngman (1986) is one of the few within radical adult education to emphasize this point and we are in agreement with him. Beyond political education, Youngman identifies general education and technical education as key dimensions for democratic socialist program planning. General education refers to knowledge and skills related to literacy and numeracy as well as the cognitive abilities of creativity, critical analysis, independent judgment, and articulate expression (p. 199). Technical training refers to the knowledge and skills necessary for running and leading social, political, and economic institutions guided by democratic and participatory principles.

Here we can see the same intersection of training as mastery of principle and skill that we saw in Chapter Four. The Sandinista National Literacy Crusade for example had as a goal the development of literacy and numeracy skills in the service of participants forming and leading agricultural and workplace cooperatives, as well as taking coordinating and leadership positions in a decentralized educational system. The training work of SNCC, inspired by the ideas and work of Ella Baker, was also based in program planning that aspired to provide people with knowledge and skills in order to run and lead local institutions.

CONCLUSION

As we look out on a world where about half of the population lives on less than two dollars per day, the program planning principles we have outlined in this chapter seem less and less like politically charged, explicitly "radical" sentiments, and more and more like commonsense planning to meet the needs of a growing majority of the world's population. We believe that addressing poverty can only happen effectively when people are educated to create and utilize a democratic, participatory, and cooperative society. These principles, as we have tried to show, are evident in the long history of social justice-oriented activism and its accompanying educational work in the U.S. When taken as a whole, these principles and goals answer the question "To what ends should we educate adults"? Planning guided by these goals and principles should not be seen as putting programs on the margins of the field, but rather as anchoring them within the best of our own traditions.

CHAPTER SIX

TEACHING ADULTS

We call this book *Radicalizing Learning* since we want our perspective to include the important learning that happens without a formally recognized teacher present. However, we also recognize that there are many situations in which the presence of an authoritative and skillful teacher is crucial to significant learning. So in this chapter we focus on the process of teaching adults and explore what makes some teachers, and some teaching, deserve to be called radical. Two ideas are central in our analysis. The first is that radical teaching is always imbued with a specific political purpose; that is, its raison d'être is to help people learn the skills, acquire the information, develop the aptitude, and solidify the commitment to create a democratic, cooperative, socialist society. If we consider the pursuit of this purpose alone to be the distinguishing feature of radical teaching, then any form of pedagogy, including the most traditional kind of lecturing with no student participation, could be considered as radical. Indeed, one of the most radical teachers who has influenced us—Herbert Marcuse—was known for his highly stylized, formal lectures (Leiss, Ober, and Sherover, 1967).

But for us radical teaching has a second definitional component, one that concerns itself with forms of practice. For us, radical teaching strives to enact forms of knowledge production and distribution that are analogous to socialist forms of production and distribution, in other words, ones that are cooperative, collective, and fully democratic. That means that radical classrooms are ones in which authority is shared and decentralized, and ones where the chief decision makers regarding what is studied and how it is learned are the chief stakeholders in the process, that is, the learners themselves. Just as we regard socialist forms of economics as those in which resources and services are owned and controlled by the producers and users of those resources and services, so we view socialist classrooms as those in which the producers and users of learning collectively decide how best to direct and allocate the resources and services available (including those of teachers' expertise and experience) for the good of the whole.

We also see radical teaching as sharing many similarities with progressive and humanist pedagogy practices. Viewing teaching as something that is always situated within the context of experience and that consequently helps people learn from experience is one similarity. Another is understanding that a dialectical relationship always exists between theory and practice, with each emerging and being shaped by the other. A third is an emphasis on teacher humility and on the importance of leading by example—of the teacher modeling for students the kinds of commitments she is looking for.

Of course, in a capitalist society such classrooms are difficult to envisage. The widespread and unquestioned acceptance of norms of hierarchical authority means that for the most part people rarely have the opportunity to practice any kind of collective decision making. A socialist form of decision making that is democratic would mean that those involved begin by generating the widest range of possible options from which choices are to be made. The most many of us have the chance to practice anything approaching this is encouraging learners to choose between options already established by an external authority. This would happen, for example, when learners are presented with a series of learning modules from which they choose one or two to explore further, or when a learning outcome is specified in advance but learners are provided with a range of different activities from which they can choose one or two in order to achieve this outcome. In an era of strong vocationalism, where education is urged to be "useful" to students' future employment prospects, there is always the pressure on students to choose subjects and teachers who will most help them "get ahead" economically.

When teachers work to subvert modes of teaching that are hierarchical, compartmentalized, competitive, and individualistic, they take responsibility for challenging teaching that mirrors capitalist economics. However, we would say that the use of an experimental approach in and of itself does not make teaching radical. It is quite possible, for example, to teach marketing or executive decision making using all kinds of role-plays, simulations, and case studies that are quite creative and experiential. No, what makes teaching radical is the deliberate and intentional attempt to help people critique capitalist ideology, envision a truly democratic future, and learn democratic socialist practices. This must always be present.

However, there is one central contradiction in our position that needs to be addressed. The concept of the producers and users of services making fully authentic choices about their usage depends on a crucial condition, namely, that they are fully aware of the range of opportunities and possibilities open to them. This is a meeting point for both liberal democrats and democratic socialists. Jürgen Habermas, who at different points in his work straddles both viewpoints, makes this a central point of his book on deliberative democracy, *Between Facts and Norms* (1996). For him a deliberative decision only has legitimacy if it is reached on the basis that those making the decision have full and accurate information regarding that decision available to them. This is the achilles heel of the "democracy as majority vote" argument. In a society in which the ideologies of capitalism, White supremacy, patriarchy, homophobia, and ableism reign supreme, any preferences expressed by the majority are likely to mirror those ideologics. In classroom terms, this means any curricular preference, selection of materials, or choice of learning methods will be made within the predefined parameters of dominant ideology unless a deliberate attempt is made to challenge this.

This is why Herbert Marcuse's argument made over 40 years ago in his essay on repressive tolerance (Marcuse, 1965) is so persuasive for us. Because of the powerful influence of dominant ideology, Marcuse mistrusts educators' instinctive preference for presenting students with a diversity of perspectives and then letting them make up their minds which makes most sense to them. The logic of his argument is that students' previous ideological conditioning will always predispose them to choose what for them are commonsense, socially sanctioned understandings. The educator's task, indeed her responsibility, therefore, is to confront—even coerce—students into engaging with troubling ideas that they would otherwise avoid. So a radical form of practice would seek to ensure that ideas marginalized as too extreme be given full prominence.

However, doing this is not as simple as it sounds. What if the marginalized ideas are marginalized because they represent far right worldviews such as those that deny the existence of the Holocaust, advocate ethnic cleansing, or advance the ideology of White supremacy? We would not wish to urge that these be given equal prominence to other ideas or to advocate that they be taken seriously as legitimate. For us, a democratic socialist curriculum privileges certain philosophies, theories, and skills. It is partisan (as is all teaching) in that it seeks to explore philosophies that concern themselves with moral, spiritual, and economic justifications for common stewardship and allocation of resources. It studies theories that explore how to provide equity of access to opportunity, how to create systems that prevent an unrepresentative elite gaining disproportionate power, and that seek to understand how a system that is blatantly unjust and skewed in favor of a certain race, class, or gender reproduces itself with a minimum of fuss. This includes understanding how mechanisms such as hegemony, disciplinary power, and repressive tolerance combine to make extreme disparity appear as normal, unremarkable, and inevitable. A radical curriculum also entails studying how people learn racism, homophobia, patriarchy, and ableism, and how they incorporate these ideologies into the microdecisions of their daily actions; in racial terms, how they learn to commit racial microaggressions. Finally, a radical curriculum develops the skills necessary for collective deliberation and decision making.

For us, the optimal form of radical teaching happens when form and function are combined, when teachers and learners use highly participatory and collaborative approaches to help learn what it takes to create democratic, cooperative, collective, and socialist forms. No doubt this is why both of us have ended up working at different times in doctoral programs (in critical pedagogy at the University of St. Thomas and in adult education at National Louis University, Chicago) that try to turn learning into community property with learners collectively deciding what objectives, materials, curricula, and forms of evaluation are in their best collective interest. It is why we have pushed for doctoral dissertations that are collaboratively written and credited to a group, not an individual. It is also why we have worked whenever possible to challenge rules that reward individual teaching and scholarship and to privilege those that emphasize team teaching and multiple authorship. In the rest of this chapter, we explore both the practices and the curriculum of radical teaching.

TEACHING AS RADICAL FUNCTION

Teaching that is radical is, as we have said, teaching imbued with purpose, or, to be somewhat redundant, teaching with a radicalizing function. That purpose or function is to encourage students to envisage and then to practice ways of living strongly opposed to the supposedly "natural" ways they have learned. For us, that is inextricably linked to teaching the theory and practice of socialism. In our Chapter One, we argued that the twin ideologies of capitalism and White supremacy were so pervasive that radical teaching had to begin by challenging them. One of the most intriguing problems radical teachers face is how "up front" they should be about this. Making full disclosure of one's intentions to students is one of the chief ways those students see a teacher acting with credibility and authenticity (Brookfield, 2006). However, in a society in which challenges to dominant ideology are mostly prohibited, announcing this project in advance provides a "heads up" to those in power that a challenge is imminent and thus enables them to squash it before it begins. In addition, students' learned conservatism often means that they will resist determinedly any teaching that appears different. This is why, for us, some of the most effective forms of radical teaching are experiential, with students learning radical ideas and practices almost without realizing this is happening.

What would be the core elements of a radicalizing adult curriculum? First, the ideology of capitalism would need to be challenged, particularly its contention that it best guarantees individual liberty and creativity. Capitalism is held by many to be coterminous with democracy, to guarantee freedom of thought and speech, and to create an economic climate that fosters free enterprise. Radical teaching punctures these pretensions by demonstrating how corporations and lobbyists have taken over U.S. democracy by controlling not only who gets nominated but also how liberal their positions can be. It illuminates the way that socialist discourse has been expunged from the language. And it explores the decline of small business and individual entrepreneurship in the age of global corporations.

Second a radical curriculum would be internationalist. It would seek to sever the link between a defensible patriotism and a knee-jerk, imperialistic jingoism that views anything produced outside one's borders as somehow suspect. This is something that Billy Bragg—one of the pop culture figures the two of us most admire—has done in his book *The Progressive Patriot* (Bragg, 2006) and in his rewriting of the socialist anthem, "The Internationale" (Bragg, 1990). An internationalist curriculum is particularly relevant in an era of global capitalism when social movements and civil society are being recast as crossing territorial as well as cultural borders. It would identify common interests among peoples in very different regions in the manner recognized by Paul Robeson over 50 years ago: "We will not forget our fight for Negro rights here is linked inseparably not only with the struggle of all American workers, but also with the liberation movements of the peoples of the Caribbean and Africa and of the colonial world in general" (Robeson, 1978/1949, p. 224).

Internationalism also means urging, as Che Guevara did in his training of African revolutionaries in Africa rather than Cuba, that learning must always reflect the culture and backgrounds of its participants. The domestication and deracination of Freire's ideas, whereby they are ripped out of their Brazilian political context and defused of revolutionary import in the manner critiqued by McLaren (2000), would be opposed by an internationalist curriculum. This internationalism would, moreover, be internal as well as external. It would recognize the chimera of a core national identity and instead explore the reality of the different ethnic and racial identities within these borders. In Minneapolis-St. Paul, where we both live, we can cross borders into areas where tribal, regional, and national identities from Asia, Central America, and Africa comprise mini-nations with their own language, family structure, and culture. To take just one example in adult education, it would mean teaching students in adult education graduate courses to be as familiar with an Africentric adult education paradigm as with a

European one. It would ask students to be Africanists, that is, to do their best to understand (admittedly from the outside) conceptions of adult learning, adult development, adult teaching, adult education history, adult educational philosophy, and so on that are grounded in African cultural values and African understandings. These would be taught as part of the mainstream curriculum to all students and not reserved only for students of the diaspora.

Third, radical teaching is teaching for diversity, which for us is teaching against racism, sexism, homophobia, and ableism. Our perspective is that diversity has been coopted by the notion of celebration. We like to celebrate diversity ourselves but that is not the same as fighting racism. The prevailing logic of diversity is a relativistic one that flattens difference and eliminates power, implying that even as people are different they are equal in their difference because "we celebrate all traditions." This neatly elides inequity and systematic disenfranchisement. Observing Martin Luther King Day, watching Spike Lee films, or voting for Barrack Obama for president is no substitute for the sustained, daily attempt to recognize and challenge racism in conversations, meetings, decision making, and micropractices. Those things mean little unless they go hand in hand with redistributing power to support local communities, or with developing international alliances to combat the Northern hemisphere's relentless exploitation of the Southern hemisphere's material and human resources.

In one of the few books on this topic, Youngman (1986) outlined what for him were the constituent elements of socialist adult pedagogy. Preeminent was political education, which focused on the development of socialist political awareness. This could be accomplished partly through theoretical immersion but was more fruitfully developed as a result of participation in struggles in the workplace or in the community for such specific projects as the right to organize or the abolition of sexist or racist hiring practices. For Youngman, "the development of a socialist political awareness involves an understanding of what needs to be done through participation in collective action" (1986, p. 198). Thus, "political education therefore regards involvement in anti-capitalist struggles as educative in itself" (p. 199). Alongside political education would go the fundamental need for universal literacy (what Youngman calls "general education") and technical training in the skills necessary for managing production processes and participatory democracy. As we contend in Chapter Four, it is sensible and accurate to talk about radical training, rather than ceding the discourse of "training" to human resource development. Likewise, we don't think there is anything inherently sinister or Taylorian about management (though we are uncomfortable with the gendered connotations of the word). The questions to ask are *what* is being managed, *whose benefit* is it being managed for, and how do we retain some kind of *democratic control* over the activity? So training in how to manage production, run committees, set up and run mechanisms for democratic decision making, bookkeeping, and so on can all be important in socialist pedagogy.

TEACHING AS RADICAL FORM

As we argued at the outset of this chapter, we believe the form of radical teaching is one with strong democratic and collective elements. But we don't believe that this removes teacher power and authority. As Rappaport (1978) points out, leadership is not the same as domination, authority is not the same as authoritarianism. For example, one of the most frequently expressed components of radical teaching is a negotiated curriculum grounded in students' experiences. But negotiation is most definitely not equivalent to teachers' capitulation in the face of whatever students wish to study. If students have uncritically internalized dominant ideologies of capitalism, White supremacy, heteronormativity, patriarchy, and ableism, then the learning needs students express will be framed by these. In such a situation teachers need to push back and insist on nonnegotiable elements of the curriculum, particularly if these don't arise from student requests.

However, a skillful teacher also needs to be able to work with students' definitions of need and to teach to their expressed interests in a way that is radical and that presents a perspective on the material very different to the one that students expect. For example, Meeropol (1978) argues for radical teachers to be ready to teach so called "traditional" economics courses but to do so with a radical perspective. In our experiences, students who volunteer for radicalized courses with a fully formed political commitment in mind are relatively rare. Far more common is a situation where we are working with students who have never really experienced an exposure to radical ideas and where we are teaching courses that assume an apolitical survey of scholarship. In such a situation, it is in the best traditions of adult education to begin where students are with the assumptions and preconceptions they have developed and then to present a very different perspective. For example, in a graduate curriculum for a master's or doctoral degree in adult education, courses on adult learning, adult education program planning and evaluation, the history and philosophy of adult education, or adult pedagogy can all be taught with a radical vein running through them. Most graduate students in adult education come into their studies with practical experience of working in the field and know only too well the ways power manifests itself in their workplaces and communities, and the ways their practice is sculpted by external forces and requirements. It requires very little stretching in our experience to begin with case studies of students' actual experiences and then to illuminate those from, say, a critical theory perspective.

For all of our careers, we have both worked in situations where the dominant logic of our employing institutions has been that of capitalism. Stephen remembers his first university teaching post where the president told him that no matter how much he published or how excellent his teaching evaluations, whether or not he stayed employed depended on how many students he brought into the doctoral program. In such environments it has been our experience that you can often go much farther in terms of getting students to engage seriously with radical ideas if you observe the surface forms of the curriculum (such as covering the central concepts, theories, or body of knowledge that has to be covered in a curriculum) and then teach this material from a radical perspective. To give just one example, a course on the history of American adult education could use Schied's (1993) study of worker education as a chief empirical text on education, O'Hearn's (2006) study of learning within Northern Ireland's H Block prisons as its historical study of learning, Loewen's (1995) content analysis of historical texts as its chief resource on historiography, and Gettleman's (2008) analysis of Communist Party adult education schools in the U.S. as an example of dissertation style research to be encouraged.

A number of writers have proposed teaching practices that are consistent with socialist theory. Youngman (1986) and Allman (2001) identify such practices as negotiating a curriculum based on the analysis of students' experiences at the workplace and in the community, breaking down disciplinary divisions, and collaboratively developing criteria used to assess learning. To Allman, dialogue is inherently revolutionary and, in a fully socialist incarnation, is absent any form of imposition and characterized by trust, humility, openness, and respect on the part of the adult educator. Yet, both she and Youngman also acknowledge that radical adult educators prescribe and direct, exerting authority. For instance, central to evaluating adult education is judging how well education prepares students to take control of the means of production and distribution. In Youngman's view, "socialist pedagogy acknowledges the authority of adult educators" (an authority derived from their expertise in such areas as critical theory or organizational skills) and then attempts to "situate this authority in a democratic context that enables leadership to function in a way that is not a form of domination" (1986, p. 207).

What is clear to a number of writers on socialist pedagogy is that focusing on the trappings of student-centered pedagogy risks reinforcing the status quo, even as this pedagogy seems to offer an alternative. One of the most powerful critiques of student-centered learning is that of Elshtain (1978) who believes that an emphasis on the process of students sharing narratives of experience "encourages a solipsistic and substanceless deep subjectivity and a strained and phony warmth which some, in moments of bland delusion, call 'community'" (p. 292). Harold (1978) likewise argues that "emphasis on the freedom and independence of the student, no matter how attractive an alternative this may seem to the drab educational authoritarianism we have had, simply cannot be counted on to create a consistently humane or valuable situation in the classroom, much less impart a politically progressive perspective" (p. 316). For Elshtain, three conditions need to be in place for teaching that deserves to be called radical: (1) training in critical theory is "the fundamental, irreducible grounding of any praxis of social liberation" (p. 304); (2) "persuasion is the only pedagogical mode consistent with the articulation of radical, critical consciousness" (p. 304), a point that echoes Gramsci's notion of the educator-activist as a permanent persuader; and (3) an acknowledgment that the teacher necessarily exerts power and authority in inculcating a critical theoretical perspective.

How can we reconcile our earlier stress on radical teaching as enacting democratic and cooperative forms of knowledge production and distribution with this emphasis on direction by an authoritative adult educator? For us, the key lies in the notion of false consciousness. A truly collaborative approach that is grounded in students' own definitions of what they need to learn and how they wish to learn it can only occur *after* students have been exposed to the full range of options for organizing society and after they have been introduced to the radically different perspective offered by critical theory. Given the Marxophobia of contemporary society, and the ideological manipulation of language to ensure that anything smacking of "socialist" is viewed as un-American, unpatriotic, morally reprehensible, and deeply suspect, students will be unable to make a free and informed choice among all possible alternatives unless a Marxist analysis and a socialist vision is fully explored. This is where the educator uses her power to force students to learn about the full range of alternatives. Once students have broken free of false consciousness, and adult education has worked as a kind of political detoxification, then the authentically democratic negotiation of curriculum and evaluation can begin. Without this required engagement with critical theory and socialist possibilities, any negotiations students enter will always be framed by the dominant ideologies of capitalism and White supremacy.

PRACTICES OF RADICAL TEACHING

It is something of a fool's errand to focus on defining the features of radical teaching, if by that effort we expect to come up with a list of standardized practices. After we searched 35 years of issues of the journal *Radical Teacher*, the thing that strikes us is how many different approaches are advocated under the umbrella of radical teaching and how varied are the contexts in which people self-identify as radical teachers. The one thing we take from the journal is the point—made again and again—that radical teaching is not the same as active learning or innovative pedagogy. Much though the two of us advocate active learning approaches, and much though we feel innovative pedagogy stands a good chance of keeping learners awake, we don't think of them as radical if they are disconnected from some fundamental purposes.

As we were writing this chapter, the *Radical Teacher*, quite coincidentally, published an issue on the theme "Radical Teaching Now." In the introduction to that issue, Jackie Brady and Richard Ohmann identify some of the most common misconceptions of radical teaching—that it is by definition unorthodox (as in teaching without texts), that it is essentially political indoctrination allowing no student dissent, and that teaching radically is an historically absurd project (http://www.radicalteacher.org/default .asp). These misconceptions are easily addressed. As is clear from the *Radical Teacher* journal, those teaching in a radical key sometimes look highly orthodox and traditional; it all depends on what approach will most help particular students at a particular time. Also, one of the most predictable features of radical practice is the ever-present and wholly predictable nature of strong student dissent. Far from working as authoritarian indoctrinators, most radical teachers are constantly making microcalculations of just how far they can push things without incurring so much dissent that learners shut down completely or complain to superiors in ways that limit what is possible. As for the idea that radical teaching is somehow historically untenable—belonging to an earlier era of clear oppression, racism, and inequity that has now passed— events during the writing of this book such as the disastrous invasion of Iraq and the total meltdown of American capitalism have demonstrated to us that such an approach is more historically justified than ever.

But once we have debunked and moved past these myths, there has to be something that unites radical teachers, something that provides a shared language for exploring how radical teaching is practiced. So what do we regard as the features of radical teaching? We propose the following:

1. *A focus that is threaded throughout all radical teaching is the illumination of power and hegemony.*

At some times this focus will be more externally directed, as the group grapples with how dominant ideologies and social structures shape consciousness, frame action, reinforce the social order, embed exploitation, and limit possibilities. At other times it will be more internally directed, as members of the group examine how they have assimilated dominant ideology and how classism, racism, sexism, homophobia, and ableism play out in their individual lives. As John has argued (Holst, 2009), Che Guevara understood how capitalist societies promote the false individualism where an individual's advancement is tied to the fall of someone else. Guevara argued "individualism as such, the isolated action of a person alone in a social environment, must disappear . . . changing the manner of thinking requires profound internal changes . . . helping bring about profound external changes, primarily social" (Guevara, 2003, p. 115). Radical teaching always questions the idea of the student as lone wolf, coming to independent judgments free of contextual influence.

It is important to say that it is individualism, not individuality, that is being critiqued here. Individualism is a learned ideology—a worldview that regards each person as disconnected from the collective and acting in an atomistic, self-propelled way in the pursuit of private self-interest. Individualism rejects any notions of collective obligation and replaces these with the pursuit of whatever objectives make the individual's life more comfortable or enjoyable. This individualistic pursuit is conducted with no regard to the effects of the individual's choices or actions on others, and without any commitment to securing the same freedom of maneuver for others. Individuality, on the other hand, is each individual's attempts to develop talents and creative abilities in ways that feel most interesting and fulfilling. But this expression of individuality is always done within a group context, with a realization that when seeking to express one's individuality, others need to be taken into account. Individuality also explores how one's unique gifts, talents, and personality can contribute to the well-being of the whole.

The focus on power and hegemony can also be intragroup, as those involved struggle with how power is being used, abused, exercised ethically, and transferred within the community, organization, institution, or learning group itself. But intra- and intergroup struggles are always shaped by a historical project of creating a new hegemony, "a fundamentally new consciousness when the prevailing and taken for granted ideas would be of a socialist nature" (Holst, 2009, p. 166). Again, we wish to emphasize as we have throughout this book that a socialist hegemony is *not* a hegemony imposed from above by an elite vanguard that has determined its agenda must be realized whether or not the majority of people want it. A socialist hegemony is one where the values we explored in Chapter One of common stewardship, fairness, inclusion, and creativity are core. A major part of radical teaching therefore is contesting the dominant stereotype of socialism as the enemy of individual creativity. Using Foucalt's (1980) idea of inversion, radical teachers strive to find ways to demonstrate that it is global, transnational capitalism, not socialism, that is the enemy of individual creativity through its tight circumscription of the channels in which people live and work.

2. *The chief curricular aim of radical teaching is to help students and teachers learn how to create a fully democratic socialist society.*

This aim will be realized when students use their understanding of how power and hegemony function as the basis for challenging and then changing dominant social and economic relations. What this will look like will differ with context. The nature of the struggle will always determine what skills need to be developed, what information needs to be assimilated, and how people should analyze their situations. A community college teacher working with a group of second-language learners from Somalia, Cambodia, and the Ukraine is not in the same situation as a guerilla leader working in the Bolivian jungle. An African National Congress leader in exile faces very different challenges than a tenants' rights organizer on the south side of Chicago or in Hackney Marshes. An Inuit leader teaching in Arctic Canada will share commonalities, but also significant differences, with a Maori leader working in Auckland. In each case, teaching for struggle and resistance will require exploring different skill sets, different bodies of knowledge, and different theoretical understandings of the world. As resistance recedes and the struggle leads into the creation of a truly democratic, participatory economy, new skills of organizing and coordinating, of inclusive decision making, and of regular critical appraisal will be needed.

3. *Teaching is always situated within and informed by particular struggles.*

This idea is found in many traditions—in Deweyian inspired progressivism, in Emersonian pragmatism, in Gramscian notions of the organic intellectual, or in Foucault's description of specific intellectuals working in specific sites. Radical teaching can certainly happen in formal classrooms, or in formal ways in fields, factories, or cyberspace, but it is always shaped by a particular struggle. Sometimes the teaching will focus on very specific situations, at other times on understanding the historical context and line of march within which highly particular situations need to be understood. Sometimes the teaching will help people learn the specific organizational skills of mobilizing a neighborhood, setting up committees, establishing food banks, or creating alternative media. But teaching situated in struggle also introduces theory and helps people learn how to analyze experience critically and collaboratively.

Teaching situated within movements and struggles privileges learning from experience, but this is always done critically. Learning from experience involves understanding and interpreting experience through new and different theoretical frames, just as much as it entails inductively deriving principles of "good practice." Learning in and from experience was a central principle for Che Guevara who believed that when it comes to learning how to struggle against an illegal and repressive regime "every minute teaches you more than a million volumes of books. You mature in the extraordinary university of experience" (Guevara, 1969, p. 386). The "teacher" here is not the experience itself; experience, after all is just that, experience. It can be interpreted in any number of ways and, depending on their personal histories, two people can interpret the same experience in wholly antithetical ways. The teachers in experiential learning are the others involved in the experience who, collaboratively and critically, try to understand the experience in multiple and complex ways.

Sometimes teaching from experience involves people with greater experience teaching others new to experience how to learn from it. To continue Guevara's example of military training, "a good battlefield instructor does more for the revolution than one who teaches a large number of raw recruits in a context of peace" (Guevara, 2000, p. 2). It may be true, as Guevara argues, that "the struggle itself is the great teacher" (1985, p. 75), but armies of every country have found that unless you set up a process by which the particular events of the struggle are analyzed, and unless you intentionally adjust strategy as well as tactics to the emerging lessons from struggle, struggle itself is not always educative. You can encourage people to occupy factories and set up workers councils, but unless people incorporate into this project the deliberate study of what their experience is teaching them and how they can learn from mistakes, there is a strong chance that their "experience" will teach them that the old autocratic way was actually much simpler and more effective. So learning from experience entails a constant dialectic in which the individual drawing of lessons from experience is often set against collective analysis of that experience. Which brings us to . . . .

4. *Learning always exhibits a dialectical relationship of theory and practice.*

A dialectical relationship is one in which two opposites face each other in struggle—proletariat and bourgeoisie, dominating teacher and dynamic learner—and, in their clash, achieve a transcendent progression. The theory-practice dialectic is usually framed as one in which academic theory, disconnected from everyday experience, is positioned in opposition to a constantly changing practice that follows no theoretical rules. Guevara (1985) describes this as an interaction between "leaders, who with their acts teach the people and the people themselves who rise in rebellion and teach the leaders" (p. 51). In terms of the theory-practice dialectic, radical teaching transcends these categories in forming (depending on your preference) theoretical practice or practical theory.

Practice—our daily decisions, actions, and judgments, and the ways these buttress or dismantle and re-create social forms— cannot be understood without a critical theoretical reading of the world. Our movement through the days of our lives is always understood in certain theoretical ways as we live out specific events in action. We ascribe meaning to the most microscopic aspects of others' actions such as their gestures, words, clothing, skin color, tone of voice, posture, and so on. These interpretations of experience are always theoretical, derived from broader meaning schemes and perspectives we use to explain what we see around us (to use the terminology of Mezirow's work on transformative learning [Mezirow, 1990, 2000]). There is very little in life that is unmediated, that is untheorized, "pure" experience. Whether we acknowledge it or not, we are all theoreticians. This is the meaning of Gramsci's oft-quoted aphorism that "all men *(sic)* are intellectuals" (1971, p. 9). In Gramsci's view "one cannot speak of nonintellectuals, because nonintellectuals do not exist" (p. 9). All people are reasoning beings and therefore theorists. Each person carries on some form of intellectual activity because she or he "participates in a particular conception of the world, has a conscious line of moral conduct, and therefore contributes to sustain a conception of the world or to modify it, that is to bring into being new modes of thought" (p. 9).

Just as everyone is an intellectual to Gramsci, so everyone is a philosopher. Whenever people use language, whenever they take action, whenever they develop guidelines of conduct, "there is implicitly contained a conception of the world, a philosophy" (1971, p. 344). Speech acts and everyday behaviors are the crucibles of philosophical thinking, not an acquaintance with abstruse texts. Gramsci wanted to destroy the idea that a cultured person is one acquainted with elite forms of aesthetic appreciation. To him "everybody is already cultured because everybody thinks, everybody connects causes and effects" (1985, p. 25) in ways framed by their culture. If this is true and everyone is indeed a philosopher, then getting them to think critically does not mean introducing them to some new form of higher order reasoning. It means, instead, adding a critical edge or dimension to their already existing forms of conceptualizing. Hence, "it is not a question of introducing from scratch a scientific form of thought into everyone's individual life, but of renovating and making 'critical' an already existing activity" (1971, p. 331). Teaching people critical thinking in this view is not an entirely new, higher order cognitive process, but a politicizing of what is already a naturally occurring process.

Theory—the attempt to develop an inclusive understanding of how ideologies and structures shape practice—can never be understood, nor its utility assessed, without a focus on how specific practices illustrate theory. Certainly, there will be times when specific practices are stressed more than a theoretical reading of a situation. For example, a group of squatters trying to fight eviction or workers threatened with dismissal for trying to join or form a union will focus on learning information and skills related to legal process, media manipulation, and building networks. But these so called "practical" efforts will always be framed in a certain reading of the world—a set of assumptions and explanatory mechanisms that illuminate the context in which they are to be used. At other times, an attempt to understand how class and race cohere deliberately and systematically to marginalize one particular group and to build a theory that might explain how other groups are marginalized in other situations will be conducted at a certain level of abstractness. But at each stage of theory building the accuracy of the theory can only be judged by constant application to experience and an understanding of how new theoretical elements spring *from* experience.

In reflecting on the Cuban revolutionary war, Guevara captures the way theory depends on and springs from practice. As the small band of revolutionaries mounted their campaign, he writes how "we began drawing theoretical conclusions in the heat of these events to create our own body of ideas" (1996, p. 412) and how "we are now speaking a language that is also new, because our thinking is not able to keep up with the speed we are traveling. We are in a state of continual motion, and theory moves more slowly" (p. 413). The theory-practice dialectic is inherently unpredictable, with each new development refining emerging understandings. Endemic to this dialectic is learning from mistakes and changing theory to account for what has been learned.

5. *Methods and curriculum are constantly negotiated and cocreated.*

Just as the central feature of a democratic socialist society is the constant negotiation of rights, responsibilities, and forms of production and distribution, so radical teaching is in a constant process of negotiation. The pace at which this negotiation is conducted will vary according to the readiness for learning of various members of the group. Negotiation depends on informed choices, and at times there may be a necessary disparity in the knowledge and skill of different group members or between learners and teacher. For a skilled and knowledgeable teacher to pretend to have no particular expertise in the subject, and to believe that learners with no knowledge of content can make as informed a choice about the focus or direction of learning as an experienced teacher, is ridiculous. There are times when a teacher saying "you know as much as me about this" is a flat out lie, as well as times when that is completely true. As a general rule, we have found that when working with groups for whom a deliberate and intentional focus on power and hegemony comes as a surprise, or with groups who have never been exposed to critical theory, we need to assume a greater degree of responsibility for setting direction than we do with groups of experienced activists, many of whom have far better powers of analysis and more knowledge than we do.

The ways any negotiation is conducted will vary according to context. At times it will be appropriate for all members to have a vote and to decide in favor of a simple majority or a two-thirds majority. At other times the major decision-making power will be with the small minority or even the individual most affected by the decision. At times a secret ballot is needed to equalize participation and prevent the powerful steamrolling of the more diffident or marginalized. At other times an open and transparent "sense of the meeting" consensus is more appropriate. A governing principle for all democratic negotiation, however, is that those who have the greatest say in a decision are always those most affected by that decision.

Authority will also be exercised differently depending on the learning task. Generally, those who have more experience, knowledge, or higher levels of skill will assume a greater share of responsibility for organizing how learning will happen. Sometimes this will be the formally credentialed teacher. Sometimes it will be one or more members of the learning group. Different people around the same decision may also exercise different kinds of authority concurrently. For example, a content specialist will exercise authority in determining the curricular terrain to be studied, while a specialist in group process will exercise authority in determining how groups can be helped to cross that terrain. Similarly, a specialist in managing computer software can help individuals or groups to appreciate when best to use wikis, Twitter, or set up discussion threads, while a specialist in disciplinary power can alert learners to the ways these techniques can be used for surveillance without students realizing it. But whatever curriculum is studied and through whatever ways it is studied, the teaching-learning process is always being appraised and renegotiated by those involved. It is never a static object and is always the embodiment of the theory-practice dialectic.

Authority is also exercised through example, through modeling of an engagement in the kind of learning necessary to build democratic socialism. Declaring "a good example, like a bad one, is very contagious" (Guevara, 1968, p. 349). Che Guevara advised his fellow Cuban trainers in the failed Congolese liberation movement that "the urge to teach should be paramount—not in a haughtily pedantic manner, but with the human warmth that goes with shared learning" (2000, p. 73). If the leader's primary function is to educate people for combat, Guevara wrote, "this is achieved when the teacher can be taken as a model for the students to follow" (2000, p. 74). He believed the commandant-leader should be the first to volunteer for difficult or dangerous tasks and in 1957 disobeyed Castro's request not to place himself in the direct line of fire. When faced with resistance to learning new skills, it was little use to crush or force people into learning "but to educate them by leading them forward and getting them to follow us because of our example" (1968, p. 349).

6. *All teaching approaches are appropriate depending on context.*

Within the project of understanding power and building democratic socialism, any number of approaches, methods, or techniques are possible. At times there will be group dialogue, at times individual reading, at times lectures from authorities, at times solitary computer-assisted learning. The learning can be conducted synchronously or asynchronously, in mass lectures or in one-on-one tutorials. Radical teaching is never fixed, never static. It is constantly self-appraising as it explores the theory-practice dialectic of how best to help people understand and challenge power and how best to help them learn the skills and knowledge of democratic socialism. Radical teaching moves beyond the simplistic bifurcation that lectures are a sign of authoritarian demagoguery and discussion a sign of liberatory purity to realize that both can be conducted in emancipatory or oppressive ways. So for us the core of radical practice is not the adoption of a particular method or technique, but the intent of the teaching, the respectful tone that is set by those in temporary authority, and the commitment to continuous critical appraisal and negotiation of what transpires.

To repeat what we argued earlier, we have seen highly creative, active, and experiential methods used in corporations. Indeed, the creative use of games and simulations by business trainers is often far more sophisticated and frequent than the use of similar techniques by university teachers. As we illustrate in Chapter Nine, one can conduct a Freirean-style problem-posing exercise and encourage learners to generate key words and pictures or skillfully use Open Space Technology to build an agenda with participants, yet do this entirely within a context focused on how to help the corporation more effectively kill off the competition in a tight marketplace. And the reverse is also true. We have been in workshops for activist teachers that profess a democratic commitment to building the curriculum from ground upward only to find them manipulative and disrespectful, essentially opportunities for egomaniacal teachers to show off their dazzling command of the lingua franca of critical theory.

In our shared contexts of working initially in community adult education and then in university teaching, we have, however, found several approaches to be valuable. First, any kind of teaching that can model collective decision making is enormously helpful to students who are struggling to break out of the learned dependency on competing individually for the best grades on a bell curve. For that reason we like team-teaching in which the team models for learners how they themselves negotiate across differences. Second, we have both been highly influenced by people we have seen who are skillful questioners and whose only "teaching" act is to ask an occasional question of an individual or the whole group. And third, we are struck with how the most influential teachers exhibit an aggressive humility toward the group. These are teachers who hold themselves subject to the same critical questioning that they apply to learners, and who, publicly and repeatedly, model this questioning of themselves in front of learners. They are teachers who always assume that learners have something important to offer the group and who are constantly seeking to encourage learners to exercise authority.

CONCLUSION

Adult educators are sometimes queasy about calling themselves teachers, as if adopting that identifier somehow marks them out as arrogant, as always "knowing better" than those whom they work with as learners. Facilitator is often the preferred term, with its implications that learners are in total control of what happens and adult educators are there to help them meet whatever learning goals they themselves set. But for us teaching is an important and irreducible part of what we do. Sometimes it's more explicitly directive than it is at other times, and sometimes our best role is indeed to help learners pursue goals they have set themselves. This is clearly the case, for instance, when we're working with activists who have far more experience than we do and who identify goals that will help them address an issue they are dealing with. At other times, we may decide to support learning goals set by learners not because we think the goals are particularly important or significant, but purely because we want learners to experience a period of being in control of their learning in the hope that this will fuel the desire to clamor for control in other parts of their lives. But these kind of contextual judgments are very far from working to support *any* goals set by learners—there are many times when we disagree with the goals proposed because they spring from an untheorized acceptance of dominant ideology. So even when we act more as facilitators, we are always working with a certain agenda, always moving in a certain direction—in other words, teaching.

CHAPTER SEVEN

GLOBALIZATION AND ADULT LEARNING

Globalization and adult learning are two concepts or processes that, to many educators and trainers of adults, seem far apart. To an educator working with a particular student or classroom or an activist working with residents or workers in a particular neighborhood or factory, globalization is a transnational process writ large, a movement of capital, factories, currency, and markets that seems far removed from any particular act of learning. Our contention, however, is that the most concrete and specific act of learning can and should be viewed through the lens of globalization. A good example of this is Youngman's (2000) description of how a computing course at a private commercial college in Harare, Zimbabwe, can be analyzed using tools of class analysis, colonialism, and the development of capitalism in Africa.

Youngman shows how the course is organized to produce the skilled labor Zimbabwe needs to compete in the global economy. The location of the course is partly a result of pressure from the World Bank and International Monetary Fund to create more private adult education organizations. The curricular materials are provided by a U.S. transnational corporation, and participation in the class is determined by the economic situation of the learners. Relations between students in the class, and between students and the teacher, are structured by patterns of class, race, gender, and ethnicity, which themselves reflect Zimbabwe's colonial heritage. Hence, to Youngman "the everyday activity and experience of the adult educator and adult learners in this class are shaped by the wider economic and political realities of Zimbabwe and its place in world economy" (p. 10).

In this chapter we want to connect some of these developments listed above to what is now seen as the irreversible tide of history—that is, globalization—and to explore what this means for the practice of adult learning. We begin this effort through a specific case example.

On the St. Paul side of the Twin Cities where we both live there is a Ford automobile assembly plant. For the last several years, this plant has been dedicated to the assembly of the Ford Ranger pick-up. The plant was built in 1924, in part because of the promise of cheap—and what we would call today, clean—energy from the hydroelectric damn build next to the plant on the Mississippi River. At the time of this writing, the plant employs about 1,900 workers who earn on average about $54,000 per year. By the time you read this, however, the Ford plant may well be closed. In January 2006, as part of Ford's "The Way Forward" restructuring plan, the company announced that it would reduce its workforce by about 30,000 employees. In April of 2006, Ford announced that the St. Paul plant was one of the two previously unnamed plants that would be closed in 2008 as a part of the company's restructuring. Then in 2008, Ford announced a delay in the closure of the plant until 2011. It should be noted that adjacent to the St. Paul plant is the site of the UAW/Ford MnSCU Training Center, a major center for adult education in the Twin Cities. Manufacturing plant closings are a common feature in the United States today and have been now for some time. These closings are commonly considered part and parcel of globalization. But, how exactly can we understand plant closings such as the Ford plant in St. Paul in the context of globalization? And, how should adult educators respond to such plant closings?

TWO ADULT EDUCATION NARRATIVES OF GLOBALIZATION

When one passes the Ford plant and sees the parking area filled with unsold Ford Rangers, the impact and nature of globalization seem evident. As the story goes, foreign competition, lack of "Big Three" auto innovation, and overly ambitious wage demands by unions have all combined to torpedo the once great manufacturing base of the U.S. Repeated wage and job concessions by the unions over the last decades and campaigns to "buy American" cannot empty the St. Paul Ford lot of its unsold Rangers; the forces of globalization are evidently too strong. For those telling this story, globalization is an inevitable process; it represents the compression of space by time through the use of modern technologies that "shrink" or "flatten" the world. Moreover, while it can cause temporary disruption of people's lives and be a painful process, its advocates contend that in the long run it promises enhanced opportunity and greater prosperity for an increasing number of people. These opportunities are not automatic, however, and it is precisely through adult education (so the argument goes) that people can and must prepare themselves for the risks and opportunities brought by globalization.

This is the central idea of lifelong education, recurrent education, permanent education, and other formulations that have become prominent in the discourse of the field. Gone are the days of the 30-year career in the same company, and thankfully so, say the proponents of globalization. This argument maintains that if one is willing to be flexible in continuously upgrading one's skills in a just-in-time fashion, in other words, to move with and at the rapid pace of the changing job market, one can enjoy the fruits of globalization. This is the position of mainstream human resource development within the field of adult education.

Positioned this way, globalization is a win-win situation: companies can prosper through greater free trade, and workers can enjoy multiple work opportunities through frequent career changes throughout their professional lives. From this perspective, St. Paul Ford workers now have the responsibility and the opportunity to retool themselves for new careers. Adult education has the responsibility to provide these workers with the right kind of retraining so that they can reenter the workforce with the skills that will make them successful in new endeavors. We can even add a humanistic orientation to this perspective by arguing that the workers have the chance to explore new opportunities, and adult educators have a chance and a professional obligation to make these opportunities a reality.

For others, the picture is not quite so rosy. Globalization is a reflection and result of the disproportionate power that large multinational or transnational corporations exert over workers, communities, and even governments. As Jarvis (2002) argues, "governments are now not only incapable of regulating the global companies, they are becoming a part of a superstructure controlled to a considerable extent by those who control capital" (p. 8). Whether globalization is inevitable is more a question of whether corporate power can still be curbed by government intervention in the economic sphere, or whether it is only an organized civil society that can take on the corporations. In the field of adult education, this latter perspective holds that it is mainly up to social movements or nongovernmental organizations (NGOs) to put brakes on the growing colonization of civil society by corporate power (see, for example, Amutabi et al., 1997; Ceballos, 2006; Cunningham 1996, 1998; Folkman, 2006; Hall, 1993a, 1996, 2000; Maruatona, 2006; Oduaran, 2000; Schmitt-Boshnick, 1995).

Globalization from this "civil societarian" perspective is a qualitatively new epoch, and it is not only marked by the resurgence of corporate control of government and communities but also by the emergence of new forms of organization or new social movements. It has been highlighted in literature in the field (Finger, 1989; Welton, 1993) that one of the most interesting characteristics of these new movements is their highly educational nature; at their core are learning processes involving the construction and reconstruction of identity and the ability of movements to move faster than the enemy and thus to "learn their way out" of repression (Finger and Asun, 2001). These new movements are often regarded as more pragmatically realistic in their demands than earlier revolutionary movements. They no longer struggle for failed utopias such as socialism, but sensibly scale down their demands to protecting or expanding civil society.

From this civil societarian perspective, St. Paul Ford workers need to engage in adult learning of a particular kind; they need to learn to organize in ways that create new opportunities for themselves. As old social movements such as the United Auto Workers union have declined in their power and relevance for people's lives, the Ford workers need to learn how to ally with new social movements such as the environmental movement and community organizations. This type of social activity has in fact happened. In January of 2007, the UAW Local 879 cosponsored a Minnesota Labor and

Sustainability Conference where several "green" proposals for alternative uses of the Ford plant were debated. There was a conscious effort at this conference to link the demands for decent paying jobs of the old social movement labor union and the ecological demands of the new environmental movement. The conference was a multifaceted learning process. The organizers had to use existing knowledge and skills to put the conference together, and the conference itself was intended to be an educational event intent on both raising awareness of the negative impact of the plant closing and brainstorming opportunities for sustainable development projects.

Both of the two perspectives outlined above have some validity. The mainstream HRD position has merit to the extent that the Ford workers are going to need some form of narrowly defined skills training if they are to have any hope of finding new employment that provides the compensation and security they once had with Ford. Thus, adult learning for new forms of work is clearly implied. The civil societarian perspective is right in considering the question of power at the heart of events such as plant closings, and it is right in recognizing the need for people to explore new forms of organizing and to create new alliances in order to fight corporate power. Here learning about new configurations of power and how best to oppose these are clearly implied. From our perspective, however, the closing of the Ford plant is illustrative of a fundamental transformation in capitalist economic relations that has very important implications for adult education. We believe that the most illuminating analysis of globalization comes from political economy, and for the next few pages, we will present a theoretical analysis of capitalism and globalization and the connections between the two, using the tools of political economy. We feel this is necessary in order to understand what are the major challenges and opportunities for adult education as we move deeper into a globalized 21st century.

A POLITICAL ECONOMY OF GLOBALIZATION

A political economy perspective understands political forms and structures as shaped by economic forces. More particularly, it regards the exercise of power and the functioning of social organization (such as education, including adult education) as determined by the logic of capitalism's unending quest for profit. The quest is aided immeasurably by the creation of new markets across the globe and by the use of ever-cheaper labor. From this point of view the ideal form of production is one involving no labor costs at all. A political economy of globalization understands the parking lot full of accumulating, unsold Ford Rangers as a reflection of what have been called the external relations of capitalism (Allman, 2001), that is, the part of capitalism dealing with large-scale market forces. But we also need to understand the internal relations of capitalism—we need to enter inside the Ford plant to see the unsold Rangers in relation to the production process. This is what Marx (1867/1967) urged when he advised leaving the noisy sphere of the market to enter the "hidden abode of production" where "we shall see, not only how capital produces, but how capital is produced" (p. 172). By standing on the outside of the plant, one sees the how the external market conditions of capitalism produce acres of unsold Rangers, an effect of globalization. Upon entering the plant, we immediately and more clearly see the internal relations of capitalism and the cause of globalization.

A single fact essential to understanding the causes of globalization is that vast areas of the plant are in near darkness. There is very little need for lighting because there are almost no human beings in these parts of the plant. Whole segments of the assembly process have been automated with robotic technology where a few workers, if any, merely oversee the operation of rows and rows of robots. Think about recent car commercials. When is the last time you saw a significant representation of hard-working autoworkers as a patriotic symbol to sell cars? Increasingly, as a reflection of the production process itself, commercial representations of autoworkers are replaced by cute or mischievous mobile robotic arms that swirl around the clean, personless factory.

Only a few decades ago, the St. Paul plant employed over 3,000 workers. In 1985, the body shop area of the plant put out 23 units per hour with about 400 workers; after the introduction of robotics in the early 1990s, the body shop began putting out about 50 units per hour with about 90 workers. The paint department went from 120 to 24 workers in a similar period and with similar outputs per hour (O'Brien, personal communication, 2007). Here we see the internal relation or contradiction between the forces and relations of production. The St. Paul plant is merely one example of the impact of robotic and microchip-based technologies in the production process. Automation is not limited to manufacturing however; one merely need travel to the Starbucks a few blocks from the Ford plant where work shifts across the country are centrally controlled by a software program. Or one can go a little further to the Kmart or the Home Depot where cashiers are being replaced by automated check out machines. The list goes on and on.

From our point of view, globalization is a new epoch in the development of capitalism characterized by and a result of robot and microchip-based technologies. In analyzing economic and human history, Marx (1967) famously argued that "it is not the articles made, but how they are made, and by what instruments, that enables us to distinguish different economic epochs" (p. 175). As the example of the Ford plant illustrates, robotic technology is qualitatively new in that it is not just labor-saving technology, but labor-replacing technology (Peery, 2002).

Globalization thus illustrates a fundamental and transformative change in the most basic of economic concepts, the labor theory of value. Initiated by classical political economists such as William Petty and Adam Smith, and developed further by Marx, this theory posits that the value of a commodity is determined by the labor time needed to produce it. The greater the amount of time it takes human labor to produce a product, the higher its value around which its price will fluctuate. As industrialization developed, machines were increasingly used to produce commodities (such as cars). These machines are, of course, themselves produced by labor. But, once it is produced, machinery is a permanent reality, what Marx called a constant form of capital. You don't need to keep remaking a piece of machinery from scratch every time you want to make another car—once the machinery is in place it keeps producing the commodity.

Labor, on the other hand, is a form of "variable capital." You can use a variety of means to make people work more productively or for longer hours thus increasing the amount of value that labor produces. In any workday, people reach a point when what they have produced covers the costs of their labor (their wages); once they work beyond that point they are producing surplus value (profit). If we think of the Ford plant, each day as the Rangers roll off the assembly line one after another, the workers reach a point when the number of Rangers assembled covers their wages and benefits for the day; if they stopped at that exact moment, Ford would break even but make no profit. The cars that roll off the line after that point represent the company's profit.

Marx identified two ways to generate surplus value or profit. One simple way is to lengthen the work day, a process Marx called absolute surplus value. Historically, people got wise to this method and began to fight for a 10-hour day and then an 8-hour day. This practice, however, is always with us and particularly in situations of vulnerability where part-time, nonunionized employees have few rights or the conditions to fight for these. The other way to create more surplus value is to make people work more productively—work "smarter" in today's terms—so that they produce more in less time. Marx called this relative surplus value, and he saw it as accomplished by organizing workers into a more specialized division of labor or by introducing more efficient machinery.

With these basic concepts of political economy in mind, let's return to the concrete example of the darkened areas of the Ford plant. Introducing new technology into the auto industry initially increased productivity as more cars were assembled in the same time and then in less time. As more complex machinery is introduced, labor is less and less a part of the production process. It is one thing to have labor-saving technology, it is qualitatively different to have labor-*replacing* technology in the way that robotics replaces human labor. The first business that introduces a new technology makes significant profit because it can actually sell the commodities at the prevailing prices but with massively reduced labor costs. As competitors develop similar technology, however, prices fall to a level that reflects the fact that few labor costs are involved in the production process. The two of us know that when a new technology appears that we desire but can't afford (because iPhones, enhanced laptops, or Blu-Ray players, when they first appear, are beyond the salary of university professors) we just need to wait it out. This is because it is only a matter of time before competitive technology brings the price down to where we can afford these toys.

The logic of capitalism—the constant generation of profit—now faces a contradiction. On a global scale, corporate products are increasingly produced by constant capital (microchip-based technologies). Businesses are thus unable to create profit by the old way of making labor (workers) work longer or more smartly or productively. Your company may get a brief, temporary advantage from discovering a new technology and producing a new and desirable product and pricing it high. But very rapidly the price will fall as other companies adopt the technology. So microchip-driven forms of production that initially offer the prospect of massive profits actually become subject to a tendency of continually falling profit. The only ways profit can then be created is (a) by expanding into new markets, (b) by monopolizing either production (you are the only company producing Blu-Ray players) or markets (no other company is allowed to sell Blu-Ray players to a particular market), or (c) by lowering wages and increased exploitation of the reduced number of workers left.

As technology replaces labor in the production process, the value of commodities drop and wages fall. Financial and speculative capital—the quick movement of money across the markets—becomes far more important than the old-fashioned productive capital represented by labor and factories. Think of the contrast between the immediate and no-questions-asked nature of the U.S. government's bailout of numerous financial firms, compared to the rejection of any immediate, no-strings attached bailout of the Big Three auto companies.

Since this is a political economy analysis, we contend that these changes at the economic level that we are describing here structure social and political life. We are increasingly living in a world that is economically, socially, and politically polarized. More and more people are finding themselves increasingly marginalized from the basic logic of capitalism where they work for a wage to buy the things they need. This marginalization manifests itself through less and less job security, the disappearance of the 30–35 year career in one job, more temporary and subcontracted work, more part-time work, and in the extreme, structural or permanent unemployment and homelessness. We are witnessing then a polarization between a tiny sector of billionaires and a growing sector of the population that increasingly finds itself unable to make ends meet. We have all heard the alarming statistics of the change in the proportions of CEO pay versus average worker pay, the astounding bonuses given to traders and brokers in the speculative or financial sector, or the fact that a little over half of the world's population lives on less than two dollars per day. In political economy, this is not a temporary state of affairs that some macroeconomic tweaking will repair, this is a historic process.

While this polarization is rightly seen as destructive, it also forces people to ask the big questions of how we organize the world in a way that is fair and humane. Alternatives that appear democratic and participatory and that address this polarization—such as democratic socialism, the recent slew of books on participatory economics (parecon), or the Green movement—are now perceived as much more viable and concrete. When people see how globalization marginalizes them, removes them from decisions that govern their lives, and creates a situation in which the basic necessities of life (a job, decent education, health care) are threatened or unattainable, it becomes clear that the only way a growing sector of humanity is going to survive is through a radical social and economic reorganization of society (Peery, 2002). Rosa Luxemburg's (1900/1970) famous admonition "socialism or barbarism" is less and less an inflammatory slogan, but rather a straightforward explanation of the concrete alternatives for a growing sector of the world's population. Although dominant ideology does its best to exclude the word *socialist* from the language or to portray it as a failed approach used only by totalitarian governments that repress any deviation from the party line, people facing the loss of certainty and security to themselves and their families are ready to consider alternative ways of organizing the world that are truly democratic and participatory, that is, socialist.

We do not live in a world of scarcity. Humanity produces more food than we can eat, and yet we have growing hunger around the world. In the United States, there is enough housing for everyone, and yet we have growing homelessness. When we look at all the basic necessities, we find the same thing. We produce more than enough of all of them, yet we have growing poverty and polarization. This is a problem then of distribution based on ability to pay rather than distribution based on need. It is a problem of production not in terms of a lack of production, but only in terms of who controls the production and distribution processes and whether or not these processes are environmentally sustainable.

ADULT EDUCATION IN THE ERA OF GLOBALIZATION

We can see how our analysis of globalization plays out specifically by linking it with the broader notion of training we developed in Chapter Four. As the reality of formal paid work becomes increasingly transformed into less stable, part-time, temporary, seasonal employment—often given a positive spin under the banner of "flexibility"—some adult educators interested in economic development are looking increasingly at education and training in the informal sector of the economy. Drawing on the International Labor Organization definition, Mitra (2005, p. 156) identifies subcontracting in small or microenterprises, home-based informal work, and independent service-type work (such as windshield washers, street vendors, domestic laborers, and so on) as the major sectors of the informal economy. It is growing clear to educators working with informal economy workers that the narrow skills transfer training paradigm developed for the formal economy does not conform to the reality facing this large and growing sector of the world's population that finds itself on the margins of stable, full-time, formal work relationships. According to Madhu Singh (2005), already in 1998, the informal economy involved approximately 500 million people globally.

Singh introduces a collection of studies titled *Meeting Basic Learning Needs in the Informal Sector* (2005) identifying the rift that has developed between vocational training and adult learning, where training is conceptually and practically restricted to narrow skill development for formal sector work. Given the serious situation that the growing informal sector faces, Singh and his colleagues argue that meeting the needs of the informal sector requires bridging the rift between training and adult learning. Workplace adult education clearly now encompasses the informal sector of the economy. And, as we tried to argue in Chapter Four, training for and in this sector can be organized in ways that are responsive to people's needs and concerns, run democratically, and infused with the kind of critical analysis we find in the best traditions of adult education.

Given our analysis of the impact of new technologies on workplaces and its accompanying economic polarization, we need to move beyond training people for economic survival. The growing informal sector is evidence that capitalist relations cannot provide decent, stable employment for the vast majority of the world's population. Those working in the informal economy face constant economic uncertainty, so enduring a series of short training programs that equip them to find work that soon will disappear is clearly not the answer. The skills needed to overcome the situation of workers in the growing informal sector—the core curriculum of informal economy training if you will—are the skills of active citizenship and organizing. They are the analytic skills necessary for people to understand the basic concepts of political economy we have outlined in this chapter and to be able to apply these to their own situations. They are the communicative skills that allow workers to connect with each other across sectors of informal employment and thus to realize their common situation. They are the organizational skills that help them form unions, create associations, and build coalitions that confront powerful and wealthy transnational corporations. They are the media skills that mean they can use existing alternative media to create a different awareness of the world than the one that the mainstream media (themselves transnational corporations) wish to promote. They are the cyberskills that are needed to sift through information available on the Internet and also to mobilize people quickly. So while vocational skills are still necessary, we need also to consider training people in the organizational, mobilizing, and advocacy skills that help them create a society in which the needs of people are put before the needs of profit.

When we look to the informal economy sector, or those most dispossessed in today's capitalist societies, we see that much of the most dynamic adult education is outside the established, traditional institutions of the left. As Wainwright (2003) notes, "when old institutions fail, people invent" (p. xx). In the United States, for example, most cutting-edge worker education is based outside labor unions such as the United Auto Workers and based instead in the kinds of worker organizations we discussed in Chapters Four and Five. Examples of these are workers' centers (Fine, 2006), nonunion worker organizations such as the Coalition of Immakolee Workers, rank-and-file action of union members outside of the union structures such as the recent Soldiers for

Solidarity movement in the auto industry, and welfare rights and poor people's movements. The recent immigration marches of historic size and scope that swept the U.S. in the spring of 2006 are probably the most powerful examples of the working class organizing outside the traditional organizations of the left.

When we look more broadly in the Americas, we also see clear evidence of innovative and powerful social movement activism outside of the traditional left institutions. Examples of this are the Zapatistas (a guerrilla of a new type), indigenous movements (Blaser, Feit, and McRae, 2004), antiprivatization struggles (Olivera, 2004), factory occupations and Piqueteros in Argentina (Adamovsky, 2002), the landless movement in Brazil (Harnecker, 2002; Kane, 2001), primary and secondary students in Chile ("Estudiantes," 2006; Vogler, 2007), and the Bolivarian Revolution in Venezuela (Chávez and Harnecker, 2005). Analyses that seem to most clearly recognize the major features of globalization today as we are outlining them here are also found in feminist literature of integrative (Miles, 1996) or structural and transformative (Shiva, 2005) perspectives. This may be because as many have argued, globalization disproportionately impacts women. Moreover, centering activism around the most negatively impacted allows for an organic integration of many struggles.

Most of this activism and popular education is based in the most dispossessed sectors of societies (Zibechi, 2005). The demands of these movements are rather basic: water, jobs, plots of land, education, and health care. Yet, demands for the basics of life made by a majority without the wages with which to pay for these necessities exposes the crisis of global capitalism. The solution to these demands is cooperative, sustainable sociopolitical economic relations that resolve the basic needs of a growing sector of humanity. As Vandana Shiva (2005) puts it, "the epic contest of our times is about staying alive" (p. 133).

A good example of educational work of emerging movements and organizations is that of Project South (2002) and their curriculum on globalization (alluded to in Chapter Five). This curriculum, what they call a "tool kit," is a comprehensive 66-page manual on how to conduct educational workshops on globalization using a participatory popular education methodology. Project South has become known in popular education circles for their successful use of a globalization timeline activity that helps workshop participants place themselves, their issues, and their organizations or movements within a historical perspective that considers the political, economic, social, and cultural impacts of globalization. Aside from the timeline, the curriculum also includes outlines for conducting educational games such as the "Globalization Gong Show" and "Globalization Jeopardy," as well as a glossary of key terms, suggested workshop agendas, and an introduction to the principles of popular education.

Another example of this kind of educational work is the Everyday Face of Globalization and the Taco Bell Boycott workshop curriculum codeveloped by the Coalition of Immokalee Workers (CIW), the Mexican Solidarity Network, and the Student Farmworker Alliance (n.d.). This education work is interesting because it was developed specifically within the CIW's campaign to get Taco Bell to pressure growers to pay farmworkers an extra one cent per pound for tomato picking. The curriculum, like that of Project South, is based in the principles of popular education and is structured like a teacher's guide with sample agendas, activities, and objectives. With the goal of advancing the boycott work of the CIW, this curriculum is directed especially to students since they are the major marketing target of Taco Bell and, therefore, the ones who can best advance the consumer boycott. The workshop is designed to raise people's consciousness of the relationships between fast food consumption and the exploitative food production processes on farms and how this relationship has been increasingly corporatized in the era of globalization.

If we refer back to our Ford plant example above, the curriculum helps people make the link between the external (market, consumption) and internal (production) relations of capitalism. The curriculum, by combining the struggles of farmworkers with people's identity as consumers, tries to show how both the labor of farmworkers and the identity of fast food consumers are dominated by corporate power. The curriculum has as its goal to "construct a new 'we' and 'they' identifying consumers with farm workers vs. consumers with corporations" (p. 2). Like the Project South curriculum, there is an emphasis on hands-on activities that personalize the issues of globalization through games relating the clothes people wear and the food people eat to global production processes, working conditions, and immigration.

GLOBALIZATION AND TRANSFORMATIVE LEARNING

Political economy holds that fundamental transformations at the economic level (such as the introduction of qualitatively new microchip technology) cause fundamental transformations at the social and political levels as well. Revolutions, which are processes that humanity has experienced throughout its history, consist of economic, social, and political transformations (Peery, 2002). Antonio Gramsci (1971) understood this process in his own time. He argued that in a revolutionary period, institutions developed in previous epochs no longer serve the needs of those for whom they were created. He also understood that one could anticipate revolutionary transformations by staying attuned to what he called the spontaneous movement of the majority of people in a given society. In other words, the rejection of old institutions and the creation of new institutions by people themselves were sure indications that fundamental transformations where afoot. We discuss this as an essential form of research in Chapter Nine.

In our view, adult educators need to be attuned to the fundamental transformations that we have outlined in this chapter. If, as we have been arguing, adult education should re-center itself around its historical roots in movements for social justice, it will find that these movements have been transformed. The cutting edge social-justice education today among the most dispossessed of society is taking place in movements and organizations that look quite different than their counterparts of the 20th century. Today, organizations such as those mentioned in this chapter and in Chapters Four and Five are of a different character than earlier movements. These organizations work with those most dispossessed by the growing displacement of human labor in the production process.

This growing sector of society is the embodiment of the decay of the basic capitalist relation that you work for a job to get a wage or salary to buy what you need. This sector does not need to be convinced of the evils of capitalism. Its very survival is based on a form of social relations that is anathema to capitalism; they need the basics of life without a way to pay for them. In other words, they need distribution of goods and services based not on the ability to pay but on the human right to live. This for us is a basic premise of democratic socialism, and it is becoming the only way to survive for a growing sector of the human species worldwide.

When adult educators talk of something being transformative, it is usual to add the descriptors "learning" or "education." We argue that adult education's discourse of "transformative" learning needs to be resituated in the context of globalization. Millions of adults are indeed being confronted with transformative social and economic developments as their jobs are lost, health care removed, savings disappear, families displaced, and training rendered irrelevant. The transformative learning and education needed in this context is characterized by the mastery of practice and principle present in historic examples of radical training and present in the new organizations emerging among the most dispossessed today. This type of adult education, which bases itself in the situation of those most impacted by globalization, will be increasingly necessary for the lives of the world's majority. Moreover, this type of adult education, based not on radical rhetoric but rather in the resolution of the basic needs of the world's growing sector of dispossessed people, inevitably leads to a serious consideration of the democratic socialism for which we are arguing, and it also returns the field to its roots in socially just and relevant educational practices.

CHAPTER EIGHT

AESTHETIC DIMENSIONS OF LEARNING

You are reading a book—an organized artifact that divides its content into neat chapters and employs academic language to analyze the topics subsumed under that focus. A book is linear and rational, with little of the immediacy and visceral nature of, say, music, art, or theater. In this chapter we attempt an oxymoronic task—to use formal academic language to chronicle how the spontaneous and passionate forces at play in artistic creativity intersect with radical learning and education. As the music critic Antonino D'Ambrosio (2004) says, art "grabs a hold of you in a place you never knew existed, shakes you to the core and shatters everything you hold as true. It is transcendent. Illuminating. Empowering. Emancipating" (p. xxiii). The potential territory to be covered is bewildering in its immensity, nothing less than the sum total of human creativity across the centuries, particularly those creative endeavors that challenge dominant ideology and envision other ways of living and being for creators and consumers.

It would be easy for us to focus on artists we grew up with and admired and to study how they intentionally used their media to highlight injustice, create solidarity, and teach us about aspects of a struggle we knew little about. We will mention some of these, but we will also try and broaden our focus to traditions and forms of expression we have little personal experience of such as hip-hop (particularly graffiti) and African music. This is, of course, perilous and problematic. But in its perils and problems it too has an aesthetic dimension. Anytime you choose to engage with a new experience or to try to appreciate the internal rules of new artistic forms, you are engaged in aesthetic learning that challenges customary ways of assigning meaning and that opens you up to the spontaneous, nonrational, and emotional elements of your being. It is these that are at the heart of the aesthetic dimension.

THE AESTHETIC DIMENSION

What exactly do we mean by the aesthetic dimension? In his small but hugely influential book *The Aesthetic Dimension* (1978), Herbert Marcuse argued that in advanced industrial societies the aesthetic dimension represents the last best hope for challenging the stifling constraints of one-dimensional thought. For him, "art subverts the dominant consciousness, the ordinary experience" (p. ix) through introducing into life a dimension of experience that does not conform to the prevailing logic. Hence, "the political potential of art lies only in its own aesthetic dimension" (p. xii). What art offers us is a chance of breaking with the familiar, of inducing in us an awareness of other ways of being in the world. Art "opens the established reality to another dimension; that of possible liberation" (Marcuse, 1972, p. 87). If radical political practice is focused on creating "a world different from and contrary to the established universe of discourse and behavior" (Marcuse, 1969, p. 73), then working to create a free society therefore "involves a break with the familiar, the routine ways of seeing, hearing, feeling, understanding things so that the organism may become receptive to the potential forms of a non-aggressive, nonexploitative world" (p. 6). Lester Bangs (2004), the American rock critic, captures what Marcuse means in one of his hyperbolic essays on punk band The Clash: "For once if only then in your life, you were blasted outside of yourself and the monotony which defines most life anywhere at any time, when you supped on lightning and nothing else in the realms of the living or dead mattered at all" (p. 90).

The political significance of art is that it helps us make this break with the ordinary and gives us new forms of visual and spoken language that open us to new ways of sensing and feeling. In Marcuse's view, learning these different forms of communication and perception is the inevitable precursor to social action. Adult education that focuses on developing artistic sensibility is, in its way, as full of revolutionary potential as Freireian culture circles, theater of the oppressed, participatory research, or education for party activism. This is why Marcuse felt that the development of the aesthetic dimension of life was as much part of political struggle as the democratizing of decision making, rejection of consumer culture, or the abolition of the exchange economy. A liberated society "presupposes a type of man *(sic)* with a different sensitivity" (Marcuse, 1969, p. 21) possessing different language, gestures, and impulses and "guided by the imagination, mediating between the rational faculties and the sensuous needs" (p. 30).

Marcuse is one of the few classic critical theorists who racialized his analysis to include artistic expression that did not mirror Eurocentric "high" culture. For him the Black Power movement was a "subversive universe of discourse" (Marcuse, 1969, p. 35). In the language of Black militants, particularly their claiming of soul—"in its essence lily-white ever since Plato" (p. 36)—and their declaration that "Black is beautiful," Marcuse detected "the ingression of the aesthetic into the political" (p. 36). Black Power represented "a systematic linguistic rebellion, which smashes the ideological context in which the words are employed and defined, and places them in the opposite context—negation of the established one. Thus, the blacks 'take over' some of the most sublime and sublimated concepts of Western civilization, desublimate them and redefine them" (p. 35). To emerging African American scholars of the time, such as Lucius T. Outlaw Jr. (1996, p. xxvii), Marcuse's work was an entry point into critical theory that connected it to Black Nationalist critiques of White supremacy.

While acknowledging that Marcuse's work has been influential on us, we are also interested in the intentionally political aspects of art, the ways that musicians, filmmakers, visual artists, writers, and sculptors deliberately include political images and messages as a way of teaching about the history of struggle or illuminating aspects of the struggle that are not well known. From Paul Robeson to Chuck D; Sweet Honey in the Rock to Sister Souljah; Patricio Guzmán to Ken Loach; Bob Marley to Joe Strummer; Woody Guthrie to Billy Bragg—artists have created art with explicit political intent. Unlike Marcuse, we view this work as revolutionary aesthetics. It is work that teaches us about struggle and the way art builds peoples' pride: the history of struggle (Patricio Guzmán's film *The Battle of Chile* or Ken Loach's *Land and Freedom*); the costs of struggle (Billie Holliday's "Strange Fruit" or Chris Menges' *A World Apart*); the centrality of art to the struggle (*Amandla!* or "We Shall Overcome"); and alternative epistemologies and ontologies (Woody Guthrie's "My Daddy (Flies That Ship in the Sky)," Mercedes Sosa's "Cambia, Todo Cambia" [Change, Everything Changes], Gil Scott Heron's "The Revolution Will Not Be Televised").

THE AESTHETICS OF LIBERATION

Building on Marcuse's analysis in the previous section, radical educators need to concern themselves with the radicalizing function of art, the way in which artistic creation politicizes artists. Marcuse himself maintained the experience of artistic creation and attention was inherently liberating. To him, trying to appreciate the creative logic embedded in an art form lifted people out of the realm of the everyday to a situation in which new forms of experience were suggested. This revolutionary awakening happened irrespective of the particular art form—to appreciate hip-hop was as inherently liberating as to appreciate Bach.

In 1982 Stephen Brookfield moved to New York City and was assailed by the sights, sounds, and smells of the city, itself a powerful experience. One of the most striking aspects of this experience was the subway system. Since he was a penniless untenured assistant professor, the subway was his chief mode of transport and, in total contrast to the London tube, he was sensorily swamped by the graffiti on the subway cars. Here was artistic creativity on a massive public scale, which, by its very nature, both constituted a challenge to authority (the canvas was the MTA subway car sides) and also escaped the commodification of the market by representing art for art's sake (the art could not be sold or traded nor could the artists receive prize money or awards for their creations). Of course, graffiti did eventually become commodified, exhibited in galleries from New York to Milan, and the MTA eventually found a way of painting cars that defied graffiti art. But for a while, it represented an art form that entailed several of the dimensions of radical adult learning.

First, the art was an original creation. Each artist had a signature or "tag" (Taki 183, Stay High 149, Lady Pink) attached to the different works each produced, and fellow artists began to recognize the art by its stylistic components to the extent that the tag became unnecessary. Second, although the art was individually created, it was produced within a collective context of an underground counterculture that observed respect for each other's creations. You never painted over another's creation, and if you did (which was necessary when graffiti mushroomed into thousands of would-be artists struggling to express themselves on train sides), you acknowledged the earlier art work. Third, the art itself could only be created under conditions that had been criminalized. As Lady Pink said, graffiti is "an outlaw art. When we train other graffiti writers we're not training fine artists to exhibit in a museum. We're training criminals. We're training kids how to take life in their own hands and go out there and hopelessly paint on some wall or some train that will do nothing for you except get you fame with other vandals and criminals" (Chang, 2005, p. 121). In this instance, artistic creativity required subversion of the established order.

At the same time as graffiti was springing up on the sides of railcars in the Ghost Yard—the giant train marshalling yard at the northern tip of Manhattan—other elements of hip-hop culture were solidifying. DJ Joseph Saddler (Grandmaster Flash) was studying new ways of mixing record breaks together and realizing that he needed MC's—rappers to improvise rhymes over the repeated breaks and to direct the crowds in clubs and at block parties. Teams of b-boys—dancers who invented furious individual stepping routines that built on accidents to incorporate new moves (including spinning round on one's back or pivoting on hands, elbows, or heads)—were devoting themselves to the most extreme physicality. All of this happened completely independent of any corporate sponsorship or even awareness. As Chang (2005) observes, "they shared a revolutionary aesthetic . . . unmediated by corporate money, unauthorized by the powerful . . . they were invisible" (p. 111); or rather, they were visible only to others who shared the obsession with "distinguishing yourself and your originality above the crowd" (p. 111).

Eventually hip-hop became controlled and commodified by the corporate record industry. However, just as all popular culture reinvents itself to escape precisely this commodification, hip-hop has branched into new forms—photography (Adler, 2006), theater (Davis, 2006), literature (Mansbach, 2006), and so on—and continues to mount a challenge to White culture's conceptions of Black life. Hanley (2007) provides vivid testimony on how it can be used in adult teacher-education in her adaptation of the hip-hop open-mic nights she attended, and Morrell (2008) calls KRS-One's album *Edutainment* "a model for critical hip-hop artists who view themselves as public entertainers and public pedagogues" (p. 225).

Stephen's New York experience piggybacked a similar experience he had in England where, during 1976 and 1977, the punk explosion had expressed a similar aesthetic to hip-hop. Reacting against the blandness and domination of mainstream record companies, and taking advantage of ever cheaper technology that placed recording and printing in the hands of anyone with even a small income, the punk rock ethic had encouraged people who could never afford expensive instruments or music lessons to plug cheap guitars into cheap amps and blow out cheap speakers as they played shorter and shorter songs with a minimal number of basic chords. In its emphasis on do-it-yourself accessibility, the punk movement echoed the "skiffle" boom of Stephen's childhood, when an acoustic guitar, a portable washboard to drag a thimble over, and an upright bass made of a box with a broom handle sticking out of it and one piece of string tied to the handle were all you needed to play two-chord American folk tunes at breakneck pace. Hip-hop, punk, and skiffle all eventually succumbed to the inevitable commodification, but, for a brief period, they represented Marcuse's aesthetic dimension—a self-invented form of artistic expression, conducted within the confines of collectively generated and understood formal structures, that temporarily estranged both creators and participants from the realm of everyday experience.

The other aesthetic dimension we are interested in as adult educators has much greater intentionality attached to it. This is the attempt by artists to use their medium educationally to inform and activate community and movement members about the history and dimensions of a particular struggle. One American example of the political-educational use of art is the University of Hip-Hop at Kenwood Academy on the south side of Chicago, which uses hip-hop crews to interest school pupils in African American history (Raven, 2008). Another is Sweet Honey in the Rock's "Ella's Song," which many assume is about Ella Fitzgerald until the group tells the audience about Ella Baker. The song's lyrics are Ella Baker's own words, particularly her reflections on her faith in young people to take the risks that adults refuse to face.

Art is also a way to express and develop subjugated knowledges and cultures in the process of fighting their subjugated status. Chilean artist Violeta Parra, Woody Guthrie, Sweet Honey in the Rock, Paul Robeson, African American filmmakers Charles Burnett and Julie Dash, and the countless participants in American Indian Pow Wow ceremonies are just a few examples of artists who research, collect, present, and re-present their peoples' cultural expressions as a way of honoring, preserving, advancing, and passing on traditions, knowledge, and beliefs that have sustained peoples. Their cultural work, however, is not a museumification of their peoples' culture but an attempt to maintain and advance it as a living and developing expression of peoples' deepest aspirations and ways of being.

Moreover, as Vetter (2000, 2003) proposes, these cultural workers often work most successfully when they emerge out of or alongside and are deeply immersed in broader social movements. The Chilean folk singer Victor Jara is a good example. Following in the footsteps of his fellow countrywoman Violeta Parra, Jara continued the resurrection and promotion of the culture—most famously music—of the Chilean popular classes (peasants and workers) within the broader social movement leading to the election of socialist Salvador Allende in 1970. The cultural manifestations of this movement (of which Jara was a central figure) in music, theater, film, poetry, literature, and murals was both a process of recuperating, promoting, and advancing the cultural expressions of the popular classes but also a barrier to the growing cultural imperialist importation of U.S. and European commodified culture. The cultural movement in Chile as a central part of a broader social movement has parallels to what Denning (1998) calls the "cultural front" during the 1930s in the U.S., when multiple cultural currents fused with broader social, political, and economic struggles during the popular front period in the era of the Great Depression. The forces of reaction clearly understand the power of these cultural currents within broader movements. Victor Jara was one of the earliest targets of brutal torture and assassination in the first few days after the Chilean military coup in 1973. In the U.S., we know that cultural workers were some of the earliest and most vehemently harassed targets of the McCarthy witch hunts of the 1950s that basically destroyed the broader socialist movement in the wake of World War II.

When artists use a particular medium to inform an audience of a struggle, we believe they act as educators, even though they would probably reject that designation themselves. But, just as educators do, they are using their position of authority and prominence to confront people with knowledge and to urge them to develop skills that they believe are in their best interests. Just as teachers do, artists also model their own public commitment to expanding their knowledge of and their involvement in projects they believe in. What artists typically don't do is the daily work of judging how well people are learning something and then giving them advice on how best to overcome specific learning difficulties. As Marcuse (1978) argues, art can raise consciousness and develop awareness; but the nuts and bolts of learning how to build an organization, broaden a movement, decide when to negotiate with authority, and when to challenge or bypass it completely— those things happen at an individual and group level between specific people in specific contexts.

THE EDUCATIONAL FUNCTIONS OF RADICAL AESTHETICS

Researcher T. V. Reed (2005) identifies the following ten functions of art in social movements: encourage, empower, harmonize, inform internally, inform externally, enact movement goals, historicize, transform affect or tactics, critique movement ideology, and make room for pleasure (pp. 299–300). As we think about the role of art in radical adult education, we discern six functions: sounding warnings, building solidarity, claiming empowerment, presenting alternative epistemologies and ontologies, affirming pride, and teaching history. Most of the works of art we will refer to cross several of these functions, so our divisions are somewhat arbitrary. It is true that many of these works and the artists who produced them can be criticized in different ways on artistic grounds alone. For our purposes we are not concerned with artistic merit, though the songs, films, and writings we have chosen are ones that speak to us. Our analysis is concerned more with the degree to which the works realized the aims they were created to achieve and whether or not they impelled action in the way the creators hoped.

Sounding Warnings

Art that sounds warnings is art that works on two social levels. First, it solidifies and encapsulates an emerging movement in a way that feels accurate and real to members of the movement. Song is particularly suited to this owing to its short gestation time. A song can theoretically be written and learned in a couple of hours, recorded and mixed in a few more, and then be available for download on the web almost immediately and on the streets a little later. It is more compact than a blog posting and works in visceral and emotional ways that an op-ed piece or blog cannot. From the Trouveres to the broadside ballads, from "Joe Hill" to "Strange Fruit," song has a directness and immediacy that appeals to memories and instincts deeper than mere prose can. This was well acknowledged by the legendary Joe Hill himself, a songwriter for the Industrial Workers of the World (the Wobblies) union who believed "a pamphlet, no matter how good, is never read but once, but a song is learned by heart and repeated over and over; and I maintain that if a person can put a few cold common sense facts in a song, and dress them in a cloak of humor to take the dryness off them he will succeed in reaching a great number of workers who are too unintelligent or too uninformed to read a pamphlet or an editorial on economic science" (quoted in Eyerman and Jamison, 1998, p. 59).

Second, art sounds warnings to members outside a movement; it lets people know "something's happening here" as Stephen Stills sang with Buffalo Springfield. A prime example of art that worked on both levels of sounding warnings and that also used two forms of media is Spike Lee's film *Do the Right Thing*, which opened with Public Enemy's "Fight the Power." The violent yet, to some, cryptic end of Lee's film was a classic warning. On the one hand, the character Mookie (played by Lee) had decided the right thing was to take sides and help destroy his employer's pizzeria; on the other hand, the closing credits quoted Malcolm X and Martin Luther King on the merits of violent and nonviolent forms of protest, with no overt indication which one Lee preferred. *Do the Right Thing* also came out when Stephen Brookfield was living in New York in the aftermath of the death in Howard Beach of Michael Griffith, Bernard Goetz's shooting of four Black teenagers in a subway car, and Michael Stewart's death after being arrested for tagging a subway car and beaten while in police custody. Public Enemy's self-description as the Black Panthers of rap had made it clear that Jesse Jackson's call for a rainbow coalition was only one of many voices in the debate about the African American future. Molefi Asante and Maulana Karenga were developing the philosophy and practice of Africentrism, the centrist David Dinkins was shaping up for a run to be New York mayor, and Minister Louis Farrakhan's Nation of Islam was emerging as the self-help model for many Black Americans. In the midst of this realignment of key players in the debate and this reconfiguration of the key issues, *Do the Right Thing* sounded a warning to a far larger audience than the New York hip-hop community that "something's happening here," and its reverberations were national, even international.

BUILDING SOLIDARITY

Radical art also has the project of building solidarity. Its creators are learning how to craft images, create melodies, develop rhythms, and tell stories that bind followers into a common cause. The purpose of art that builds solidarity is to encourage someone to signify a commitment to a struggle. Great speeches do this, but speeches emanate from one person and, while one can invoke resonant phrases ("I have a dream"), it is hard to internalize a speech, to claim it as one's own. Song is particularly suited to this, particularly song that follows the "zipper" format described by Lee Hays of the Weavers (quoted in Eyerman and Jamison, 1998, p. 42). This format establishes a basic lyrical and melodic structure that is then repeated as much as people want with a new word or phrase being inserted each verse. The civil rights song "We Shall Overcome" is a classic example of this. Sung at the Highlander Folk School as the police broke up a workshop there, a new verse was added with the refrain "We are not afraid." The song endures across multiple contexts, and every time it is sung in the midst of a struggle (on a picket line or at a demonstration rather than in a folk club or concert hall), people are publicly committing themselves to a particular project as well as expressing solidarity.

The documentary film *Amandla!* is another good example of how movement intellectuals learned how to use song, systematically and intentionally, to bind members, affirm commitment, and build solidarity. Chronicling the role of music in the South African struggle against apartheid, from Vuyisile Mini's "Watch Out Verwoerd" to "Nkosi Sikelel' iAfrika" ("The People's Anthem"), the film shows how songs of protest became radicalized as the Nationalist government's control measures became more and more extreme. Commissars and freedom fighters in the ANC pay eloquent testimony to the intentional use of song to keep up morale even as killed comrades were being mourned.

Cultural workers also demonstrate solidarity across socially constructed differences in the creative act of their cultural work. The aforementioned "We Shall Overcome" was originally a labor movement song adopted for the Civil Rights Movement. In this particular case of expressing the aspirations of the African American Freedom Movement, activists drew on an affiliated social movement tradition. Joan Baez famously directed her creative talents to the Freedom Movement. In his master work *El Canto General* ["The General Song"], the book-length epochal poem which documents the history of the peoples of Latin America, Pablo Neruda (1988) dedicates a section to the United States. While he sounds a warning against aggressive and imperialist U.S. foreign policy, he first appeals to the natural solidarity that ought to exist between the peoples of the entire American continent. He speaks directly to the people of the United States:

> open your ear to the vast human world,
> it is not the elegant gentleman of the State Department . . .
> speaking to you
> but a poet from the extreme south of America
> son of a railroad worker from Patagonia. . . .
> You are not the idol
> who carries gold in one hand
> and in his other the Bomb.

You are
what I am, what I was, what we must
protect, the fraternal sub-soil
of pure America, the simple
men of streets and roadways.
My brother Juan sells shoes
just like your brother John,
my sister Juana peels potatoes
just like your cousin Jane,
and my blood is of miners and sailors
like your blood, Peter. (pp. 30–31)

One of Victor Jara's most famous songs and scathing critiques of the narrow-minded lifestyle of the Chilean middle and upper classes, "Las Casitas del Barrio Alto" ["The Little Houses of the High-Class Neighborhood"] has an interesting history. The song's origins began in California with the U.S. folk singer and daughter of Jewish immigrants Malvina Reynolds. In the early 1960s, she wrote the song "Little Boxes." This became one of her most famous songs and was popularized by Pete Seeger and Phil Ochs. Phil Ochs befriended Victor Jara on a trip to Chile in the early 1970s. It was through his contact with Phil Ochs that Victor Jara learned of "Little Boxes" and wrote a Chilean version.

There are countless examples of song swapping, artistic influence, and joint performances across genres and socially constructed differences. In the U.S., the musical mixing in the South between gospel, blues, country, bluegrass, and folk music are often at the heart of musical innovation and inspiration. At the level of individual artists in noncommercial settings, these encounters are often solidarity building encounters of cultural workers. It is generally larger commercial interests that intervene to make these encounters ones of exploitation.

CLAIMING EMPOWERMENT

Augusto Boal's (2006) theater of the oppressed is one of the most well-known approaches to using aesthetics to challenge the status quo. Boal attempts to overturn traditional divisions between audience and actors by encouraging people to switch between those roles. At a theater of the oppressed event, participants develop scenes and stories based on their own experiences fighting oppression, or those who begin as actors act out situations in public contexts (a demonstration, a bus queue, a subway platform) as a catalyst to civic conversation. In forum theater, the audience intervenes to stop the action and suggest new possibilities. Picher (2007) notes how Boal's approaches have moved into community organizing with centers in India, New York, and France. The ethic of empowerment at the heart of theater of the oppressed— the notion that the future is open and waiting for us to create it—is central to community organizing and to what Habermas (1979) called "political will formation." In political will formation, a shared concern crystallizes into a pressure group or movement and can even lead to the forming of a political party. In the U.S., there are also longstanding theatrical traditions linked with social movements. Popular theater, for example, was a major cultural force within the broader farmworker and Chicano/Mexican American movement upsurge of the 1960s and 1970s (García, Gutiérrez, and Nuñez, 2008).

In 1984, John Holst began some of his earliest political activity through participation in the guerrilla theater group Macho Nerds for Reagan at the University of Wisconsin-Madison. In the fall of 1984, the new national leadership of the College Republicans, which included Ralph Reed and Jack Abramoff, planned the nationwide Student Liberation Day on the first anniversary of the U.S. invasion of Grenada. The College Republicans were particularly interested in staging events on campuses such as UW-Madison with a history of student radicalism; more audacious still was their plan to hold their rally on the steps of the student union, a historic spot for progressive student rallies. A group of local and student activists, once hearing of this invasion celebration, hurriedly begin planning a response. Typically, they planned to hold a counter-rally in which speakers would denounce the imperialist nature of the invasion and the moral bankruptcy of celebrating a military attack on another sovereign nation.

Another group of students, however, decided that typical protest tactics would not be sufficient. They needed to not just denounce this act but mock and expose its fundamentally immoral and reactionary nature; they had to go even further to the right, to the most extreme xenophobic, conservative positions to expose the Republicans. The Macho Nerds for Reagan, along with their loyal and supportive ladies auxiliary the Girl Geeks for the Gipper, would show the university community what true Republicans were like and stage an even more celebratory demonstration in favor of the president and U.S. imperialism. On the day of the event, the Nerds, dressed in outlandishly nerdish and patriotic red, white, and blue clothing, gathered in the symbolic center of campus (Bascom Hill) and marched to the student union chanting "Macho nerds for Reagan, punch out the weak." Dutifully following behind their men, the ladies auxiliary politely provided support by chanting slogans such as "Mommies, mommies, don't be commies, stay at home and fold pajamies." Since the College Republicans planned to have a medical student speak who had been "rescued" by the U.S. invasion of Grenada (an official justification for the invasion), the Nerds staged their own medical student rescue in the middle of the Liberation Day celebration. As the contingent of Nerds and Girl Geeks reached the student union and the medical student rescue was launched with military music and a fake contingent of brave commandos, chaos broke out and the College Republicans simply gave up on their celebration. Their effort to transform Madison student political culture, at least for the moment, was a complete failure. The gathered crowd was thrilled with the arrival of the Nerds as a new, creative political force on campus.

These types of guerilla theater tactics make people laugh but also teach at the same time. The Nerds were able to take college republicanism to its ultimate conclusions to expose its reactionary nature. A few years later, a group of postmodernist-inspired student activists turned the tables on progressive activists with the formation of the Nihilist Workers Party. They would hold "demonstrations" where they would march in circular picket lines with blank placards and blank "leaflets" chanting slogans such as "Nobody, nowhere, nothing, not a god damn thing." While some progressive activists felt offended by this affront to their righteous political activity, the Nihilist Workers Party did expose the limitations of typical protest activity. They did, then, following Reed (2005), critique the student movement itself and make it question its tactics. In addition, Graeber (2009) documents the activities of the Revolutionary Anarchist Clown Bloc at recent antiglobalization/global justice protests who use meta-chants such as "Call! Response! Call! Response!" and "Three-word chant! Three-word chant!" Their actions are in solidarity with others as their outrageous costumes and seemingly senseless chants help disorient the police, thus allowing fellow activists to better position themselves for actions during extended protests and mobilizations.

In the skiffle, punk and hip-hop movements the do it yourself (DIY) ethic prevailed strongly over the ethic of formal skill. In terms of musicianship, both skiffle and punk were basic, relying on a small number of major chords. In terms of formal language, the MC'ing of hip-hop (which evolved into rap) did not use the "high" culture language taught in English classrooms but a mixture of Ebonics and street slang. The point of skiffle, punk, and hip-hop was their accessibility. Anybody, potentially, could participate without an extensive (and often expensive) period of formal training in technique. This is not to say that technique was not involved. In hip-hop the battles between freestyling MC's were dazzling in their virtuosity. In her essay on using hip-hop in adult education professional development, Hanley (2007) writes how "black and white teachers express amazement at the ability of black male emcees to command language, rhythm, rhyme, and complex concepts in an improvisational form known as freestyle" (p. 39). Yet, freestyling is theoretically open to anyone quick enough to jump in and improvise. Being a hip-hop DJ did not involve training in a vocational-technical institute, nor a degree in broadcast communications, just access to a turntable and a power source. Grandmaster Flash had only style, not a big record collection.

ALTERNATIVE EPISTEMOLOGIES AND ONTOLOGIES

Artistic expression, because of its often concise presentation in mediums such as songs or film, can present very effective, distilled versions of alternative epistemologies or ontologies. In other words, the arts can take what could be presented in a semester-long philosophy class and condense it in a page of song lyrics or a two-hour movie. In songs, these philosophical mini-treatises can seem deceptively simple. The Woody Guthrie children's song "My Daddy (Flies That Ship in the Sky)" for example is a clever and sophisticated presentation of the socialization of labor. The song, through the voice of children mentioning their fathers' occupations, shows how the safe and successful flight of airplanes is dependent upon a whole network of labor, from the plane's construction to its piloting and the flight control systems at airfields.

> Well, a curly-headed girl with a bright shining smile
> Heard the roar of a plane as it sailed through the sky
> To her playmates she said, with a bright twinkling eye
> My Daddy flies that ship in the sky. . . .
> Then a button-nosed kid, as he kicked up his heels
> He said, My Daddy works in the iron and the steel
> My Dad builds the planes and they fly through the sky. . . .
> Then a freckled-faced kid pinched his toe in the sand
> He says, My Daddy works at that place where they land
> You tell your mama, don't be afraid
> My Dad'll bring your daddy back home again

Cuban filmmaker Tomás Gutiérrez Alea's *The Last Supper* is a fictionalized account and expansion on the brief historical reference in a text on Cuban history to a sugar plantation owner's decision to reenact the last supper with 12 of his slaves as a form of Christian instruction. The film as a whole, and in particular the near hour-long dinner scene, is an excellent depiction of Hegel's ontological conceptualization of the master-slave relationship foundational to later dialectical conceptualizations such as Marx's proletariat-bourgeois, Fanon's colonizer-colonized, Freire's oppressed-oppressor, and bell hooks' margin-center. The film clearly and graphically depicts the master's complete inability to understand the slave and the slaves' ability to understand the role of the master and that of the slave in the relationship. The slaves' rebellion at the end of the film is their effort to overturn the relationship, and the successful escape of the most militant slave prefigures future struggles to permanently overthrow the master-slave relation.

The opening scenes of Charlie Chaplin's film *Modern Times* is a brilliant and hilarious depiction of the impact of technology on the pace of industrial work. As Chaplin's character desperately attempts to keep up with the speeding pace of the factory line, he is literally absorbed by the machinery. While spinning through the gears of the giant machine, he continues repetitively to use his wrench to tighten any nut that crosses by him. While audiences around the world laugh, they also realize the devastating impact of industrialization on the body and psyche of workers. The subsequent scenes find Chaplin's character being obligated to test out the lunch eating machine which employs scientific efficiency to shorten the worker's lunch break in order to increase the exploitation of labor. The eating machine is so clearly designed from the perspective of the bosses, and Chaplin's struggles with trying to avoid being choked and punched by the machine expose for audiences the asymmetrical relations embedded in capitalist production.

AFFIRMING PRIDE

An important part of radical aesthetics is to affirm pride, to build self-respect for a race, group, class, or movement that has historically been marginalized and the recipients of systemic brutality. This is seen throughout the gay rights movement, from Tom Robinson's English hit "Glad to Be Gay" to the highly stylized floats and costumes in numerous gay pride parades. Act Up, the Aids Coalition to Unleash Power, is an organization that uses deliberate cultural provocation to mobilize communities to highlight the AIDS crisis and to demand funding, action, and education to address it. It conducts widespread adult education around nonviolence training involving affinity training, consensus decision making, building a campaign, and becoming familiar with legal procedures around arrest and protest. In diversity training, a familiar element is helping participants become explicitly aware of the pride they take in their racial and cultural identity.

The African American entertainer and activist Paul Robeson devoted a substantial part of his life to using mass culture to develop race pride among African Americans. This project had two dimensions: educating adults about the richness of the African cultural heritage and educating them about the values and practices that lay at the heart of authentic African culture. Like DuBois, Robeson believed that a commitment to Pan-Africanism and a commitment to socialism were compatible. While in London, he conducted a series of substantial adult learning projects, studying at the School of Oriental Languages and learning a number of

African languages such as Swahili, Yoruba, Efik, Benin, Ashanti, and Tivi. Indeed, he often said that it was in England that he became an African, partly as a result of his language studies and partly through his conversations with African seamen in London, Liverpool, and Cardiff. Increasingly he became a passionate advocate of African Americans' learning about the rich heritage of African culture, believing that a lack of knowledge of their culture meant they were denied a potent source of race pride. As early as 1934 he declared that "in my music, my plays, my films I want to carry always this central idea: to be African" (Robeson, 1978/1934, p. 91). The next year he declared that "for the rest of my life I am going to think and feel as an African—not as a white man. . . . To me it seems the most momentous thing in my life" (p. 91). In common with the contemporary Africentric turn away from Eurocentrism he maintained, "it is not as imitation Europeans, but as Africans, that we have a value" (p. 92).

The heritage Robeson sought to educate people about was that of Africa's "great philosophy and epics of poetry" (Robeson, 1978/1953, p. 352) which he maintained were comparable to the achievements of Greek and Chinese poetry. He celebrated what he felt was the "great precision and subtlety of intonational structure" to be found in African languages, the "rich oral folklore . . . distinctive decorative art" of African culture and the "highly developed and original musical art distinguished by an extraordinary wealth of rhythm" (p. 352) he found in his studies of Africa. Yet, he lamented, none of these were evident in the "savage and cannibalistic" images of half-naked Black people presented as examples of Africans "as the newspapers, radio, book and lecture propagandists would make them" (Robeson, 1978/1949, p. 228). In the pursuit of an authentic Africentrism, he urged an educational campaign to make African Americans aware of their African roots. The following statement, made in 1934, is typical of this: "The dances, the songs, and the worship perpetuated by the Negro in America are identical with those of his cousins hundreds of years removed in the depths of Africa, whom he has never seen, of whose very existence he is only dimly aware. His peculiar sense of rhythm alone would stamp him indelibly as African" (1978/1934, p. 90). As Robeson conducted this educational project, he become more and more aware of the political underpinnings of his work. As he put it, "there was a logic to this cultural struggle, and the powers-that-be realized it before I did. The British Intelligence came one day to caution me about the political meanings of my activities. For the question loomed of itself: If African culture was what I insisted it was, what happens to the claim that it would take 1,000 years for Africans to be capable of self-rule? Yes, culture and politics were actually inseparable here as always" (1978/1953, p. 352).

So, after reflecting critically on his earlier assumptions regarding the significance of education about African culture, Robeson switched his emphasis to advocating cultural adult education as a central political component in the Black liberation struggle. What was particularly frustrating for Robeson was the fact that African Americans shared the White supremacist stereotypes of Africans as uncultured savages lacking even language. Hence the major purpose of his studies of African language and folk music was "to dispel this regrettable and abysmal ignorance of the value of its own heritage in the negro race itself" (Robeson, 1978/1953, p. 87). His decision to sing only Negro spirituals in concert, to charge low admission prices to his concerts, and to make independent films financed outside of the studio system were all manifestations of this project. These were political statements, not just cultural choices. As his career evolved, he learned more and more the importance of integrating the cultural and political dimensions of educating people about African culture. This became reframed as an important element in the anticolonial struggle rather than an act of purely aesthetic or anthropological education.

TEACHING HISTORY

This is probably the radicalizing function of art that most people think of first, and it is probably the most common. Song has tried to do this, often in the folk ballad form with multiple verses describing particular struggles or injustice. Bob Dylan's early work such as "The Lonesome Death of Hattie Carroll," "Oxford Town," or "Only a Pawn in Their Game" built on the ballad form to the extent of sometimes claiming old ballad melodies. Bob Marley's "Buffalo Soldier" is a well-known example of an explicit teaching song. Marley sings to potential inquirers (and maybe to himself as well) "if you know your history then you would know where you were coming from" about the former slaves and freemen "stolen from Africa, brought to America" to fight in the U.S. 9th and 10th cavalry regiments.

Perhaps the most successful aesthetic forms for teaching history are visual. Murals, quilts, and frescoes all constitute visual records of struggle, from the murals on 124th Street in Manhattan celebrating the Irish Republican Army's (IRA) Bobby Sands hunger strike, to the ornate and storied banners of British Trade Unions, to the quilts in Minneapolis-St. Paul produced by Hmong refugees detailing their flight from the mountains of Laos and Cambodia. But film currently trumps all those forms and is the way many learn narratives of struggle. The English film director Ken Loach has a five-decade career of filmmaking, with no major commercial success to his name, in which narratives of struggle have consistently played a central part. Although often set in the United Kingdom, these have ranged beyond those borders to include the Irish Republic, Nicaragua, Los Angeles, and Spain. A familiar theme that threads its way through his narratives is the means-ends dilemma, the ever-present conundrum of deciding when ends justify means and which tactics work best for a marginalized group facing a superior force. Typically, Loach locates these dilemmas in the context of an individual narrative, so that the protagonist's choices are emblematic of broader dilemmas facing a movement.

In *Bread and Roses*, his account of the Los Angeles janitor's strike, there are explicit teaching sections, as when the central character, a White union organizer, describes the origins of the phrase "Bread and Roses." Less overtly pedagogic are Loach's depictions of the choices made by two Hispanic sisters, one an immigrant with documents and one without, who find their choices narrowed by class and race. This is a central theme in Loach, the daily necessity working people face of making choices from only bad alternatives. Another theme concerns Loach's belief—or rather our reading of his implied belief—that the ends should never justify the means. In *The Wind That Shakes the Barley*, the readiness of Irish Republican rebels to compromise with the British in accepting dominion status (as against full independence) is dramatized through one brother ordering the execution of another brother for refusing to follow the official Republican line. In *Land and Freedom,* the central character—an Englishman who goes to fight for the Republican cause and joins the POUM in the Spanish Civil War—vacillates between the wisdom of staying true to collectivist ideals or trading independence of action for superior weaponry and allying with the Soviet-supplied Communist Party of Spain. For educators interested in the dynamics of discussion, by the way, we recommend the extended segment in *Land and Freedom* where villagers and Republican forces together debate the wisdom of collectivizing and abolishing private ownership.

We want to mention another film with teaching functions. This is *The Battle of Chile,* Patricio Guzmán's three-part documentary on the Popular Unity Government in early 1970s Chile and the military coup against it. The film is a powerful demonstration of the development of working-class hegemony as a highly pedagogical grassroots process. In part three of the documentary titled "People's Power," the film shows how peasants, poor, and working-class people, through their various organizations and political parties, build organs of people's power in workplaces, neighborhoods, and the countryside. As the right wing forces (with support from the U.S.) take measures to sabotage the production and distribution of goods and services and to provoke daily street violence, people self-organize to maintain and expand production and its fair distribution, while also exerting greater and greater control over the basic social institutions. The film documents how the popular classes themselves, through their own day-to-day activities and political work, begin to see how the very nature of institutions of capitalist society do not allow for full democratic participation and distribution of the basics of life. Their response to this realization is to create their own parallel institutions to build, step-by-step, a new sociopolitical economic order based on their confrontations in meeting the basic demands of the country's majority.

SUBVERTING FROM WITHIN: PAUL ROBESON

Paul Robeson was one of the towering American public intellectuals of the 20th century. His biographer claims that at one point in his life he was the most well known and most admired Black man alive (Duberman, 1988). For many people in the U.S., Robeson is known mostly for his pop culture fame as the singer of "Old

Man River" from the musical *Showboat* and as the theatrical star of *Othello, The Emperor Jones,* and films such as *Sanders of the River* and *The Proud Valley.* U.S. football fans also remember "Robeson of Rutgers," the first African American, All-American football player. Less well known, perhaps, are his tireless efforts at organizing, building mass movements, working within a radical presidential campaign, singing to and supporting labor unions, cultural work within the Hollywood studio system, supporting colonial struggles across the globe, and his long-standing involvement in the antinuclear movement. Most people who have heard of him are probably dimly aware that he was caught up in the McCarthy-ite witch hunt of communists in the 1950s and that he famously refused to name names when called in front of the House on Un-American Activities Committee (HUAC). To the end of his life, he refused to buckle under pressure to denounce the Soviet Union, which, for him, represented the best hope of providing support for anti-imperialism.

At the height of his mainstream popularity, Robeson was one of the best-known U.S. entertainers in the world, pulling down an enormous six figure salary in the 1940s. As he became a target of the HUAC, that rapidly dwindled to $6,000 per year. In addition, the State Department's confiscation of his passport denied Robeson the chance to earn a living overseas where he remained hugely popular. Although the White establishment tried to separate Robeson from the Black community by portraying him as a wealthy dilettante, he built an impressive record of involvement in union organizing. He was particularly active in trying to persuade African Americans to join mainstream labor unions, which he saw as the chief and best hope for advancing Black interests. He also played a major role in the Progressive Party's campaign to elect Henry Wallace as president in 1948. Like Gramsci, he felt that the interests of the working class needed to be represented by a revolutionary party.

Robeson maintained a strong interest in popular culture throughout his adult life and was suspicious of the way it represented mainstream interests and disseminated dominant ideologies of capitalism and White supremacy. For Robeson, popular culture was a site for struggle (another similarity he shared with Gramsci), and he strove to use the Hollywood studio system against itself by promoting films that he felt could help undermine White supremacy. Robeson became an expert on musicology, studied a number of African and Asian dialects, and explored African cultural values, philosophy, art, music, and spirituality. This eclecticism was evident in his internationalism. He traveled the world constantly, initially as a singer, and then as a political activist concerned to connect the disenfranchised and dispossessed of different countries and racial groups. As a socialist, Robeson was used to thinking both politically and internationally and constantly argued that workers and racial minorities always had more that connected them than divided them. This was true linguistically and musically but, even more importantly, it was true politically. Robeson was consistent in his efforts to point out the international dimensions of, for example, the struggle for racial equality.

Robeson was one of those rare examples of a successful, admired, and feted leader who sees through the sham of ideological manipulation and risks everything to move to the left. His growing wealth, fame, and international acclaim did not soften his growing criticism of U.S. imperialism and its hostility to the Soviet Union (which Robeson thought was grounded in the Soviet Union's championing of anticolonial struggles across the globe). The more his fame propelled him into international tours and travel, the more he learned of the growing anticolonial movements across the world and the link these had to fighting White supremacy in the U.S. (and vice versa). Robeson's influence on U.S. affairs was tempered by his growing public and private commitment to socialism (which grew concurrent with the advent of the Cold War) and his refusal to disavow the Soviet Union, even after Khrushchev's 1956 address publicizing Stalin's repression. When the State Department confiscated his passport as he faced the House on Un-American Activities Committee he was, in effect, an exile in his own country.

His work with popular culture is probably the area of his life that is known to the broadest number of people. Beginning as a singer, Robeson expanded his activities to include film and theater, starring as Othello at Stratford-on-Avon in the United Kingdom once the State Department had returned his passport to him. For him art was always politically charged, and he famously declared at a rally in support of the antifascist forces in the Spanish Civil

War "the artist must take sides. He must elect to fight for freedom or slavery. I have made my choice. I had no alternative" (Robeson, 1978/1937, p. 119). He tried to work in the commercial studio system to develop race pride by providing historically accurate representations of Africans in films such as *Sanders of the River*. After disavowing the film as "a piece of flag-waving, in which I wasn't interested . . . total loss" (Robeson 1978/1938, p. 121), he declared "the big producers insist on presenting a caricature image of the Black, a ridiculous image, that amuses the white bourgeoisie, and I am not interested in playing their game" (p. 126). He did not lose confidence in film as a medium of social change, however, arguing in Gramscian mode that film "is the medium through which to express the creative abilities of the masses" and that "only on the screen can the Negro's real place in the building of the United States be properly shown" (Robeson, 1978/1939, p. 39).

In 1937 he complained (Robeson, 1978/1937 p. 120) that "things were twisted and changed and distorted" whenever he worked with film and said again in 1942 (regarding *Tales of Manhattan*) "I thought I could change the picture as we went along . . . . but in the end it turned out to be the same old thing— the Negro solving his problem by singing his way to glory. This is very offensive to my people. It makes the Negro child-like and innocent and is in the old plantation tradition" (1978/1942, p. 142). Because of his disillusionment with Hollywood's White bankrollers, he gradually moved away from commercial films and ceased to target his appeal to a broad audience. Increasingly, he aimed his acting at members of labor unions, believing that art could help demonstrate the common economic interests of poor working-class Whites and Blacks and thus play a part in creating a viable mass, working-class movement (his film *The Proud Valley* is the best example of this). He elevated the singing of Negro spirituals to the status of serious, socially committed art—and hence made it a political act—believing that it was one way to educate African Americans and Whites of the rich heritage of African culture. Robeson thus viewed popular culture as a powerful medium through which millions of adults outside formal education could be reached.

When it was clear that the Hollywood studio system as then comprised could not be subverted from within, Robeson reappraised his commitment to film. In 1937, he concluded "one man can't face the film companies. They represent about the biggest aggregate of finance capital in the world. . . . So no more films for me" (1978/1937, p. 120). Declaring "what I won't do is work for the big companies, which are headed by individuals who would make me a slave, like my father, if they could" (1978/1937, p. 126), he came up with two strategies. First, he proposed an alternative mode of film production and distribution that totally bypassed the major studios. Such films would be financed by unions, cultural associations (such as the Council on African Affairs), or wealthy independent backers and would allow him to make films on such topics as the life of a Black commander of the Lincoln Brigade in the Spanish Civil War (a project he was never to realize). Second, he suggested that African Americans, union members, and progressive Whites boycott studio-produced films, hoping that such a stand would inspire similar boycotts in international markets. It was his conviction that "the mounting of the right kind of campaign could shake Hollywood to its foundations" (1978/1938, p. 126) and seriously affect its members. Consistent with his internationalism, he argued that if elements of the U.S. public took the lead, "help would be forthcoming from all over the world" (p. 126).

As already mentioned, in 1937 at a Spanish Civil War rally, he made one of his earliest and most renowned declarations of how he had come to place his art—his cultural work—in the service of struggle. In declaring that a choice was forced on all artists to work for freedom or slavery, he was making a broad philosophical commitment. Ten years later, this abstract commitment solidified into a concrete commitment to abandon his lucrative singing and film career for direct political action: "In 1947, on an NAACP picket line in St. Louis, I decided to retire from the concert stage and enter the day-to-day struggle of the people from whom I spring" (1978/1952, p. 319). Having learned of how his success was being used to justify White supremacy, Robeson turned the ideological tables and decided to use it to fight that same supremacy. In contemporary terms, this would be as if Michael Jordan or Michael Jackson—at the height of their fame and their ability to secure millions of dollars in recording contracts and lucrative sponsorships—had announced that they were devoting their talents and energies to forging a mass movement between Blacks and labor unions to fight capitalism, or to reviving the Black Panther Party. Perhaps the closest equivalent is the world champion boxer Cassius Clay converting to Islam and becoming Muhammad Ali, conscientious objector to the Vietnam War. Robeson's artistic and political trajectory was the opposite of the typical tale of early radicalism transmogrifying into mainstream co-optation and commodification, and constitutes a vivid example of political principle maintained within, and sometimes transcending, the confines of the mainstream market.

CONCLUSION

Art is one of the ways social movements educate new members, raise awareness, communicate urgency, teach history, and bind people together in common cause. As such, its educational and aesthetic dimensions are sometimes inseparable. Any radical understanding of adult learning needs to investigate how provocateur art is taught within social movements and how people learn to use existing mainstream forms of expression and subvert them to their own agendas. We have mentioned only a minute sample of possible genres, expressive forms, and artists in this chapter, and the examples we have chosen represent our own autobiographies more than anything else. Other educators would, of course, choose vastly different examples based on their identities and backgrounds. Our intention in including this chapter is to ensure that any analysis of radical adult education place the aesthetic dimension at its center.

CHAPTER NINE

RESEARCHING LEARNING

It is commonplace to state that we engage in research in order to better understand the world. We would add to this that radical educators do research in order to better the world. Most educators, however, we believe, would say that they educate or research in order to better the world. This for us raises three questions: What are the changes that we think would make the world better? From where do we develop our list of changes? Do there exist real chances to make these changes a reality?

We can *a priori* dream up a laundry list of things that we would like to see in the world. Many social change organizations, in fact, operate in this manner. They draw up a policy proposal of some sort and then try to rally around it as many people as possible. They can even use their laundry list to criticize others as being too utopian by demanding the impossible or too timid by not demanding enough. We, however, come to this from a particular perspective, and surprisingly, given its origins in Marxism, we believe it is a particularly nonsectarian way of operating. Marx and Engels (1948) insist that communists "do not set up any sectarian principles of their own, by which to shape and mould the proletarian movement" (p. 22). They go on to say that "[t]he theoretical conclusions of the Communists are in no way based on ideas or that have been invented, or discovered, by this or that would-be universal reformer" (p. 23). This certainly does not sound like the communism they taught us about in school in which a maximum ruler through an iron rule imposed a laundry list of ideas upon an oppressed citizenry. From where then do these firebrands propose we develop our proposals and our ideas in general? They tell us that the goals of communists "merely express . . . actual relations springing from an existing class struggle, from a historical movement going on under our very eyes" (p. 23). If we pay careful attention to reality—in other words, if we engage in research—we will find demands already in existence. There is, however, an important caveat to this idea. If we pay particular attention to the reality faced by a given society's oppressed sectors, we will find a list of demands for changes; they may not be our own, but they will be demands that require fundamental social transformation for their fulfillment.

What we are proposing here from an epistemological and a metaphysical standpoint is that research for a democratic socialism critically promotes the knowledge of oppressed people and shows that reality itself is revolutionary. In other words, embedded in reality are demands that require a radical transformation of society. These demands do not need to be, nor should they be, compiled from the fiery rhetoric of militant speeches. Instead, they represent the daily reality of society's most oppressed sectors. Radical adult educators do not need to dream up an agenda that is then disseminated; the agenda is already there, waiting to be noticed.

So how is the agenda noticed? Through research. We have already made this point in Chapter Five on program planning and in Chapter Seven on globalization. In both instances, we drew on Antonio Gramsci's (1977) idea that a given society's majority "indicate the precise direction of historical development" (p. 173). Gramsci insisted that democratically minded socialists must be constantly co-researching with the oppressed their own reality in order to keep up with the ever-changing nature of social reality. Once one becomes distant from the lives of the oppressed, one loses touch with the development of a society. To help clarify what we mean, we will provide examples from the history of adult education of the type of research we are proposing. We will then follow up these examples by outlining the general principles of research for a radical adult education.

EXAMPLES OF RESEARCH FOR RADICAL ADULT EDUCATION

ELLA BAKER'S PARTICIPATORY ACTION RESEARCH

In 1946, Ella Baker returned to her Harlem apartment on St. Nicholas Avenue and West 133rd Street having just finished five intense years as assistant field secretary and later director of branches of the NAACP. These years (which we highlighted in Chapter Four) were spent traveling throughout the South building the organizing and leadership capacities of local branches. Upon returning to New York, Baker became active in the local branch of the NAACP, eventually becoming elected as its branch president in 1952. A major issue for Baker at this time was school segregation and inequality in New York City. Baker came to an understanding of these issues through a participatory form of action research.

Well before participatory action research was formally named as an approach to research (Hall, 1993b), Baker was engaged in the co-construction of knowledge with parents of African American students in New York's public school system. As education chair of the NAACP branch, she worked with parents on a survey called "Check Your School." Among other issues, this survey involved parents in an investigation of their children's own schools. Parents collected data on the physical condition of the schools, classroom size, teacher professional experience, and student achievement. As Grant (1998) documents, this participatory research was a part of and helped lay the foundation for a wider parent-led movement that worked to improve the schooling conditions for African Americans. The movement also related schooling issues to broader issues such as housing segregation. Baker continued this work until the emerging Civil Rights Movement would call her back to the South in mid-January 1958 to begin work for the recently formed Southern Christian Leadership Conference (SCLC).

NELSON PEERY AND REVOLUTIONARY PARTICIPATORY ACTION RESEARCH

Almost exactly one year later after Ella Baker left Harlem to head south, Nelson Peery (2007) arrived in New York City with all his possessions in his canvas satchel and bricklayer's tool bag and headed to Harlem. He found a place to stay in a rooming house on St. Nicholas Avenue and 155th Street, one mile up from Ella Baker's apartment. Peery arrived in Harlem after the culmination of his first decade as a revolutionary. He had joined the Communist Party USA (CPUSA) in 1946 in his home state of

Minnesota after returning from World War II as a solider in the Pacific. A bricklayer by trade, his work in the CPUSA would take him from Minnesota to the underground in Detroit and eventually to Cleveland. During his time in Cleveland, the increasing FBI infiltration and resulting internal disorientation within the party, coupled with Peery's defense of the Negro Labor Council, led to his expulsion from the CPUSA in 1953. By 1959, revolutionary groups that had left or were expelled from the CPUSA were regrouping and forming new organizations. Peery was drawn to New York in order to build one such organization called the Provisional Organizing Committee (POC). Peery would stay in New York until 1964, bricklaying and building the POC.

In 1964 he, along with his wife and son, moved to the Watts neighborhood of Los Angeles to build a West Coast organization of the POC. It was through his political work in Watts, and particularly after the Watts rebellion of 1965, that Peery began to realize that this rebellion marked the beginning of a fundamental transformation of capitalism. Peery and his fellow comrades came to this understanding through what Gramsci insisted upon: longtime and intimate contact with the most oppressed sectors of society. Together, through an educational process of co-investigation, they began to realize that the new technologies emerging in the last decades of the twentieth century were pushing people out of the production process and transforming the working class into a class with decreasing ties to full-time, stable employment. This understanding grew as Peery participated in the founding of other revolutionary organizations of a more national scope that incorporated members from various parts of the country. Here, collective co-investigation of the realities of working-class people across the country drove this point home even more clearly. From Los Angeles to Chicago, Detroit and beyond, the conditions of working-class people have been deteriorating. At the core of this deterioration, and this sector of the working class, is the growing homeless population.

The examples of Ella Baker and Nelson Peery, two African Americans who nearly crossed paths in Harlem, provide examples of the type of research we are advocating. By this point, it is probably clear that participatory research is as much pedagogical as it is investigatory (Freire, 1974; Gaventa, 1989; Maguire, 1987; Kassam,

1982). Moreover, it is an engaged research that seeks collectively developed answers which resolve collectively identified problems (McKnight, 2009). As an engaged research, it also constitutes the foundation for participatory and democratic forms of program planning and curriculum creation in specifically educational settings. The interconnectedness of pedagogy, investigation, program planning, and action will be very apparent in the following examples.

PAULO FREIRE AND THE EMERGENCE OF PARTICIPATORY ACTION RESEARCH

While Nelson Peery was preparing to move from Harlem to Watts in November of 1964, the Brazilian pedagogue Paulo Freire was preparing to leave La Paz, Bolivia, for Chile. Freire had been jailed after the April 1964 military coup in Brazil and then received asylum from the Bolivian government where he spent the first months of what would be his 16 years of political exile. In November of 1964, however, there was a military coup in Bolivia. With another coup and his inability to withstand the altitude of La Paz, Freire sought and gained permission to move to Chile. He arrived in Chile at a time when the country was beginning a reform process under the newly elected Christian Democratic president Eduardo Frei Montalva. Freire arrived in Chile with more than 15 years of experience in adult education practice among poor and working-class people in the northeast of Brazil. He also brought with him the beginnings of his efforts to theoretically sum up his practice in the form of notes that would form the basis of his first book, *Education as the Practice of Freedom.*

It was not adult education work that led to the Brazilian military government's decision to jail him however, but the particular way in which Freire approached this work. Freire's literacy method, in terms of the actual mechanics of teaching literacy, was not particularly innovative or threatening. Since Portuguese and Spanish are phonetic languages, it is relatively easy to teach reading and writing with a few dozen short generative words which can be broken up into syllables and rearranged into new words. For several decades before Freire, Latin Americans had been learning to read and write by breaking up words into syllables and rearranging the syllables to form words. For example, the Chilean *Silabario* [literacy primer] by Claudio Matte Pérez (2004) was first published in 1884 and was used throughout Latin America to teach literacy to children. The Matte silabario features generative words such as *mano* [hand] and *lana* [wool] that are broken up and rearranged to form words such as *mala* [bad]. In Freire's literacy work, these "benign" words are replaced with words such as *favela* (the Portuguese word for shantytown) and *arado* (plow). It is not even the word choice, however, that makes Freire's work innovative or threatening, but the fact that these words are derived from an in-depth research process that precedes the act of teaching literacy. Moreover, this process of research is both innovative and participatory and the essential basis of his literacy work.

For Freire, the starting point for the educational process is the existential condition of the oppressed. Moreover, Freire conceptualizes education as the re-presentation of things about which people want to know more. The re-presentation of things, however, should be done in a way that poses things as problems to be critically considered and acted upon; this is the idea of problem-posing education. In the dialectical perspective from which Freire operated, phenomena should be conceptualized as interrelated and in contradiction. So, for example, the poor conditions of peasant life are related to and in contradiction to the wealthy conditions of the upper classes. Therefore, the educational process is a process of problem-posing the contradictions of the oppressed's situation for reflection and action.

In Freire's pedagogy, generative themes capture the existential condition of the oppressed. Generative themes represent the aspirations, ideas, and values of a given time period and a given group of people. Taken as a whole, the themes of an epoch constitute a thematic universe. Themes are contained in what Freire calls "limit-situations" that can be overcome through reflection and "limit-acts." For example, the landless state of some peasants is a limit-situation to their aspiration (generative theme) of owning and working their own land. Themes move from the universal to the particular. Each epoch has a universal theme. Freire believed that the universal theme of the 1960s and 1970s was domination and its opposite, liberation. The landless state of peasants was a particular theme within the larger universal theme of domination. The overcoming of this limit-situation through reflection and the limit-act of struggling for agrarian reform and land distribution was a part of the larger theme of liberation.

In *Pedagogy of the Oppressed*, Freire (1970/2001) outlines the steps in the participatory research process preceding literacy work. The selection and discovery of generative themes of the political-economic context of a specific group must involve participants as co-investigators. When participants investigate generative themes, they create the foundation for problem-posing literacy work. Before beginning what we would generally consider the education process, Freire identified five research stages necessary for an understanding of the thematic universe of the community with whom an educator works.

Stage 1: Informal meeting of invited specialists with volunteers from the community

- Volunteers with specialists begin "decoding" the area through qualitative research methods: observations, interviews, with extensive field notes.
  - Investigators should record as much as possible.
  - They should see the community holistically.
  - They should discover the "idiom" (how people communicate and relate to one another) of the community.
  - The goal is to discover major themes (contained in limit-situations) facing the community.
  - After each observation, the researcher should write a narrative report reflecting upon what was observed.

Stage 2: Evaluation meeting of co-investigators to discuss research findings

- Here the interpretation spirals from the individual to the team.
- Data is coded to discover the themes of the community.
- The team should organize themes into a thematic fan that reveals the interconnectedness of themes.
- Themes should be "codified."
  - The codifications (visual or audio representations of the themes) should not be too easy or too difficult to "decode."
  - The codifications should represent something familiar to the community.

Stage 3: Thematic Investigation Circles
- Here the team presents the codifications to groups of individuals in the community.
- They begin a dialogue on the codifications.
- The effectiveness of the codifications is evaluated.
  - Are they challenging without being too difficult?
  - Do they reflect issues of interest in the community?
  - Do they elicit dialogue organically tied to the interests and issues of the community?
  - Do they lead from the particular to the universal and back again?
- These meetings are recorded for later assessment.

Stage 4: Interdisciplinary study of the findings that emerge from the evaluation of Stage 3
- Each researcher suggests the themes that emerge from Thematic Investigation Circles.
- An effort is made to find a "hinged theme," a theme that ties together all the others. For Freire, the hinged theme was often "culture."

Stage 5: Recodification of themes
- New "didactic" materials that codify the themes are developed. These may be pictures, dialogues, skits, films, etc.

In the case of literacy work, it is after Stage 5 that literacy instruction begins in what Freire called "cultural circles." The first activity of the cultural circles is to begin dialogues on the final codifications. From these dialogues emerge generative words from which the skills of reading and writing are taught. The generative words are broken down on discovery cards. So, for example, if the generative word *favela* mentioned above is chosen, then the word is broken up into its syllable groups for further literacy work: fa, fe, fi, fo, fu / va, ve, vi, vo, vu / la, le, li, lo, lu. During Freire's years in Chile, he used these research stages both in literacy work to understand the thematic universe of illiterates and in agrarian reform work in order to understand the thematic universe of peasants and farmworkers.

Some readers will know that in Chile the period from 1964 to 1969 preceded the election of socialist Salvador Allende of the Popular Unity coalition of left-wing political parties. Freire's time in Chile was marked by a rapid process of political radicalization among workers, peasants, and youth leading up to the historic election of Allende. Since Freire's main work in Chile was concentrated in agrarian reform in the countryside and in the national literacy campaign among the poor throughout the country, his research process put him and the young Chilean collaborators that he worked with in direct and sustained contact with the realities of working-class and peasant life in Chile.

The projects that Freire worked on were not of a revolutionary nature and were openly reformist in their goals. The agrarian reform project was wholly sanctioned by the United Nations and endorsed by the United States as exemplary of what the U.S.'s Alliance for Progress was trying to accomplish in Latin America, namely reform societies in order to prevent another Cuban-style revolution in the region. The literacy campaign was intended to use adult education to integrate poor people into the capitalist modernization process that was the overall political project of the Christian Democratic government. Nevertheless, the close contact with the popular classes at the heart of Freire's approach to research, combined with the inability of the reform process to resolve the problems of poverty it highlighted, accelerated a process of politicalization and radicalization of Freire, his collaborators, and those with whom they worked. This is what Freire (in Freire and Guimarães, 1987) says of himself during this period: "It is not that Chile made me a completely different man from the person I was before, but what it did exactly was to deepen in me a radicalization that was already in process" (p. 127, our translation). This radicalization would lead Freire to write his most famous text, *Pedagogy of the Oppressed*, and would lead his Chilean collaborators to become active protagonists in the movement for a socialist transformation of Chilean society.

EXAMPLES OF PARTICIPATORY RESEARCH IN THE U.S. CIVIL RIGHTS MOVEMENT

While Freire's approach to participatory research is recognized as a forerunner (Torres, 1995) to what became formalized as participatory action research in the 1970s, there is, as many have recognized, a long-standing practice of participatory forms of research in social movements around the world (Darcy de Oliveira and Darcy de Oliveira, 1975; Gaventa, 1989; Heaney, 1993; Quigley, 1997); the U.S. is by no means an exception to this fact. In Chapter Four we detailed the democratic nature of training within the Civil Rights Movement in the work of the Highlander Folk School, the Citizenship Schools of the Southern Christian Leadership Conference (SCLC), and the Student Nonviolent Coordinating Committee (SNCC). Since, as we mentioned above, participatory forms of social movement practice combine program planning, investigation, and pedagogy, we will describe a few examples of participatory research practices within the civil rights work we highlighted in Chapter Four.

The Citizenship Schools that were first organized through Highlander and later by SCLC were exemplary of the participatory action research (PAR) principle of combining education, investigation, and action. In a Highlander Folk School (n.d.) document titled "Training Leaders for Citizenship Schools: Outline of Training Workshop," we see that participants in the training were asked to engage in community mapping in preparation for establishing a Citizenship School. The document contains a "Questionnaire on Community Background" that asks participants to investigate issues related to the logistics, content, and voter registration outcomes of the Citizenship School they were being trained to establish. For example, the questionnaire asks participants to investigate seasonal employment patterns and hours of work of potential school participants in order to determine the best time of year and hours of the day for scheduling purposes. How many adult education programs still today face low and inconsistent enrollment because they fail to engage in this essential program planning research? In terms of the content of the school curriculum, participants are asked to investigate the level of existing voter registration, what the requirements for registration are in the particular locality, whether there are numerous barriers to registration, and what specifically the barriers are. This background research conducted by the trainee in conjunction with local contacts and future Citizenship School participants forms the basis for the school curriculum. Here school participants and the Citizenship School teacher are then expected to continue co-investigating these voter registration issues and other community issues.

Under the auspices of SCLC, Citizenship School training continued the practice of asking trainees to engage in community mapping research. In the section titled "Planning a Voter Registration Campaign" of SCLC's (n. d.) *Citizenship Workbook*, participants are given a list of nine questions to help them map their community. For example, participants are asked to research the size of the African American population in their area, the number of African Americans of voting age, and the area of concentration of the African American population. The next section of the workbook provides a "Canvass Your Neighborhood" table that participants, and others they involve in the voter registration drive, should use in order to map their community. The canvass table has columns for the specific house number, names of citizens, and then a series of indicators to check regarding their registration status and willingness to register and vote.

Heavily influenced by the participatory practice of Ella Baker, the Student Nonviolent Coordinating Committee (SNCC) engaged in participatory forms of research in at least two areas. First, the organizing strategy of SNCC was a form of participatory action research. As Ransby (2003) describes, SNCC activists would begin their work by making contact with elders or established activists in a particular locality. They would ask these local residents to analyze the local reality and begin to engage them in a co-investigation of local problems and strategies to address these problems. Second, the SNCC Freedom School curriculum was organized around a participatory action research case study method. The report from the meeting of the Subgroup of the Leadership Development and Current Issues Committee (1964) charged with developing the Freedom School curriculum shows that the committee proposed using case studies of local issues as the basis for the curriculum. Specific academic content would be introduced as it helped participants in their co-investigation and organizing efforts to resolve the local issue under investigation. The report lists six reasons for using this curriculum strategy.

- Each case is related to the life experiences of the students.
- The co-investigation of a case study allows for creative teaching methods.

- The case study allows participants to see the interrelatedness of the various social, political, economic, and cultural forces at play in any given case.
- The case study helps compensate for any lack of teaching experience.
- The case study allows for a creative experience.
- The case study allows for, what we call today, differentiation.

PARTICIPATORY RESEARCH IN THE LABOR MOVEMENT

Similarities to the community mapping for voter registration in the Civil Rights Movement are evident in Wigmore's (2005b) description of how collective workplace mapping can be used as a way to build worker power. First, in union organizing campaigns, the collective creation of a workplace map builds worker consciousness, creates or strengthens networks among workers, and provides a visual representation of the relations of power or powerlessness in a given workplace. A workplace map makes, as Wigmore argues, the ordinary day-to-day workplace extraordinary. Through a visual representation, it brings workplace power relations to the forefront of people's thinking. A workplace map is also helpful in situations of low literacy levels or multilingual worksites. With a collectively created map, a union organizing committee of workers, for example, can see where they have the most support, which workers they need to build support among, where they have contacts with whom they can build networks across the workplace, which workers are under the most and least supervisory surveillance, and so on.

Second, Wigmore (2005a) suggests that collectively created workplace maps can be particularly useful in organizing around health and safety issues. Wigmore describes two types of maps for this purpose. The creation of body maps with which a group of workers can identify common aliments. When combined with workplace maps which identify where workers are experiencing specific problems, workers can identify the specific source of health and safety issues. These maps help turn what some might think of as personal health issues into collectively experienced problems in need of collective solutions.

In *Teaching Defiance* Michael Newman (2006) describes a problem-solving training model he developed based on the following straightforward questions:

- What's wrong?
- What will we do?
- What can we do?

As much as this is a training model, like the previous examples, this is also a model for participatory action research. Newman describes how these three simple questions allow for a collective investigation of workplace issues and for their collective resolution. This participatory approach combines collective learning, investigation, and action to identify an issue, understand its root causes, and develop a strategy to resolve the issue.

A model such as Newman's may raise some concerns that these three questions, like the methodologies outlined in the other examples, do not necessarily lead toward creating a genuinely democratic, cooperative, socialist society. The issue of the potential to co-opt participatory forms of research for mainstream goals has been raised in the literature on participatory research (Heaney, 1993, Kassam, 1982; Mulenga, 1999), and Quigley (1997) reminds us that action research has its origins in Kurt Lewin's corporate-based training and development. We recognize the potential for co-optation and agree with Heaney (1993) that beyond a collection of specific techniques, participatory research is an epistemological critique of mainstream notions of knowledge production. As with program planning, in order for participatory research to play a central role in the struggle for a democratic socialism we should evaluate our research practices based on the criteria we listed in Chapter Five.

PRINCIPLES FOR A PARTICIPATORY RESEARCH

In this last section of the chapter, we will outline what we consider to be the essential epistemological and methodological principles of a research practice for radical adult education. We derive these principles from an analysis of the research practices of social movements and from the existing literature on participatory research.

EPISTEMOLOGICAL PRINCIPLES

Epistemology is the philosophical way of labeling how we understand the nature of knowledge. Participatory research has a particular epistemology. First, metaphysically speaking, reality is interconnected; nothing exists or can be understood in isolation. Second, as Freire (1974) argues, research needs to consider the objective and the subjective aspects of reality. By subjective we mean our understanding of the world, and by objective we mean the concrete material reality in which we live. Third, the objective and the subjective are understood as always being dialectically related. In other words, there is a relationship between the objective and the subjective in which one cannot be understood outside of the relationship with the other. Fourth, since we live in a dialectical world, we understand reality to be interrelated and in a state of constant motion and change driven by internal contradictions. This change is quantitative (incremental) and becomes qualitative (fundamental) when something new is added or subtracted (Peery, 1993). So, for example, moisture can build incrementally in storm clouds, but it is the addition of dust particles or ice crystals upon which moisture coalesces that sparks the qualitative change to rain.

Since a goal of radical adult educational research is to understand the constantly changing relationship between the objective and the subjective, people must be involved in exploring how this process manifests itself in their lives (Freire, 1974). A world in constant motion and change necessitates continuous research and assessment of conclusions we have drawn about reality. If reality is not static, neither is knowledge. Rather, knowledge is actively created as we engage the material world and each other. Knowledge becomes critical when it captures the dialectical interrelatedness of the world and its change and motion.

As our social, political, and economic world is dominated by capitalism and the asymmetrical relations it produces, the control and production of knowledge is not a neutral process.

A fundamental question then becomes "Who has the right to create knowledge?" (Hall, 1977). In this context, radical research is openly partisan in siding with those on the losing end of prevailing asymmetrical relations. It actively promotes the legitimacy of the knowledge of the oppressed, while at the same time critiquing the assumption of the unearned legitimacy of knowledge produced by powerful groups and institutions (Heaney, 1993).

At this point, we should state that the epistemological principles we are outlining here are largely within the Marxist tradition. We do not wish, however, to emphasize the divisive dichotomy that has been documented in the literature on participatory research (Kassam, 1982; Mulenga, 1999) between Marxist perspectives and more pragmatic and reformist perspectives. While we agree that this dichotomy exists, we are cognizant of the wide variety of contexts in which readers work and research. In this sense, we agree with Gaventa (1989) that there is a continuum of participatory research approaches from pragmatic and reformist to revolutionary.

Following our epistemological principles, however, and drawing on the work of Peery (2002) and Allman (1999), we can say that there is a dialectic of reform and a dialectic of revolution. A dialectic of reform is when the struggle is to better one's position within a relation such as that of the labor movement. A dialectic of revolution is when something new is added to the relation that allows for the relation itself to be overcome. Nelson Peery (2002) argues that we are now moving into a period where a dialectic of revolution is emerging. His participatory research practice within the organizations among the most oppressed sectors of society demonstrates, in his opinion, that the new microchip-based technologies are a qualitatively new addition to the prevailing relations of production. As we described in Chapter Seven, this makes reform struggles less winnable and revolutionary struggles for a qualitatively new relation more possible. In the golden age of capitalism in the post–World War II period, technology allowed for the expansion of manufacturing-based production and employment, laying the foundation for the reform struggles of the trade union movement and the creation of a stable working class. The new technologies replace labor in the production process creating a new growing dispossessed sector of society outside the prevailing relations and laying the foundation for a struggle for a new form of social and economic organization of society. It is within this epistemological framework that we can begin to address the question as to whether there exist real chances for reform or revolutionary changes to become reality.

METHODOLOGICAL PRINCIPLES

In an analysis of participatory research in North America, Gaventa (1989) provides a useful typology that considers the relationship between forms of research and the extent of control exercised over the process of knowledge production. The first level Gaventa calls "Research by the People: The Reappropriation of Knowledge." This refers to research in which people affected by an issue or problem seek existing knowledge in an effort to overcome the problem. In the labor movement, for example, workers will do extensive research on a company before entering into contract negotiations. In John's experience with the union of adult educators at City Colleges of Chicago, the union engaged in extensive research over how much monies the City Colleges received for the adult education programs. The union knew exactly how many student attendance hours it took for the colleges to receive enough funding to support the salary of an adult educator. Through research, the union knew, for example, that the colleges received more monies for the adult education program than were going into the program. As Gaventa argues, this type of participatory research is both empowering and educational. The union went into contract negotiations knowing that the colleges were receiving enough monies to meet its demands. It was an empowering experience for union negotiators to disprove the college's arguments with data they had collected on the funding levels for the program.

The second level Gaventa calls "Research by the People: Developing the Peoples' Knowledge." An example of this level of research can be found in the recovered factory movement in Argentina that we discussed in Chapter Four on training. Here, workers themselves discovered through their own research that they could find ways to produce goods in their factories without the need for bosses. Out of necessity the workers, through participatory research, developed a whole new body of knowledge and skills about production, distribution, marketing, and sales.

Gaventa calls the third level "Research by the People: Popular Participation in the Social Production of Knowledge." This level describes a fundamental transformation in the control and production of knowledge and its social use. Level three goes beyond expanding the access to existing knowledge and the participatory development of knowledge in particular situations to include direct participation by community members in crucial matters. Ordinary people are centrally involved in the deciding how public monies will be allocated for research and in determining the purposes for which knowledge will be used. Gaventa cites as an example of level three the Appalachian Land Ownership Study that involved local people in all levels of the research and decision making regarding the public determination of land use.

In terms of specific research practices, the Society for Participatory Research in Asia (Kassam, 1982) presents a list of useful techniques in its introductory text on participatory research. This list includes: group discussions, public meetings, research teams, open-ended surveys, community seminars, fact-finding tours, collective production of audio-visual materials, popular theater, and educational camps. These practices can be used along with what can be considered more traditional forms of qualitative or quantitative data collection techniques. As we stated above, while specific techniques such as these lend themselves to participation and democratization of the data collection and analysis process, standard research techniques can also be used; it is important to see specific techniques, like the methodology as a whole, along a continuum of practices of ever-increasing participation.

KEY QUESTIONS FOR RESEARCHERS

We will conclude this chapter with a list of questions drawn from the work of the Society for Participatory Research in Asia (Kassam, 1982), the work of feminist researcher Patricia Maguire (1987), and indigenous researcher Linda Tuhiwai Smith (1999). These questions are designed to clarify the necessarily partisan nature of radical research, its relation to social change and asymmetrical power relations, and its pedagogical nature.

Who initiates and controls the research process?
- Do all those involved or affected have equal say in initiating and controlling the process?
- Are there constraints to some people's participation, and how are these constraints addressed?
- Are there funding issues or outside forces impacting the direction of the research?

What is the content of the research?
- Are the issues being researched framed in a way that considers exactly how all people are affected by the issues?
- What is not being researched, and does what is left out leave anyone out?

Is social location considered in the collection and analysis of data?
- Do data collection methods consider the multiple ways of knowing based on different people's social location?
- Is social location considered when determining who collects data?
- Are the limits of each data collection technique considered and compensated for?

What is the pedagogical nature of the research process?
- Is the research constructed in a way that maximizes collective learning?
- Is the learning process accessed equally across all those involved?

How are the results used for action?
- Are the benefits of the research equitably shared?
- Do the results advance the interests of the oppressed?
- Is social location considered in how the results impact all people?

The research we advocate is partisan, participatory, and dedicated to the development of knowledge aimed at fueling a struggle for a truly inclusive, democratic socialism. The specific data collection techniques are not all that important. While we recognize that the popularization of qualitative research methods marks a step toward a democratization of research by emphasizing the voices and perspectives of those from whom data are being collected, quantitative forms of research can play an equally important role in participatory and democratic research (Peters, 1997). The main point for us is the partisan nature of research; in other words, the research process begins with the reality of the oppressed. Depending on the specific context, qualitative or quantitative techniques may be the most appropriate. But the goal of radical research is unchanging—an ever-expanding and critical understanding of people's own reality with the intent of resolving problems at the root of people's oppression. The "political" nature of the reality will emerge from a robust investigation of reality in its dialectical totality, or more plainly stated, by investigating the interrelatedness of people's social, economic, political, and cultural realities.

CHAPTER TEN

ADULT LEARNING IN
A DIVERSE WORLD

Diversity is, arguably, the zeitgeist of our time. The need to recognize and then celebrate diversity is trumpeted throughout adult education and in the world beyond its boundaries. Politically, the election of a biracial U.S. president is claimed to have ushered in an era of postracial politics. Academically, the winds of postmodernism have blown away the cobwebs of Eurocentric Enlightenment certainty. In adult education, "outlawed" or subjugated discourses such as Africentrism and queer theory are moving center stage. College catalogs regularly display a rainbow of racial identities on their front covers in ways that suggest that European Americans are a minority of faculty and students on campus. Right-wing ideologues, politicians, and pundits regularly bemoan the un-Americanization of the United States, but in adult education it would be strange indeed to hear of an academic program, a community organization, or a research paper that advocated racial insensitivity and cultural unresponsiveness. In fact, in an era that is supposedly postmodern, the "grand narrative of diversity"—once we were blinkered and racist, then the scales dropped from our eyes and now we celebrate diversity—is remarkably compelling.

Given the centrality of the "celebrating diversity" narrative, it may seem unsurprising that we devote a chapter to this theme. However, our position is one that questions the accuracy of this narrative, even as we acknowledge its powerful presence and recognize the important and hard-fought struggles that have transformed the formal field of adult education from a mainly

White and male endeavor. Nevertheless, hegemony is skilled at absorbing challenges to its legitimacy and appearing to cede territory while subtly co-opting insurgencies and superficially reconfiguring itself so that structures of inequity are left intact even as transformation seems to have occurred. So what seems to be an acceptance and celebration of the different backgrounds and identities of adult learners, and the need for a plethora of programs grounded in racial, cultural, and gender identities, can sometimes be interpreted as a strengthening of Eurocentric, heterocentric, ableist, upper-class, dominant cultural values. We argue that we need to be ever vigilant to the power of hegemony in our struggles to transform the field. We begin this chapter by articulating our critique of mainstream accounts of diversity using as our heuristic Herbert Marcuse's notion of repressive tolerance. We will follow this up with examples of alternative practices and conceptualizations of diversity.

In the 1960s Marcuse, a refugee from Nazi Germany who settled in the U.S., wrote a small essay on repressive tolerance (Marcuse, 1965). The long-lasting effect of this is so incendiary to conservatives that if you go to the Marcuse home page (http://www.marcuse.org/herbert/index.html) and click on the link "Haters Page" (http://www.marcuse.org/herbert/booksab out/haters/haters.htm), you will find contemporary fulminations against this 42-page essay written almost half a century ago. In the essay, Marcuse argues that that an all-embracing tolerance of diverse views in media, politics, curriculum, and classroom discussions always ends up legitimizing an unfair status quo. Such all-embracing toler- ance for Marcuse is repressive, not liberating—exclusive, not inclu- sive. How can this be so? Doesn't broadening the perspectives and intellectual traditions reviewed in a curriculum so that equal weight is given to radical ideas represent a qualitative progression forward? No, according to Marcuse. His argument is that whenever radical ideas or excluded racial traditions are incorporated into a curriculum, placing them alongside mainstream ideas always dilutes the radical qualities of the newly added perspectives.

Not only is radicalism blunted, according to Marcuse, repres- sive tolerance ensures that adults believe they live in an open society characterized by freedom of speech and expression while in reality their freedom is being constricted further and further.

Marcuse criticizes educators who painstakingly spend time presenting students with a diversity of perspectives and then let them make up their own minds which makes most sense to them. His argument is that students' previous ideological conditioning is so strong and enduring, it will always predispose them to choose what for them are "commonsense" socially sanctioned understandings. The radical educator's task, indeed her responsibility, therefore, is to confront—even coerce—students into engaging *only* with troubling ideas that they would otherwise avoid.

The contemporary logic of diversity assumes that exposing students to the widest possible array of views is inherently educative. Understood this way, diversity legitimizes (in the name of freedom of speech and academic freedom) all viewpoints, no matter how bigoted or pernicious. It gives the same weight and consideration to perspectives that are racist as it does to those that are antiracist and argues that a liberal education should expose students to both and then allow them to make up their minds as to which is the most accurate. In Marcuse's opinion, those who proclaim tolerance for all viewpoints only reinforce an unfair status quo and give succor to antieducational practices. This is because people's previous ideological conditioning has been so successful in socializing them into accepting mainstream conservativism that establishment views will always prevail.

A number of contemporary education debates in the United States are examples of the dynamic Marcuse describes. One is the call for creationism to be given equal weight in the curriculum alongside the theory of evolution, with the implication that both have roughly equal scientific credibility. Such a position implies that a valid choice exists between one or the other argument and that it is fine for students to choose which to believe is the more scientifically accurate. Another is teaching that global warming is a contested theory, as if it were a viewpoint roughly equally supported by some scientists but dismissed by others. A third is the idea of the bell curve as applied to the study of intelligence, in which the innate superiority of Europeans is proposed as an intellectually tenable proposition. In all three cases, the logic of diversity requires that we frame classroom discussions of these issues in terms that give equal and serious consideration to both or multiple sides of an argument. Marcuse's point is that in giving equal consideration to views that reinforce the interests of White supremacy, global capitalism, and religious fundamentalism teachers end up undercutting their own intention of developing students' powers of critical thinking.

Repressive tolerance further neutralizes dissenting views and efforts for democratic social change while appearing to support them. How does it achieve this? Essentially it ensures the continued marginality of minority views by placing them in close, comparative association with dominant ones. When a curriculum is widened to include dissenting and radical perspectives that are considered alongside the mainstream perspective, the minority perspectives are always overshadowed by the mainstream one. This happens even if the radical perspectives are scrupulously accorded equal time and space.

Whitestream is a term employed by contemporary critical race theorists to describe the way that Whiteness and the desirability of White identity are subtle White supremacist elements at the heart of Eurocentric philosophy. As long as the dominant, Whitestream perspective is included as one of several possible options for study, its presence inevitably overshadows the minority ones which will always be perceived as alternatives, as others—never as the natural center to which students should turn. Irrespective of the educator's viewpoint (which may be strongly opposed to dominant ideology), the mere inclusion of that ideology as one option ensures its continued dominance. This is because the Whitestream ideology has so seeped into our "structures of feeling" (Williams, 1977) that it operates at a preconscious level shaping our responses to alternatives that are proposed to it. The only way to promote real tolerance—liberating or discriminating tolerance in Marcuse's terms—is to deny learners the chance to consider mainstream perspectives as one possibility among many. Instead of exposing people to a smorgasbord of mainstream and radical perspectives, educators practicing true tolerance will allow students exposure only to alternative views, to dissenting traditions.

Marcuse argues that repressive tolerance is hard to detect because it masks its repressive dimensions behind the façade of open, evenhandedness. Alternative ideas are not banned or even censored. Critical texts are published and critical messages circulated. Previously subjugated knowledges and perspectives (Africentrism or queer theory for example) are inserted into the curriculum. The defenders of the status quo can point to the existence of dissenting voices (such as Marcuse's) as evidence of the open society we inhabit and the active tolerance of a wide spectrum of ideologies. But the framing of meaning accomplished by hegemony is all. Sometimes the meaning of radical texts is diluted by the fact that the texts themselves are hard to get or incredibly expensive. More likely the radical meanings are neutered because they are framed as the expressions of obviously weird minority opinion. As Marcuse writes; "other words can be spoken and heard, other ideas can be expressed, but, at the massive scale of the conservative majority . . . they are immediately 'evaluated' (i.e. automatically understood) in terms of the public language—a language which determined 'a prior' *(sic)* the direction in which the thought process moves. Thus the process of reflection ends where it started: in the given conditions and relations" (Marcuse, 1965, p. 96). Marcuse cites Orwell's analysis of language in illustrating how the meaning of peace is redefined so that "preparing for war *is* working for peace" (p. 96).

The contemporary discourse of diversity, of opening up the field of adult education to diverse voices, perspectives, and traditions, can be analyzed quite effectively using the idea of repressive tolerance. An honorable and emancipatory position to take is that adult education research, theorizing, and practice needs to include alongside the grand narrative of Eurocentric rationality work that draws on other cultural traditions and represents different racial perspectives. Providing an array of alternative perspectives and sensibilities seems to be a major step in moving away from a situation in which White, male, European voices dominate. Yet Marcuse alerts us to the possibility that this apparent broadening of voices can actually reinforce the ideology of White supremacy that it purports to undercut. By widening curricula to include a variety of traditions, we appear to be celebrating all positions. But the history of White supremacy, and the way that language and structures of feeling frame Whiteness as the natural, inevitable conceptual center, means that the newly included voices, sensibilities, and traditions are always positioned as the exotic other. Adult educators can soothe their consciences by believing progress is being made toward racial inclusivity and cultural equity and can feel they have played their small but important part in the struggle. But as long as these subjugated traditions are considered alongside the dominant ideology, repressive tolerance ensures they will always be subtly marginalized as exotic, quaint, and other than the natural center. The logic of liberating or discriminating tolerance would require an immersion only in a racial or cultural tradition that diverged radically from mainstream ideology—for example, an adult education graduate program that allowed only the consideration of Africentric ideas and perspectives or a program in which the mainstream was presented for what it is, namely a perspective that has gained prominence through the exclusion of alternative and better perspectives with more explanatory power and alternative practices. The logic of repressive tolerance holds that as long as a perspective such as Africentrism is considered as one of many possible perspectives, including Eurocentrism, it will always be positioned as the marginal alternative to the White supremacist center.

REPRESSIVE TOLERANCE IN ACTION

In this section we want to explore case studies of repressive tolerance in action. These are, in turn, Marcuse's own analysis of how repressive tolerance distorts discussion-based classrooms, case studies by Gary Cale and Sue Huber of how teaching against dominant cultural values in a community college classroom only served to entrench those same values, Ian Baptiste's proposal for a pedagogy of ethical coercion, and the antiracist work of the People's Institute for Survival and Beyond of New Orleans.

A crucial component of repressive tolerance is the metanarrative of democracy. This narrative is ideologically embedded in the way higher educators sometimes think of the discussion method, where the intent is to honor and respect each learner's voice (Brookfield and Preskill, 2005). But the implicit assumption that in good discussions all contributions carry equal weight can easily lead to a flattening of conversation. Dignifying each student's personhood can result in a refusal to point out the ideologically skewed nature of particular contributions, let alone saying someone is wrong. In Marcuse's view, the ideology of democratic tolerance in higher education seminars means that

> the stupid opinion is treated with the same respect as the intelligent one, the misinformed may talk as long as the informed, and propaganda rides along with falsehood. This pure tolerance of sense and nonsense is justified by the democratic argument that nobody, neither group nor individual, is in possession of the truth and capable of defining what is right and wrong, good and bad." (1965, p. 94)

Additionally, the airing of a radical perspective as one among many possible perspectives on a situation always works to the detriment of that perspective, since participants' ideological conditioning disposes them to view that perspective with skepticism or hostility. Thus "persuasion through discussion and the equal presentation of opposites (even where it is really equal) easily lose their liberating force as factors of understanding and learning; they are far more likely to strengthen the established thesis and to repel the alternatives" (Marcuse, 1965, p. 97).

The only way to make democracy a reality, in Marcuse's view, is to have its participants in full possession of all relevant information; "the democratic argument implies a necessary condition, namely that the people must be capable of deliberating and choosing on the basis of knowledge, that they must have access to authentic information, and that, on this basis, their evaluation must be the result of autonomous thought" (1965, p. 95). In stressing autonomous thought, Marcuse takes us right to the idea of self-directed learning, but it is a politicized interpretation of that idea that avoids equating it with the self-indulgent reiteration of familiar ideas. Autonomous individuals are "freed from the repressive requirements of a struggle for existence in the interest of domination" (p. 105) and able to choose where best to exercise their creativity. In exhibiting the capacity to think autonomously, people are demonstrating their maturity. Marcuse invokes J. S. Mill's argument that democracy only works if those involved are "human beings in the maturity of their faculty . . . capable of being improved by free and equal discussion" (p. 86).

An interesting educational case study of repressive tolerance in action is Cale's analysis of his attempt to work critically and democratically in a community college freshman composition class teaching writing through the analysis of race, class, and gender in the U.S. (Cale, 2001; Cale and Huber, 2001). Cale and his coauthor Huber draw on Marcuse to illustrate the danger of providing an array of philosophical and ideological perspectives and assuming that these have rough parity in students' eyes. Hence, despite his giving lectures critiquing the concept of meritocracy and outlining capitalism's deliberate creation of an underclass, Cale notes that "once I allowed the 'common sense' of the dominant ideology to be voiced, nothing could disarm it" (Cale and Huber, 2001, p. 16). It did not matter that a disproportionately large amount of time was spent in criticism of this ideology. As long as Cale allowed his White students (the majority in the class) to voice their own opinions regarding racism—opinions based on their own experiences as adults—the focus was continually shifted away from White privilege and toward discussions of reverse discrimination and Black "problems." Cale refreshingly and courageously admits that his past efforts to work democratically by respecting all voices and encouraging the equal participation of all learners "has in many cases actually helped to silence some of my students, to reinforce the dominance of the status quo, and to diminish my own ability to combat racism, sexism, and classism" (Cale and Huber, 2001. p. 16). He concludes that his use of "democratic" discussion achieved little effect other than to provide "opportunities for students to attack and silence oppositional thinkers, including myself" (p. 17).

Another contemporary analysis of repressive tolerance—which, unlike Cale's is not explicitly grounded in Marcuse's work—is the outlining of an ethical pedagogy of coercion conducted by Trinidadian born adult educator Ian Baptiste (2000). In Baptiste's view, educators often function as persuaders and organizers but choose not to acknowledge this. He argues that they already use forms of justifiable coercion but are queasy about admitting to that reality. To Baptiste it is naïve and empirically inaccurate for educators to insist that their job is not to take sides, not to force an agenda on learners. Like it or not (and Baptiste believes most of us do not like to acknowledge this), educators cannot help but be directive in their actions, despite avowals of neutrality or noninterference.

One of the most contentious aspects of Baptiste's writings is his insistence on the morality of coercion. Citing George S.

Counts in his support, Baptiste believes that educators cannot avoid imposing their preferences and agendas on learners and that in certain instances it is important that they do this. Sometimes, in furtherance of legitimate agendas or to stop the perpetration of illegitimate ones, Baptiste argues that the educator must employ coercion. At other times, and for reasons that have to do with the educator's wish to stop any challenge to his authority, coercion is used but masked by a veneer of passive-aggressive, nondirective facilitation. We all know of situations in which we or our colleagues have said that "anything goes," while concurrently making it very clear (often through subtle, nonverbal cues) that the "anything" concerned needs to reflect our own preferences.

In Baptiste's view, a pedagogy of measured coercion is justi- fiable if it uses "force sufficient to stop or curb the violence or injustice. The aim is not necessarily to annihilate the perpetrators but rather to render them incapable of continuing their pillage" (p. 43). To support his case he describes a situation in which he worked with a number of community groups on the south side of Chicago to assist them in reviving an area ravaged by pollution and migration. As the neutral, independent facilitator he was supposed to stay free of forming alliances with any of the groups involved. Citing his liberal humanist sensibilities, he describes how, in trying to stay neutral, "I succeeded only in playing into the hands of the government officials (and their lackeys in the community). They played me like a fiddle, pretending in public to be conciliatory, but wheeling and dealing in private" (p. 47).

In hindsight, Baptiste argues, the experience taught him that in situations where there is a clear imbalance of power, educators should take uncompromising stands on the side of those they see as oppressed. An inevitable consequence of doing this will be the necessity for educators "to engage in some form of manipulation— some fencing, posturing, concealment, maneuvering, misinforma- tion, and even all-out deception as the case demands" (pp. 47–48). He points out that if educators do admit that manipulation is sometimes justified, then an important learning task becomes researching and practicing how to improve one's manipulative capacities. Through studying ethically justified manipulation, educators can "build a theory that can legitimize and guide our use of coercive restraint" (p. 49).

Finally, an interesting example of practice against repressive tolerance is provided by the People's Institute for Survival and Beyond of New Orleans, an organization dedicated to antiracist education. The institute advocates what is an extended, workshop-long commitment to a liberatory perspective that involves the suppression of critique regarding the pervasiveness of racism. Chisom and Washington (1997) emphasize how institute workshops insist that certain assumptions will not be debated. Examples of these unchallengeable assumptions are that White supremacy prevails, that such supremacy is the basis of all other inequalities, and that attempts to overcome other oppressions must begin with antiracist efforts. Why can't these assumptions be debated? Partly, this is because if debate of these is allowed valuable time for antiracist work will be lost. But, chiefly, it is because if these assumptions are debated the previous ideological conditioning of participants (which says that the Civil Rights Movement means race is no longer an issue and that affirmative action now discriminates unfairly against White males) will cause the workshop's central purposes to be marginalized and obfuscated. Hence a tolerance of the viewpoint that racism is no longer a central fact of U.S. life—even if this view is vigorously critiqued by the institute's facilitators—will sabotage a serious analysis of participants' own collusion in White supremacy. Such a tolerance would be, in Marcuse's terms, repressive.

PRACTICING LIBERATING TOLERANCE

In Marcuse's view, the only way to break the sort of logjam identified in the previous section by Cale, Huber, and Baptiste is to practice liberating tolerance. The educator must try to "break the established universe of meaning (and the practice enclosed within this universe)" so that people are "freed from the prevailing indoctrination (which is no longer recognized as indoctrination)" (Marcuse, 1965, pp. 98–99). In a society living under false consciousness, people "are indoctrinated by the conditions under which they live and think and which they do not transcend" (p. 98). To help them emerge from this, they need to realize that truth is manipulated, that the "facts" "are established, mediated, by those who made them" (p. 99). They need to shed the tolerance for multiple truths, each of which is presumed to have its own integrity and internal validity, and realize instead that "there *is* an objective truth which can be discovered, ascertained only in learning and comprehending that which is and that which can be and ought to be done for the sake of improving the lot of mankind" (p. 88). This objective truth is a liberatory truth concerning the need to overthrow the dominant ideology of capitalism and White supremacy, and it must always take precedence over a supposedly respectful, but ultimately repressive, tolerance of all viewpoints.

To Marcuse "tolerance cannot be indiscriminate and equal . . . it cannot protect false words and wrong deeds which demonstrate that they contradict and counteract the possibilities of liberation" (1965, p. 88). Providing a smorgasbord of alternative perspectives in the name of a pluralist tolerance of diversity only ensures that the radical ones are marginalized by the dominant consciousness. The only way to break with the face of spurious impartiality is to immerse students fully and exclusively in a radically different perspective that challenges mainstream ideology and confronts the learner with "information slanted in the opposite direction" (p. 99). After all, "unless the student learns to think in the opposite direction, he will be inclined to place the facts into the predominant framework of values" (p. 113). This rupture with mainstream reality will inevitably be castigated as undemocratic censorship, but this criticism is to be expected as the predictable response of organized repression and indoctrination; "the ways should not be blocked on which a subversive majority could develop, and if they are blocked by organized repression and indoctrination, their reopening may require apparently undemocratic means" (p. 100).

Here Marcuse is proposing a kind of community-sponsored intellectual positive discrimination; "withdrawal of tolerance from regressive movements, and discriminating tolerance in favor of progressive tendencies would be tantamount to the 'official' promotion of subversion" (1965, p. 107). For him the end of learners' access to objective, liberatory truth justifies the means of censorship of dominant, mainstream ideas and of discrimination in favor of outlawed knowledge. Realizing the objective of tolerance calls "for intolerance toward prevailing policies, attitudes, opinions, and the extension of tolerance to policies, attitudes, and opinions which are outlawed or suppressed" (p. 81). An intolerance of certain teaching practices (Marcuse does not specify which) may also be called for if students are to develop autonomous thought:

> The restoration of freedom of thought may necessitate new and rigid restrictions on teachings and practices in the educational institutions which, by their very methods and concepts, serve to enclose the mind within the established universe of discourse and behavior—thereby precluding a priori a rational evaluation of the alternatives. (pp. 100–101)

As can be imagined, Marcuse's vigorous assertion of the need to censor conservative viewpoints proved highly contentious and was responsible for much of the hostility directed toward him. But he often responded by pointing out that his own life demonstrated the consequences of repressive tolerance. He wrote that "if the Nazi movement had not been tolerated once it revealed its character, which was quite early, if it had not enjoyed the benefits of that democracy, then we probably would not have experienced the horrors of the Second World War and some other horrors as well" (Marcuse, 1970, p. 99). For him the example of Nazi Germany provided a powerful illustration of "an unequivocal position according to which we can say: here are moments that should not be tolerated if an improvement and pacification of human life is to be attained" (p. 99).

Marcuse's analysis has considerable utility for practicing adult educators and suggests a number of adult learning projects. In the rest of this chapter we sketch out what it looks like to celebrate diversity from a radical perspective. We argue that this entails recognizing that the "celebrating diversity" approach can obscure the need to focus on antiracism and divert attention from the fact that permanent material inequity and racial identity are inextricably intertwined.

IDEOLOGICAL DETOXIFICATION

Concurrent with exploring diverse ideas, traditions, and practices must go the analysis of how dominant ideology is learned. When a belief seems natural and obvious and when it serves to reproduce existing systems, structures and behaviors, it is ideological. Ideology is the system of ideas and values that reflects and supports the established order and that manifests itself in our everyday actions, decisions, and practices, usually without our being aware of its presence. Its function is to normalize and legitimize a situation that is untenable—the co-opting of the power to decide on the allocation of societal resources by an unrepresentative minority and the deliberate structuring of society to maintain economic and cultural disparity. In the United States, the refusal to engage in an open and fair consideration of anything that could be described as socialism is a dominant ideological value that works very powerfully to deflect any revolutionary change. When we are faced with choices in life and find ourselves turning without conscious deliberation to what seem like obvious, commonsense forms of reasoning, the chances are good that there is an ideological basis to these. The fact that these forms of reasoning seem almost effortless, suggesting themselves in the same instant that we are confronted with the choice, is an important indication of their ideological nature.

These seemingly natural, obvious ideas have not just forced themselves onto our consciousness from some compartment in the brain labeled "decision-making center." Their immediacy springs from the fact that they represent the commonsense wisdom accepted by the majority in our class, race, and culture. In their apparent obviousness lie their subtle seductiveness and their hidden power. The truth is that these supposedly obvious ideas always serve some interests and oppose others. What seem like wise choices based on transparent truths often end up hurting us without our knowing quite how this has happened. Because ideology is so soaked into our existence, it seems objective and neutral, rather than partisan. This helps to explain how it manages to obscure the injuries it does us.

A radical approach to diversity tries to clarify what comprise dominant ideological values and to illuminate how these are learned. It would show the dominance of White supremacy, heterosexism, democracy as majority vote, patriarchy, ableism, and class inequality. The intent would be to show how these belief systems intersect to justify structural inequity whereby access to opportunity and the ability to utilize resources that should be available to all is rigidly stratified by class, race, gender, sexual preference, and physical capability. An adult educational program that addresses diversity from a radical standpoint will often begin with a deliberate uncovering of how normality is learned and how diversity is "othered." This is the first phase of ideological detoxification.

Such a program could involve several elements. One would be to understand how popular "grand narratives" support ideology. For example, the narrative of "freedom" that holds we live in a society in which the right to free speech is constitutionally protected would need to be deconstructed. Challenging this narrative would lead to challenging the narrative of "capitalism" that holds that capitalism destroyed authoritarian feudalism and ushered in an era of entrepreneurial freedom and a free marketplace that somehow help guarantee the exercise of free speech. Ideological detoxification would require teaching how the opportunity to construct access to communication and to define the parameters of acceptable debate are the prerogative of corporations controlling cyberspace and media. So teaching people media literacy—how to "read" the news distributed through print, TV, and cyberspace as a constructed reality—would be paramount.

The narrative of "White supremacy" that portrays the development of the U.S. as the result of the civilizing influence of White European invaders and that views forms of thought derived from the Enlightenment (such as hypothesis formulation and testing) as the dominant rubric producing legitimate, trusted knowledge would also be laid bare. This would require identifying forms of privilege that being a White European-American confers and the way racist structures are buttressed by this narrative. Heteronormative views of sexuality, ableist deficit models of what comprises a fully functioning person, and patriarchal classifications of male and female stereotypes would all be examined for the ways they help construct the grand narrative of "normality." The narrative of democracy would be examined for the ways that a conservative majority vote works as a tyranny of the majority to prevent all kinds of progressive change.

The narrow and ideological perspective of diversity itself so often present in educational discussions of diversity must be confronted. Far too often, diversity is seen from one side and in what Paula Allman (2001) would call an uncritical and reproductive way. Diversity, however, following Allman, more accurately should be seen critically, dialectically, and therefore, internally related to unity. In Chapter Seven on globalization, we discussed external and internal relations in terms of the market and production and the Ford plant in St. Paul. In mainstream conversations of diversity, differing groups are generally seen as externally related. When they come in contact with one another, they each have an influence on the other. The idea then, and this is how diversity is often posed in terms of its economic value, is that it is advantageous to know other groups so as to be better able to work with them. As commerce internationalizes, for example, it is important to be bi- or multicultural in order to be successful in sealing deals and contracts with diverse peoples around the world.

From what Allman calls a critical and revolutionary perspective, diversity should be seen as internally related to unity. Recall from Chapter Seven that when things are internally related one cannot be understood outside of the relationship with the other. In more concrete terms, our humanity itself cannot be understood outside of its diverse manifestations. In other words, to understand ourselves, we must understand the multiple manifestations of the human experience. From this critical perspective, the celebration of diversity is a celebration of humanity's diverse manifestations. Celebrating diversity is not a discovery of an other, but an encounter with another fellow human being with differing ways to express our common humanity. Since, as we know, the relations between people across differences are asymmetrical relations, the process of encountering another can only be done when it is also a process of making the relations symmetrical. In Freirean terms, the oppressed can recognize the oppressor as a fellow human being when, and only when, they meet within relations in transformation where there is no longer an oppressor or an oppressed but rather two human beings transformed by the process of reconstructing new relations. The celebration of diversity, then, cannot be an intellectual learning exercise detached from social movements that challenge the very asymmetrical power relations preventing people from authentic recognition. It is in acts of solidarity, where people are willing to make real sacrifices across socially constructed differences, where recognition begins; these acts involve powerful learning and transformation. Exemplary of this type of solidarity is John Brown of whom Frederick Douglass said, "although a white man, [he] is in sympathy a black man, and is deeply interested in our cause as though his own soul has been pierced with the iron of slavery" (as cited in Nelson, 2009, p. 28).

CONFRONTING DIFFERENCE

If ideological detoxification deconstructs normality and shows how consent to permanent material inequity is manufactured by dominant ideology, then confronting difference requires an immersion in ideas and practices that challenge this ideology. A radical approach to adult education for diversity would insist that learners engage seriously with ideas and practices that provide alternative conceptions of normality. Narratives of democratic socialism stand in opposition to the narrative of monopoly capitalism; narratives of critical race theory or Africentrism stand against that of White supremacy; narratives of feminism oppose patriarchy; queer theory que(e)rics heteronormativity; a narrative of inclusion contrasts to ableism. Confronting difference does not stop, however, with academic study. It requires extended contact and immersion in radically different practices. Sometimes this involves moving from a social location of privilege and sameness into one where members of dominant, privileged groups are stripped of this power (as far as this is realistically possible) and forced to live as a member of the dispossessed. Educationally this obviously poses a serious problem, since few of the dominant class are ready to abandon power and privilege.

There are, however, already avenues in formal education in which variations on this theme are apparent and that provide openings for people to confront different practices. One is the growth in games and simulations that have become more and more popular as teaching techniques. Some, such as "StarPower," "BaFa BaFa," or "What Is No?" are fairly benign; others, such as Boal's theater of the oppressed, more intense. Of course games and simulations can be dismissed and forgotten as soon as people leave the classroom and reenter the "real" world. But we believe practicing educators seize every opening to advance difference, and our own informal observations have convinced us people often remember participating in games and simulations long after they forget reading they have done.

Participatory research has a considerable history in adult education, mostly through the intersections of the field with popular education and the work of Paulo Freire (Cammarota and Fine, 2008), both of which place learning and education within the context of purposeful social change. Participatory research projects are ones in which "expert" researchers, who are usually from the dominant class or racial group, typically work with racially diverse community members to address problems that the community members themselves identify (McIntyre, 2007). As part of the research, experts and members are required to learn how to communicate across race and cultural difference and how to move the community's interests forward in ways that negotiate the different agendas and that combat intergroup racism.

DISMANTLING PRIVILEGE

Dismantling privilege of all forms—economic, class, racial, sexual— is at the heart of radical education and is central to adult education. Privilege is enshrined within contemporary racism as a system of beliefs and practices (i.e., an ideology) embedded in the institutions and conventions of everyday lives that legitimizes the power of one racial group and justifies it viewing all others as inherently inferior. Racism is simultaneously overt (in law, the economy, political participation, education) and covert (in the media, social mores, fashion). When threatened it responds with overt force (torture, police brutality, political imprisonment, murder) and covert manipulation (symbolic festivals, media, prominent "success" stories). When threatened, racism is extremely adept at reconfiguring itself by appearing to have ceded important territory while in reality maintaining its power.

In the context of diversity, the focus tends to be on race rather than gender and sexuality, with White privilege and White supremacy usually generating the most attention. Dismantling privilege calls for action on all fronts. Economically, it means overturning the influence of first-world multinational corporations and first-world dominated fiscal institutions such as the World Bank, as well as working to create and nurture worker cooperatives and people's banks in communities of color. In terms of dominant ideology, it means naming White supremacy as it emerges in all walks of life, from a clearly racist mass media to the racial microaggressions committed on the smallest scale in private interactions. In terms of immediate practice in the field of adult education, the contributors to the recent *Handbook of Race and Adult Education* (Sheared, Johnson-Bailey, Colin, Peterson, and Brookfield, 2010) explore how curricula, classroom practice, and research and scholarship in the field can address racism. One of the most elusive projects facing members of the dominant class who support a radical agenda is to learn how their own behavior directed at dismantling privilege actually secures its continuance.

For over 10 years the European-American Collaborative Challenging Whiteness (ECCW), a San Francisco-based group of White Euro-Americans, has regularly met, studied, talked, and written perceptively about the traps Whites fall into as they promote an antiracist agenda. In its essay in the *Handbook of Race and Adult Education*, the ECCW explores how proselytizing (declaiming the importance of being antiracist) and disdaining (condescendingly pointing out the lack of race cognizance shown by apparently less enlightened Whites and urging them to change) can effectively shut down dialogue in the very moment people are trying to develop it. Through a case study of one particular conversation, members of the collaborative show how even after 10 years they fall into the traps of seeking the approval of people of color and of exuding condescension as they "explain" racism to other Whites.

Racial microaggressions are the daily examples of racism that are expressed in small-scale interactions—the tone of voice people use as they interact publicly and privately, gestures that ignore or demean another person, meeting behaviors that shut out certain voices on the basis of race, conversational speech in which slurs and stereotypes glide by unnoticed, and so on (Sue, Bucceri, Lin, Nadal, and Torino, 2007). Given adult education's traditional concern with small-group discussions as democratic laboratories and the more recent emphasis on cohort and collaborative learning models, calling out microaggressions represents an immediate antiracist practice. White adult educators can take the lead in monitoring their comments and behaviors as a way of modeling for White students a strike back against the insidious nature of racism.

Understanding the way racism is normalized in daily routines and embedded in institutional practices is the concern of critical race theory (CRT). CRT assumes, like critical theory, that a state of permanent inequity has become accepted as normal in the U.S. (Delgado and Stefancic, 2001). However, whereas critical theory traditionally focuses on exclusion by class, critical race theory is concerned with racism and the dominant ideology of White supremacy. Critical race theory views racism as *the* enduring, all-pervasive reality of U.S. life and suggests adult educators acknowledge this and make its analysis and confrontation a central feature of study and practice. CRT assumes that racism is endemic, and that as legal measures restrict its overt expression (as in the existence of Whites-only clubs or organizations), it reconfigures itself in racial microaggressions and aversive racism (Dovidio and Gaertner, 2000). Racial microaggressions, as we have seen, are the subtle, daily expressions of racism embodied in speech, gesture, and actions. Aversive racism comprises the racist behaviors that liberal Whites enact even as they profess sincerely to be free of racism. Peterson's (1999) early analysis of critical race theory in adult education describes how these subtle forms of racism endure and the conversations African American adult educators need to have to confront class, power, and language in the fight for dignity.

CRT places considerable emphasis on the use of narrative, particularly counter-storytelling. Counter-storytelling encourages people of color to recount their experiences of racism in ways that reflect their own culture, a process that challenges not just what Whites consider to be racial reality (that civil rights has made racism a nonissue) but also what constitutes appropriate forms of classroom expression or scholarship. Using hip-hop as a means of counter-storytelling, for example, stands in contrast to mainstream forms of narrative such as formal autobiographies or memoirs (Guy, 2004). The process of counter-storytelling is complex, however, as Merriweather-Hunn, Manglitz, and Guy's (2006) tale of a White adult educator's involvement with the African diaspora pre-conference of the Adult Education Research Conference illustrates.

Attempting to work as an ally in support of colleagues of color and to promote counter-storytelling illuminating how White supremacy operates, a White researcher—Elaine Manglitz—coauthored a paper with an African American colleague that was accepted for the African diaspora adult education pre-conference. Neither researcher was aware of the stipulation that only scholars of African descent could present at the conference. Both presenters arrived at the conference and were told that the White presenter could attend the session at which her paper was presented but that she could not speak. She agreed to this restriction, but her African American coauthor refused to present if her White coauthor could not speak and left the conference the next day. As the White author reflected, "I believe this story fits well with a theme of whom can speak for whom, the power of counter-storytelling and the importance of having a safe space, but I am left at a loss for how we can move forward" (Merriweather-Hunn, Manglitz, and Guy, 2006, p. 246).

Critical race theory argues for a curriculum that stresses the analysis of how White supremacy is permanently embedded in educational texts, practices, and forms of student assessment. It places racism as *the* central factor of U.S. life and requires adult educators to explore how they collude in its perpetuation. Although originated by scholars of color in critical legal studies, the CRT perspective enjoins White adult educators to explore their own racism. Whites need to scrutinize publicly their own racial microaggressions, such as regularly overlooking the contributions of students of color, dismissing the jargon of some groups while employing that of the dominant White culture, citing examples and authors that are exclusively White, or grading students of color differently because they are held to lower expectations. CRT also explores the notion of discriminative justice, echoing Marcuse's (1965) argument that "discrimination is good when it reveals processes of oppression and privilege in classrooms, funding and policies" (as cited in Rocco and Gallagher, 2006, p. 39).

A PRESCRIPTION FROM HISTORY

We end this chapter by looking back to one of the most provocative statements regarding the connections between the fight for racial equality and the establishment of democratic socialism in the United States. This comes from the towering African American intellectual, W.E.B. DuBois who in the 1930s was contracted by a subsidiary of the American Association for Adult Education to author one in a series of booklets (that came to be known as the "Bronze" booklets) exploring the state of African American adult education. DuBois was asked to write an essay on social and political aspects of African American adult education in the wake of Franklin D. Roosevelt's New Deal legislation. He decided to write something that stressed adult education's need to create economic as well as political democracy. As DuBois grew older, his views became increasingly radical and controversial which served to marginalize him not only from mainstream liberal-minded Whites but also among the Black intellectual community. During the depression years, DuBois was reformulating his ideas concerning race progress away from the NAACP's platform of civil rights reform toward a more radical view (Marable, 1982). Whereas he previously believed that racism was primarily due to ignorance, he had begun to conceptualize the stronger relation of economic factors to racism based on the analytical tools of Marxism (DuBois, 1971). By 1935 DuBois had formulated a concrete plan for race progress and Black liberation through political activism, group solidarity, community involvement through education, and through an explicit commitment to socialism.

The second of DuBois' volumes of autobiographical reflections *Dusk of Dawn* (DuBois, 1971) mentions in four fascinating pages (pp. 319–322) his being commissioned in 1936 by the American Association for Adult Education to undertake a study titled *Negro and the New Deal*. DuBois mentions how at that time he was ready to put in permanent form "that economic program of the Negro which I believed should succeed, and implement the long fight for political and civil rights and social equality which it was my privilege for a quarter of a century to champion" (p. 319). He recounts how the invitation to prepare this study came from "the colored 'Associates in Negro Folk Education' (ANFE) working under the American Association for Adult Education" (p. 319). DuBois mentions how the then African American president of the AAAE, Alain Locke, pressed him for the manuscript and how he was paid for his work. In DuBois' estimation *Negro and the New Deal* "made a fair and pretty exhaustive study of the experience of the Negro from 1933 to 1936" (p. 319). As part of his study, DuBois included "a statement and credo which I had worked out through correspondence with a number of the younger Negro scholars" (p. 319), though who these scholars were is not mentioned. This work comprised four statements summarizing the current condition of the Negro race followed by an eleven-item Basic American Negro Creed.

Three pages later, *Dusk of Dawn* contains three fascinating sentences that identify one of the most puzzling and provocative omissions in the history of U.S. adult education. DuBois writes of his Basic American Negro Creed, "this creed proved unacceptable both to the Adult Education Association and to its colored affiliates. Consequently when I returned home from abroad the manuscript although ordered and already paid for, was returned to me as rejected for publication. Just who pronounced this veto I do not know" (p. 322). DuBois does not speculate in *Dusk of Dawn* why the creed was considered unacceptable, but a reading of it (it is reproduced in *Dusk of Dawn* on pages 319–322) gives strong clues. The creed is a typically uncompromising indictment of the American ideology of democratic equality of opportunity, arguing that Whites exclude Negroes from economic and political decisions and relegate them to a status as "disenfranchised peons" (p. 319), "disinherited illiterates" (p. 320) and "parasites" (p. 320). In DuBois' estimation, the way to create a truly democratic America is not through "the escape of individual genius into the white world" (p. 320) but through "unity of racial effort, so far as this is necessary for self-defense and self-expression" (p. 320). This stands in stark contrast to the "enervating philosophy of Negro escape into an artificially privileged white race which has long sought to enslave, exploit and tyrannize over all mankind" (p. 320).

In his research on Alain Locke, Guy (1993) traces the correspondence between Locke and Lyman Bryson. As series coeditor, Locke envisioned the Bronze booklets to be used in Negro adult education programs across the country. However, there always existed tension between what the AAAE leadership was willing to support and what the Negro adult education leadership wanted to do. Guy quotes a 1932 letter that Morse Cartwright, executive director of AAAE, wrote to Locke: "The Negro adult education experiments were yet in such early stages that to propagandize for them at the present time might be dangerous" (Guy, 1993, p. 150). Specifically, Cartwright's concern had to do with sanctioning a racialist curriculum that was relevant to the special needs of African Americans in a racist society.

AAAE's role in circumscribing permissible Negro adult education was replayed in the development of the Bronze Booklets. In a careful analysis of the correspondence between Locke and Bryson, Guy (1993) notes how when writing to Bryson in February 1935 Locke indicated that DuBois had taken several editorial suggestions to heart but asked in the letter "Do you agree with me that it is debatable about printing DuBois' summary creed?" Locke proposed either printing a summary of the creed or omitting it entirely. In June 1936 Locke further wrote to Bryson saying he had paid DuBois for the manuscript and that he had curbed DuBois' style (to DuBois' evident annoyance). But he goes on to say, "I do not agree that we were or can be committed to purely neutral subject matter dealing with 'what was fine and worthy in Negro culture and in the contributions which they have made to American culture.' It was clear to me from the beginning, and I hope I made it clear, that part of the series would treat contemporary social and economic issues and their connection with the problems and the programs of the Negro." As Guy (1993) points out, Locke characterized his disagreements with Du Bois as ones of style and balance, not of perspective, and defends DuBois' position as a necessary counterbalance to that of Ralph Bunche (author of *World Aspects of the Race Problem*). In Guy's (1993) view, Bryson's presence as a White person on the ANFE committee compromised the freedom of action of the organization. "Locke's experience with ANFE underscores the dependent nature of the relationship between the ANFE and the (Carnegie) Corporation. His authority over the affairs of the organization was in name rather than fact" (Guy, 1993, p. 166).

It is not difficult to see which aspects of the creed made it unwelcome at the American Association for Adult Education. First, as has already been argued, the creed identifies the idea and practice of White supremacy as the enemy of the Negro race. DuBois states that the pursuit of economic equality has been forced upon the Negro race "by the unyielding determination of the mass of the white race to enslave, exploit and insult Negroes" (DuBois, 1971, p. 322). In response to this he urges "unity of racial effort, so far as this is necessary for self-defense," a framing that anticipates

Malcolm X's emphasis on the defense of Black interests by any means necessary. Second, the creed clearly situates racial advancement within a broader working-class movement, in which trade unions will play a substantial role. DuBois states, "we believe that Negro workers should join the labor movement and affiliate with such trade unions as welcome them and treat them fairly" (p. 321). In this he echoes the sentiments of Paul Robeson, an unjustifiably neglected adult educator, who over many years worked to influence American trade unions to make the fight against White supremacy a priority. Through workers' councils organized by Negroes, DuBois believed that "interracial understanding should strive to fight race prejudice in the working class" (p. 321).

Third, and perhaps most controversially of all, DuBois linked the advancement of the Negro race and the abolition of racism to socialism. The creed calls for the establishment of "a co-operative Negro industrial system in America" that might serve as a model for the "reconstruction of the economic base of the nation which must sooner or later be accomplished" (DuBois, 1971, p. 321) The sixth element of his creed states baldly, "we believe in the ultimate triumph of some form of Socialism the world over; that is, common ownership and control of the means of production and equality of income" (p. 321). This equalizing of work and wealth is urged as "the beginning of the rise of the Negro race in this land and the world over, in power, learning, and accomplishment" (p. 321). The equalization of wealth is to be achieved through taxation and through "vesting the ultimate power of the state in the hands of the workers" (p. 321), a situation that will be accompanied by the working class demanding their "proportionate share in administration and public expenditure" (p. 322). Du Bois ends the creed with an expansive appeal to people of all races to join in fighting White supremacy and creating socialism. In his words "to this vision of work, organization and service, we welcome all men (*sic*) of colors so long as their basic subscription to this basic creed is sincere and proven by their deeds" (p. 322).

Was it the focus on White supremacy as the enemy of racial advancement that made the creed unacceptable to the overwhelmingly White American Association of Adult Education? Did the emphasis on Negroes participating in a broad-based labor movement prove too politicized a strategy for the editorial board of the Associates in Negro Folk Education? Or was it the unabashed advocacy of socialism that tipped the balance against publication, even though the Cold War and McCarthyism lay 10 to 15 years in the future? Guy and Brookfield (2009) argue that the AAAE was practicing repressive tolerance, appearing to encourage Black adult education while simultaneously (and covertly) circum-scribing it. As a consequence the Bronze Booklets—though lauded as an important landmark in African American adult education scholarship—had their full impact blunted by the forced removal of DuBois' work from their catalog.

Dubois wrote his Basic American Negro Creed in the mid-1930s at a time when the Communist Party USA (CPUSA) was putting forth the slogan of "Black and White, Unite and Fight" as a summation of its desire to build crossracial unity in the struggle for socialism, to which DuBois was increasingly drawn as reflected in the creed. Nelson Peery (2002) presents an important critique of the CPUSA strategy of the 1930s and 1940s based on a historical and materialist analysis of racism. In Chapter Seven on globaliza-tion, we presented a similar analysis based on considering the objective (real, material) and subjective (consciousness) realities prevailing in a particular time period. At the time the CPUSA was putting forth the subjective slogan of crossracial unity, the vast majority of White workers and Black workers were objectively living different realities. Moreover, the trajectory of these differ-ing objective realities was for Whites to garner increasing skin-color–based privileges through the post-World War II period.

DuBois, for his part, as we mention above, was seeking inde-pendent Black cooperative strategies with an understanding that the hopes for crossracial unity were not likely, or at least could not be central to an overall strategy to address the needs of African Americans in that period. Today, however, we are in a very differ-ent period than that of the creed. As we argued in Chapter Seven on globalization, today we are witnessing a fundamental trans-formation of the objective realities facing us all. Moreover, the economic transformations today are eroding the economic basis of White privilege for a growing sector of the poor and working class (the majority of people in the U.S.). In the period of DuBois' creed, economic expansion meant that Whites could disproportionately attain access to good-paying, stable employment in an expanding economy. This is the process through which the urban White ethnic working-class enclaves transformed into the White middle-class suburbs in the post-World War II boom.

Today, the possibilities for sustained economic growth through which major sectors of the working class of any race or ethnicity can rise economically are no longer present. Today, given the dominance of financial capital, any economic recovery is a jobless recovery largely benefiting smaller and smaller sectors of society, leaving the majority of society in a downward trajectory, and leaving a diminishing objective basis for White privilege.

The importance of this brief foray back into political economy is to argue along the lines of Heagerty and Peery (2000) that the objective basis for White privilege is weakening. This is exceedingly important for educators. Ideas emerge and can flourish when they have a solid relationship to people's objective experience. If a set of ideas (an ideology such as racism) has some explanatory power for people's experience, they may take it on as their way to explain what they see and experience. This has been the history of White supremacy in the United States given the objectively unequal realities lived by Whites in comparison to "nonwhite" groups. Ideologies lose their hold on people's thinking when, and only when, the ideology loses this link to people's objective realities and when new ideas are present that offer reasonable alternative explanations for people's experience. Racism, as an ideology, can only be successful challenged pedagogically (subjectively) when the objective basis upon which it can flourish wanes. In the 1930s, you could preach all you wanted about racial unity, but it was simply not an objective reality, and in fact, the objective reality taught people the opposite. In the 1930s and through the post-World War II boom, the objective reality was that Whites could use race as a weapon for individual and collective advancement.

Today, while White privilege is by no means absent, the objective reality is that a growing sector of Whites is being economically driven downward. White supremacy as a subjective explanation of the objective reality has decreasing explanatory power for the lived reality of a growing sector of Whites. To put it bluntly, whiteness has decreasing value. In the extreme, if you are White, jobless, and homeless, what privileges do you have over the Black person lying in the bunk next to you in the homeless shelter? What explanatory power does White supremacy have for your lived experience? If you think you can cash in your whiteness to get a job to get out of the shelter, you are facing increasingly fragile hopes in cycle after cycle of jobless economic recoveries. In today's reality, unity along common basic needs, regardless of race or ethnicity or gender or any other element of diversity, is an objective necessity if a growing sector of humanity is to resolve its growing unmet demands for the basics of life. This is the objective climate within the sector of society with whom antiracist pedagogy has the best chance to take hold. This growing sector of humanity increasingly finding itself on the margins of society is disproportionately present in the classrooms of many adult educators who work in adult basic education and community-based education settings.

CONCLUSION

As we argued in Chapter One, a radical adult education must place diversity at its core. The more diverse are our work and educational practices, the more that social arrangements reflect the widest possible range of preferences and the more that the people's different passions and individual interests are encouraged, then the healthier a society will be. The point of common control of resources to meet basic survival needs is to free people to develop themselves to the fullest in whatever way they see fit, with the proviso that this must not diminish the development of others. So, diversity is both a democratic and a socialist imperative. Unlike the stereotypical notion of socialism as bland conformity, a properly socialist system celebrates difference. But this is not to argue for diversity for diversity's sake. We don't want an entrenched diversity of wealth, nor a diversity represented by a collection of island mini-states contained within one larger society that have little or no communication with one another. Fairness and inclusion and the common stewardship of material resources cannot happen when individuals and communities only look inward rather than outward. Learning to communicate across difference is a major learning task adult education must engage with.

Epilogue

In the formally recognized and accredited field of adult education, radical practice is today a marginalized tradition. But if we move beyond formal programs to consider the whole range of human experiences and practices, particularly those that are consciously oriented toward advancing social relations based in the principles we outlined in Chapter One, radical practice is exploding. By placing our frame of reference for adult education squarely in the traditions of progressive social movements in many countries, we can identify vibrant theories and practices that have at times outdone the formal institutions of adult education. For example, the party schools of the Communist Party USA in the mid-1900s were, as Gettleman (2008) argues, the largest network of adult education institutions in the country.

For us the vitality of a tradition such as radical adult education should not be measured solely by a count of references to it in the formalized field's journals or conference proceedings. As academics we do look with favor upon radical adult education's continued presence in the literature and discourse and hope this text will further that presence. But for us, ultimately the vitality of radical adult education is better measured by the strength of social movement activity in any given time and place. What then can we say of the status of radical adult education? We end this text with an effort to place the current situation in context and to look to the future.

Throughout most of the decade of the 1990s, it was widely held that socialist politics were, if not outright dead, at least in near fatal crisis. At the beginning of the decade, marking 10 years of Reaganism-Thatcherism, the European socialist camp was quickly disintegrating. Revolutionary movements in power or on the verge of power in Central America were in retreat. Neoliberal structural adjustment programs were the norm for the

Third World as welfare states were dismantled in the First World. Postmodernism, that was in many ways an attack on the ideals and philosophical foundations of democratic socialism, was all the rage in academia. In 1992, Francis Fukuyama's *The End of History and the Last Man* declared the world to be forever capitalist, as many leftists and Marxists were finishing their journey from neo-Marxism to post-Marxism and on to anti-Marxism. The field of adult education was not immune to this retreat from traditional left politics. Jane Thompson's (1993) ironic and sad "open letter to whoever's left" captured the sense of defeat among radical adult educators.

Nevertheless, all of the capitalist euphoria over neoliberal globalization and postmodern-inspired smug cynicism did not last long. In 1992, Los Angeles erupted in one of the largest urban revolts in the history of the United States. On January 1, 1994, the Zapatista Army of National Liberation (EZLN) greeted the implementation of the North American Free Trade Agreement (NAFTA)—a codification of transnational neoliberalism—with an armed seizure of major cities in the southern Mexican state of Chiapas. The year 1995 was witness to, among other events, the Million Man March of African American men in the United States and the most massive strikes in France since 1968. The grand narrative of postmodernism began to lose steam by the mid-1990s—helped along in no small part by Alan Sokal's parody that slipped by the postmodernist editors of *Social Text* in 1996—and today stands merely as a trend within many fields including adult education. The global justice movement, with antecedents at least as far back as the anti- International Monetary Fund protests in Venezuela of 1989 (Katsiaficas, 2004), reached a certain plateau and coalescence in the United States when the growing student movement, environmental movement, and reform trends within the labor movement converged for the dramatic World Trade Organization (WTO) protest in Seattle in 1999. Subsequent antiglobalization or global justice protests, including the first World Social Forum attended by over 12,000 in Porto Alegre, Brazil, in January of 2001, have occurred in major cities across the world (Mojab, 2004).

In the United States, the US Social Forum in Atlanta in 2007 marked for many a potential new era in democratic socialist politics. These forums show a leadership of poor and working-class people emerging in new and existing movements for social justice and peace. Victories of part-time UPS workers in the late 1990s, the successful boycotts of Taco Bell, McDonald's, and Burger King by the Coalition of Immokalee (farm) Workers from 2001 to 2008, the strong presence and leadership of poor and working-class people and organizations in the protests against the Free Trade Agreement of the Americas meeting in Miami in 2003 and again in the Poor People's Marches at the Republican National Conventions in New York City in 2004 and St. Paul in 2008, and the several million strong immigrant rights marches of May 2006, all showed the emergence and growth of social movement organization and activism among some of the most dispossessed sectors of U.S. society. The US Social Forums, largely educational in nature, provide opportunities for a consolidation of this leading role for poor and working-class people in the emerging upsurge in social movement activism. While the crisis of democratic socialism is far from over, we are now in a very different political conjuncture 17 years on from the so-called end of history.

This brief review of some major trends brings us to our current position marked by a growing social, political, and economic polarization. This process causes tremendous social and political disruption in communities and countries around the globe. Many of Michael Moore's films have documented the socially destructive nature of this polarization in places such as his hometown of Flint, Michigan. From a philosophical standpoint, central to any polarization is the destruction of the middle; that which binds the two poles in the process of polarizing. In social class terms, polarization in the U.S. means the often talked about disappearance of the middle class and the destruction of the complementary American Dream. With the destruction of the middle class, there is also the loss of the social service professions and institutions that have historically provided a buffer against the worst effects of economic change and polarization. Adult educators are aware of this process through the cutting, consolidating, and curtailing of many of the more generously funded community-based adult education programs of previous periods. The heyday of publically funded, community-based adult education, which brought so many of us into the field and upon which the late 20th century formal field of liberal or progressive-oriented adult education was built, is long past with no real hopes of any resurrection.

Today, with the destruction of the middle, the side of increasingly unjustifiable wealth faces a growing sector of the world's majority who are finding it harder and harder to make ends meet or to even survive. In adult education, the destruction of the middle puts increasing pressure on the formal field to put itself at the service of capital accumulation through ever-changing learning for earning schemes. As the dialectic of reform is surpassed by the dialectic of revolution, the choice, to paraphrase Rosa Luxemburg, is between educating for socialism or barbarism. To educate for a social order based on peaceful, sustainable, and cooperative relations or for one in which increasing numbers of people are simply determined not to have a right to the basics of life such as food, shelter, health care, and education. For us, the choice is clear; our field's own history points us in the direction of working toward a democratic socialist alternative.

There is no reason not to state frankly that this current process of polarization through which we are passing, like all processes of polarization, is very destructive. Polarization is, however, the only process through which qualitative or fundamental social change becomes possible. Every instance of fundamental transformation is preceded by and embedded within a process of polarization. In the U.S. as we know, the defeat of slavery was only possible once the society polarized on the issue culminating in the Civil War. The Civil Rights Movement was also the culmination of a similar process of polarization, which like that of the Civil War period had economic, social, and political manifestations. These processes of polarization are historic processes for which adult educators need to be prepared for two main reasons. First, polarizations of societies do not automatically lead to progressive advances as the victory of fascism in parts of Europe and Asia in the mid-20th century teaches us. Second, processes of polarization create the conditions for qualitative transformation, but the direction of this transformation is in no way predetermined. This means adult education in and around social movements can and will play a vital role in determining the direction of social change in the coming years.

What we have tried to do in this text is to take the basic concepts of adult education as evident in the chapter titles and present our understanding of these concepts when considered from a democratic socialist orientation. We think this to be a very timely presentation precisely because we have entered into a period of prolonged and deepening polarization in which progressive and democratic socialist adult educators can, should, and will inevitably be involved. As competing visions for the future are put forth from specific social and political quarters, we feel it necessary to begin to consciously stake out a position within adult education that offers an alternative vision based on meeting the basic needs of the majority of humanity that increasingly finds itself dispossessed of the necessities of life. Since the field is framed by the basic concepts of learning, training, teaching, program planning, and so on, we have dedicated a chapter to each of these topics in an effort to present what we consider are the practices and theories understood from a radical perspective. We know our ideas are on the margins of the formal field, yet we believe that unless the formal field begins to address the pressing demands of growing sectors of society that make these ideas necessary, the field will find itself increasingly on the margins of the growing struggles for cooperative and sustainable relations between people and the planet.

REFERENCES

Adamovsky, E. "Argentina's Social Movement Goes Global." ZNet, 2002. Retrieved February 9, 2007, from www.zmag.org/content/showarticle .cfm?ItemID=2283

Adler, B. "Who Shot Ya: A History of Hip-Hop Photography." In J. Chang (Ed.), *Total Chaos: The Art and Aesthetics of Hip-Hop*. New York: Basic Books, 2006, pp. 102–116.

Albert, M. *Parecon: Life after Capitalism*. London: Verso, 2003.

Allman, P. *Revolutionary Social Transformation: Democratic Hopes, Political Possibilities and Critical Education*. Westport, CT: Bergin and Garvey, 1999.

Allman, P. *Critical Education Against Global Capitalism: Karl Marx and Revolutionary Critical Education*. Westport, CT: Bergin and Garvey, 2001.

Altenbaugh, R. J. *Education for Struggle: The American Labor Colleges of the 1920s and 1930s*. Philadelphia: Temple University Press, 1990.

American Friends Service Committee. (1997). *Coyuntural Analysis, Critical Thinking for Meaningful Action: A Manual for Facilitators*. Chicago: American Friends Service Committee.

Amutabi, M., Jackson, K., Korsgaard, O., Murphy, P., Quiroz Martin, T., and Walters, S. "Introduction." In S. Walters (Ed.), *Globalization, Adult Education and Training: Impacts and Issues*. London: Zed Books, 1997, pp. 1–12.

Argyris, C. *Flawed Advice and the Management Trap*. Oxford: Oxford University Press, 2000.

Arnove, R. F. *Education and Revolution in Nicaragua*. New York: Praeger, 1986.

Asante, M. K. *Afrocentricity: A Theory of Social Change*. (Revised edition). Trenton, NJ: Africa World Press, 1998a.

Asante, M. K. *The Afrocentric Idea*. Philadelphia: Temple University Press, 1998b.

Auerbach, E. R., and Wallerstein, N. *ESL for Action*. Reading, MA: Addison-Wesley, 1987.

Avila, E. B. et al. "Learning Democracy/Democratizing Learning: Participatory Graduate Education." In P. Campbell and B. Burnaby (Eds.), *Participatory Practices in Adult Education.* Toronto: Erlbaum, 2000, pp. 221–236.

Baker, E. "Bigger Than a Hamburger." *The Southern Patriot,* 1960, *18*(5), 4.

Baker, E. "Developing Community Leadership." In G. Learner (Ed.), *Black Women in White America.* New York: Vintage, 1972, pp. 345–352.

Baker, E. "Organizing for Civil Rights: Interview with Ellen Cantarow and Susan Gushee O'Malley." In E. Cantarow, *Moving the Mountain: Women Working for Social Change.* Old Westbury, NY: The Feminist Press, 1980, pp. 52–93.

Bangs, L. "The Clash." In A. D'Ambrosio (Ed.), *Let Fury Have the Hour: The Punk Rock Politics of Joe Strummer.* New York: Nation Books, 2004, pp. 69–118.

Baptist, W., and Theoharis, L. "Who are the Poor?" Retrieved September 1, 2008, from http://universityofthepoor.org/?page_id=8

Baptiste, I. "Beyond Reason and Personal Integrity: Toward a Pedagogy of Coercive Restraint." *Canadian Journal for the Study of Adult Education,* 2000, *14*(1), pp. 27–50.

Baptiste, I., and Brookfield, S. D. "Your So-Called Democracy Is Hypocritical Because You Can Always Fail Us: Learning and Living Democratic Contradictions in Graduate Adult Education." In P. Armstrong (Ed.), *Crossing Borders, Breaking Boundaries: Research in the Education of Adults.* London: University of London, 1997, pp 26–30.

Basseches, M. *Dialectical Thinking and Adult Development.* Norwood, NJ: Ablex, 1984.

Belenky, M. F., Bond, L. A., and Weinstock, J. S. *A Tradition That Has No Name: Nurturing the Development of People, Families, and Communities.* New York: Basic Books, 1999.

Bellah, R. N., Madsen, R, Sullivan, W. M., Swidler, A., and Tipton, S. M. *The Good Society.* New York: Alfred A Knopf, 1992.

Bellah, R. N., Madsen, R., Sullivan, W. M., Swidler, A., and Tipton, S. M. *Habits of the Heart: Individualism and Commitment in American Life.* Berkeley: University of California Press, 1996.

Bierema, L. L. "Moving Beyond Performance Paradigms in Human Resource Development." In A. L. Wilson and E. R. Hayes (Eds.), *Handbook of Adult and Continuing Education.* San Francisco: Jossey-Bass, 2000, pp. 278–293.

Blaser, M., Feit, H. A., and McRae, G. (Eds.). *In the Way of Development: Indigenous Peoples, Life Projects and Globalization.* London: Zed Books, 2004.

Bloom, A., and Breines, W. (Eds.). *"Takin' It to the Streets": A Sixties Reader.* New York: Oxford University Press, 1995.

Boal, A. *The Aesthetics of the Oppressed.* New York: Routledge, 2006.

Bragg, B. *The Internationale.* (CD) London: Utility Records,1990.

Bragg, B. *The Progressive Patriot: A Search For Belonging.* London: Transworld Books, 2006.

Brigham, S. A. "Our Hopes and Dreams Enrich Its Every Corner: Adult Education With an Africentric Focus." In L. Servage and T. Fenwick (Eds.), *Learning in Community: Proceedings of the 48th Annual Adult Education Research Conference.* Halifax, Nova Scotia: Mount Saint Vincent University, 2007, pp. 79–84.

Brookfield, S. D. *Independent Adult Learning.* Unpublished doctoral dissertation, University of Leicester, 1980.

Brookfield, S. D. "The Concept of Critically Reflective Practice." In A. Wilson and E. Hayes (Eds.), *Handbook of Adult and Continuing Education.* San Francisco: Jossey-Bass, 2000a, pp. 33–49.

Brookfield, S. D. "Self-Directed Learning as a Political Idea." In G. A. Straka (Ed.), *Conceptions of Self-Directed Learning: Theoretical and Conceptual Considerations.* Berlin/New York: Waxmann, 2000b, pp. 9–22.

Brookfield, S. D. *The Power of Critical Theory: Liberating Adult Learning and Teaching.* San Francisco: Jossey-Bass, 2004.

Brookfield, S. D. *The Skillful Teacher: On Technique, Trust, and Responsiveness in the Classroom.* (2nd Ed.). San Francisco: Jossey-Bass, 2006.

Brookfield, S. D., and Preskill, S. *Discussion as a Way of Teaching: Tools and Techniques for Democratic Classrooms.* (2nd ed.). San Francisco: Jossey-Bass, 2005.

Bryson, L. *Adult Education.* New York: American Book Company, 1936.

Caffarella, R. S. *Planning Programs for Adult Learners.* (2nd Ed.). San Francisco: Jossey-Bass, 2002.

Cale, G. *When Resistance Becomes Reproduction: A Critical Action Research Study.* Proceedings of the 42nd Adult Education Research Conference. East Lansing: Michigan State University, 2001.

Cale, G., and Huber, C. "Teaching the Oppressor to be Silent: Conflicts in the 'Democratic' Classroom." In *The Changing Face of Adult Learning,* Proceedings of the 21st Annual Alliance/ACE Conference. Austin, TX, 2001.

Cammarota, J., and Fine, M. (Eds.). *Revolutionizing Education: Youth Participatory Research in Motion.* New York: Routledge, 2008.

Cardenal, F., and Miller, V. "Nicaragua 1980: The Battle for the ABCs." *Harvard Educational Review,* 1981, *51*(1), 1–26.

Ceballos, R. M. "Adult Education for Community Empowerment: Toward the Possibility of Another World." In S. B. Merriam, B.

C. Courtenay, and R. M. Cervero (Eds.), *Global Issues and Adult Education.* San Francisco: Jossey-Bass, 2006, pp. 319–331.

Centro de Investigaciones y Estudios de la Reforma Agraria. *Participatory Democracy in Nicaragua.* Managua: Author, 1984.

Cervero, R. M., and Wilson, A. L. *Planning Responsibly for Adult Education.* San Francisco: Jossey-Bass, 1994.

Cervero, R. M., and Wilson, A. L. *Working the Planning Table.* San Francisco: Jossey-Bass, 2006.

Cervero, R. M., Wilson, A. L., and Associates. *Power in Practice: Adult Education and the Struggle for Knowledge and Power in Society.* San Francisco: Jossey-Bass, 2001.

Chang, J. *Can't Stop, Won't Stop: A History of the Hip-Hop Generation.* New York: St. Martins Press, 2005.

Chávez, H., and Harnecker, M. *Understanding the Venezuelan Revolution.* (C. Boudin, Trans.). New York: Monthly Review Press, 2005.

Chisom, R., and Washington, M. *Undoing Racism: A Philosophy of International Social Change.* (2nd Ed.). New Orleans: The People's Institute Press, 1997.

Clark, S. P. *Echo in My Soul.* New York: E. P. Dutton, 1962.

Clark, S. P. "Literacy and Liberation." *Freedomways,* 1964, *4*(1), 113–124.

Clark, S. P. *Ready from Within: A First Person Narrative.* (C. Stokes Brown, Ed.). Trenton, NJ: Africa World Press, 1996.

Coady, M. M. *Masters of Their Own Destiny.* New York: Harper & Brothers, 1939.

Coalition of Immokalee Workers. (n. d.). Consciousness Commitment Change: How and Why We Are Organizing. Retrieved September 1, 2008, from www.ciw-online.org/about.html

Coalition of Immokalee Workers, the Mexican Solidarity Network, and the Student Farmworker Alliance (n.d.). The Everyday Face of Globalization and the Taco Bell Boycott. Retrieved April 18, 2010, from http://cjtc.ucsc.edu/globallocalpoped/downloadable/CIW/msn_ciw_workshop.pdf

Colby, A., and Damon, W. *Some Do Care: Contemporary Lives of Moral Commitment.* New York: Free Press, 1994.

Colin, S.A.J. III. "The Universal Negro Improvement Association and the Education of African Ameripean Adults." Doctoral dissertation, Department of Adult Education, Northern Illinois University, 1988.

Colin, S.A.J. III. "Adult and Continuing Education Graduate Programs: Prescription for the Future." In E. Hayes and S.A.J. Colin III (Eds.), *Confronting Racism and Sexism.* New Directions for Adult and Continuing Education, No. 61. San Francisco: Jossey-Bass, 1994.

Colin, S.A.J. III. "Marcus Garvey: Africentric Adult Education for Selfethnic Reliance." In E.A. Peterson (Ed.), *Freedom Road: Adult Education of African Americans.* (Revised Edition). Malabar, FL: Krieger, 2002, pp. 41–66.

Colin, S.A.J. III, and Guy, T. A. "An Africentric Interpretive Model of Curriculum Orientations for Course Development in Graduate Programs in Adult Education." *PAACE Journal of Lifelong Learning,* 1998, 7, 43–55.

Colin, S.A.J. III, and Heaney, T. "Negotiating the Democratic Classroom." In C. A. Hansman and P. A. Sissel (Eds.), *Understanding and Negotiating the Political Landscape of Adult Education.* New Directions for Adult and Continuing Education, No. 91. San Francisco: Jossey-Bass, 2001, pp. 29–38.

Collins, M. *Adult Education as Vocation: A Critical Role for the Adult Educator.* New York: Routledge, 1991.

Commission of Professors of Adult Education. *Standards for Graduate Programs in Adult Education.* Washington, DC: Author, 1986.

Cotton, D. F. "Letter to Mr. James O. Scott." SCLC Papers, Part IV, Reel 11, 1961, March 30, 932.

Cotton, D. F. "Citizenship School Report." SCLC Papers, Part IV, Reel 12, 1963, November, 324–327.

Cranton, P. M. "Transformative Learning" In L. M. English (Ed.), *International Encyclopedia of Adult Education.* New York: Palgrave Macmillan, 2005, pp. 630–637.

Cunningham, P. M. "Making a More Significant Impact on Society." In B. A. Quigley (Ed.), *Fulfilling the Promise of Adult and Continuing Education.* New Directions for Continuing Education, No. 44. San Francisco: Jossey-Bass, 1989, pp 33–45.

Cunningham, P. M. "Adult and Continuing Education Does Not Need a Code of Ethics." In M. W. Galbraith and B. Sisco (Eds.), *Confronting Controversies in Challenging Times.* New Directions for Adult and Continuing Education, No. 54. San Francisco: Jossey-Bass, 1992, pp. 107–113.

Cunningham, P. M. "Conceptualizing Our Work as Adult Educators in a Socially Responsible Way." Paper presented at the International Adult and Continuing Education Conference, Seoul, Korea. ERIC Document Reproduction Service No. ED 401 410, 1996.

Cunningham, P. M. "The Social Dimension of Transformative Learning." *PAACE Journal of Lifelong Learning,* 7, 1998, 15–28.

D'Ambrosio, A. "Introduction." In A. D'Ambrosio (Ed.), *Let Fury Have the Hour: The Punk Rock Politics of Joe Strummer.* New York: Nation Books, 2004, pp. xxi–xxix.

Darcy de Oliveira, R., and Darcy de Oliveira, M. *The Militant Observer* (IDAC Document #9). Geneva, Switzerland, 1975. Retrieved from: www.vidyaonline.net/arvindgupta/TheMilitantObserver.htm.

Darkenwald, G. G., and Merriam, S. B. *Adult Education: Foundations of Practice.* New York: Harper & Row, 1982.

Davis, A. Y. *Women, Culture, and Politics.* New York: Vintage Books, 1990.

Davis, A. Y. *The Angela Y. Davis Reader.* Blackwell: Malden, MA: 1998.

Davis, E. "Found in Translation: The Emergence of Hip-Hop Theater." In J. Chang (Ed.), *Total Chaos: The Art and Aesthetics of Hip-Hop.* New York: Basic Books, 2006, pp. 70–77.

Delgado, R., and Stefancic, J. *Critical Race Theory: An Introduction.* New York: New York University Press, 2001.

Denning, M. *The Cultural Front.* London: Verso, 1998.

Dovidio, J. F., and Gaertner, S. L. "Aversive Racism and Selection Decisions." *Psychological Science,* 2000, *11*(4), 315–319.

Duberman, M. B. *Paul Robeson.* New York: Knopf, 1988.

DuBois, W.E.B. *Dusk of Dawn: An Essay Toward an Autobiography of a Race Concept.* New York: Schocken Books, 1971.

DuBois, W.E.B. *John Brown.* New York: International, 1972.

DuBois, W.E.B. *The ABC of Color.* New York: International, 2001.

Ehrenreich, B. *Bait and Switch: The (Futile) Pursuit of the American Dream.* New York: Holt, 2006.

Ehrenreich, B. *Nickel and Dimed: On (Not) Getting By in America.* New York: Holt, 2008.

Elshtain, J. B. "The Social Relations of the Classroom: A Moral and Political Perspective" In T. Mills and B. Ollman (Eds.), *Studies in Socialist Pedagogy.* New York: Monthly Review Press, 1978, pp. 291–313.

Engels, F. "Socialism: Utopian and Scientific." In K. Marx and F. Engels, *Selected Works. Volume 2.* London: Lawrence and Wishart, 1950.

English, L. M. (Ed.). *International Encyclopedia of Adult Education.* New York: Palgrave Macmillan, 2005.

"Estudiantes hacen temblar al modelo" [Students Make the Model Tremble]. *Punto Final,* 2006, *40*(616), 1–2, 4–5, 16–17.

Eyerman, R., and Jamison, A. *Music and Social Movements: Mobilizing Traditions in the Twentieth Century.* New York: Cambridge University Press, 1998.

Fenwick, T. J. "Putting Meaning into Workplace Learning." In A. L. Wilson and E. R. Hayes (Eds.), *Handbook of Adult and Continuing Education.* San Francisco: Jossey-Bass, 2000, pp. 294–311.

Fenwick, T. "Conceptions of Critical HRD: Dilemmas for Theory and Practice." *Human Resource Development International,* 2005, *8*(2), 225–238.

Fine, J. *Worker Centers: Organizing Communities at the Edge of the Dream.* Ithaca, NY: Cornell University Press, 2006.

Finger, M. "New Social Movements and Their Implications For Adult Education." *Adult Education Quarterly,* 1989, *40*(1), 15–22.

Finger, M., and Asun, J. M. *Adult Education at the Crossroads: Learning Our Way Out.* New York: Zed Books, 2001.

Foley, G. *Learning in Social Action: A Contribution to Understanding Informal Education.* London: Zed Books, 1999.

Folkman, D. V. "Framing a Critical Discourse on Globalization." In S. B. Merriam, B. C. Courtenay, and R. M. Cervero (Eds.), *Global Issues and Adult Education.* San Francisco: Jossey-Bass, 2006, pp. 78–94.

Foner, P. S. (Ed.). *The Black Panthers Speak.* Philadelphia: J. B. Lippincott, 1970.

Foucault, M. *Power/Knowledge: Selected Interviews and Other Writings, 1972–1977.* New York: Pantheon Books, 1980.

Freire, P. "Research Methods." *Literacy Discussion,* Spring 1974, pp. 133–142.

Freire, P. *Pedagogy Of The Oppressed.* (M. Bergman Ramos, Trans.). New York: Continuum, 2001. (Originally published 1970).

Freire, P., and Guimarães, S. *Aprendendo Com a Própria História* [Learning With One's Own History]. Rio de Janeiro: Editora Paz e Terra, 1987.

Fromm, E. *The Sane Society.* London: Routledge, Kegan and Paul, 1956.

Fromm, E. *The Revolution of Hope: Toward a Humanized Technology.* New York: Harper and Row, 1968.

Garcia, A. C. (2005, Nov./Dec.). "Government Bureaucracy Affecting Humanitarian Efforts to Save Katrina Victims." *People's Tribune.* Retrieved April 12, 2008, from http://peoplestribune.org/ PT .2005.11/PT.2005.11.5.html

García, L. E., Gutiérrez, S. M., and Nuñez, F. (Eds.). *Teatro Chicana.* Austin, TX: University of Texas Press, 2008.

Gastil, J. "Adult Civic Education Through the National Issues Forums: Developing Democratic Habits and Dispositions Through Public Deliberation." *Adult Education Quarterly,* 2004, *54*(4), 308–328.

Gaventa, J. (1989). "Participatory Research in North America." In *An Approach to Education Presented through a Collection of Writings.* New Market, TN: Highlander Research and Education Center, 1989, pp. 246–262.

Gboku, M., and Lekoko, R. N. *Developing Programmes for Adult Learners in Africa.* Hamburg: UNESCO Institute for Lifelong Learning, 2007.

Gelpi, E. *A Future for Lifelong Education: Volume 1, Lifelong Education Principles, Policies and Practices.* Manchester: Manchester Monographs 13, Department of Adult and Higher Education, University of Manchester, 1979.

Gettleman, M. E. "Defending Left Pedagogy: U.S. Communist Schools Fight Back Against the SACB and Lose (1953–1957)" *Reconstruction: Studies in Contemporary Culture*, 2008, *8*, 1. Retrieved from http://reconstruction.eserver.org/081/gettleman.shtml

Grace, A. P., and Rocco, T. S. (Eds.). *Challenging the Professionalization of Adult Education: John Ohliger and Contradictions in Modern Practice.* San Francisco: Jossey-Bass, 2009.

Graeber, D. *Direct Action: An Ethnography.* Oakland, CA: AK Press, 2009.

Gramsci, A. *Selections from the Prison Bibbooks.* (Q. Hoare and G. N. Smith, Eds.). London: Lawrence and Wishart, 1971.

Gramsci, A. *Selections from Political Writings, 1910-1920.* (Q. Hoare, Ed. and J. Mathews, Trans.). London: Lawrence and Wishart, 1977.

Gramsci, A. *Selections from Cultural Writings.* (D. Forgacs and G. Nowell-Smith, Eds.). Cambridge, MA: Harvard University Press, 1985.

Gramsci, A. *Pre-prison Writings* (R. Bellamy, Ed. and V. Cox, Trans.). New York: Cambridge University Press, 1994.

Gramsci, A. *The Antonio Gramsci Reader.* New York: New York University Press, 2000.

Grant, J. *Ella Baker: Freedom Bound.* New York: Wiley, 1998.

Guevara, E. *Venceremos!* New York: Macmillan, 1968.

Guevara, E. *Che.* Cambridge, MA: MIT Press, 1969.

Guevara, E. *Guerrilla Warfare.* Lincoln, NE: University of Nebraska Press, 1985.

Guevara, E. *Episodes of the Cuban Revolutionary War, 1956–1958.* New York: Pathfinder, 1996.

Guevara, E. *The African Dream: The Diaries of The Revolutionary War in The Congo.* (P. Camiller, Trans.). New York: Grove Press, 2000.

Guevara, E. *Che Guevara Reader.* Melbourne, Australia: Ocean, 2003.

Guskin, J., and Wilson, D. L. *The Politics of Immigration.* New York: Monthly Review, 2007.

Guy, T. C. *Prophecy From the Periphery: Alain Locke's Philosophy of Cultural Pluralism and the American Association of Adult Education.* Unpublished Doctoral Dissertation. DeKalb, IL: Northern Illinois University, 1993.

Guy, T. C. "Gangsta Rap and Adult Education." In L. G. Martin and E. Rogers (Eds.), *Adult Education in an Urban Context.* New Directions for Adult and Continuing Education, No. 101. San Francisco: Jossey-Bass, 2004, pp. 43–57.

Guy, T. C., and Brookfield, S. D. "W.E.B. DuBois' Basic American Negro Creed and the Associates in Negro Folk Education: A Case Study of Repressive Tolerance in the Censorship of Radical Black Discourse on Adult Education." *Adult Education Quarterly,* 2009, *60*(1), 65–76.

Guy, T. C., and Colin, S.A.J. III "Selected Bibliographic Resources for African American Adult Education." *PAACE Journal of Lifelong Learning*, 1998, *7*, 85–91.

Habermas, J. *Communication and the Evolution of Society*. Boston: Beacon Press, 1979.

Habermas, J. *The Theory of Communicative Action, Volume One: Reason and the Rationalization of Society*. Boston: Beacon Press, 1984.

Habermas, J. *The Theory of Communicative Action: Volume Two, Lifeworld and System—A Critique of Functionalist Reason*. Boston: Beacon Press, 1987.

Habermas, J. *Moral Consciousness and Communicative Action*. Cambridge, MA: MIT Press, 1990.

Habermas, J. *Between Facts and Norms: Contributions to a Discourse Theory of Democracy*. Cambridge, MA: MIT Press, 1996.

Hall, B. *Creating Knowledge: Breaking the Monopoly*. Participatory Research Project, Working Paper #1. Toronto: ICAE, 1977.

Hall, B. "Learning and Global Civil Society: Electronic Networking in International Non-governmental Organizations." *International Journal of Canadian Adult Education and Training*, 1993a, *3*(3), 5–24.

Hall, B. "Introduction." In P. Park, M. Brydon-Miller, B. Hall, and T. Jackson (Eds.), *Voices of Change: Participatory Research in the United States and Canada*. Westport, CT: Bergin & Garvey, 1993b, pp. xiii– xxii.

Hall, B. "Adult Education and the Political Economy of Global Economic Change." In P. Wangoola and F. Youngman (Eds.), *Towards a Transformative Political Economy of Adult Education: Theoretical and Practical Challenges*. DeKalb, IL: LEPS Press, 1996, pp. 105–126.

Hall, B. "Global Civil Society: Theorizing a Changing World." *Convergence*, 2000, *32*(1–2), 10–32.

Hanley, M. C. "Old School Crossings: Using Hip-Hop in Teacher Education and Beyond." In E. J. Tisdell and P. M. Thompson (Eds.), *Popular Culture and Entertainment Media in Adult Education*. New Directions for Adult and Continuing Education, No. 115. San Francisco: Jossey-Bass, 2007, pp. 35–44.

Hardin, G. "The Tragedy of the Commons." *Science*, 1968, *162*(3859), 1243–1248.

Harnecker, M. *Sin Tierra: Construyendo Movimiento Social* [Landless: Building Social Movement]. Madrid: Siglo XXI, 2002.

Harold, B. "Beyond Student-Centered Teaching" In T. Mills and B. Ollman (Eds.). *Studies in Socialist Pedagogy*. New York: Monthly Review Press, 1978, pp. 314–334.

Harrington, M. *Socialism: Past and Future*. New York: Signet, 1992.

Harvey, D. *A Short History of Neoliberalism.* New York: Oxford University Press, 2005.

Heagerty, B., and Peery, N. *Moving Onward: From Racial Division to Class Unity.* Chicago: People's Tribune, 2000.

Heaney, T. W. "If You Can't Beat 'Em, Join 'Em: The Professionalization of Participatory Research." In P. Park, M. Brydon-Miller, B. Hall, and T. Jackson (Eds.), *Voices of Change: Participatory Research in the United States and Canada.* Westport, CT: Bergin & Garvey, 1993, pp. 41–46.

Heaney, T. W. "Adult Education and Society" In A. L. Wilson and E. R. Hayes (Eds.), *Handbook of Adult and Continuing Education.* San Francisco: Jossey-Bass, 2000, pp. 559–572.

Highlander Folk School. (n.d.). *Training Leaders for Citizenship Schools: Outline of Training Workshop.* Monteagle, TN: Author. (SCLC Papers, Part IV, Reel 13, 502–524).

Hill, R. J. "What's It's Like to Be Queer Here?" In R. J. Hill (Ed.), *Challenging Homophobia and Heterosexism: Lesbian, Gay, Bisexual, Transgender, and Queer Issues in Organizational Settings.* New Directions for Adult and Continuing Education, No. 112. San Francisco: Jossey-Bass, 2006, pp. 7–16.

Hirshon, S. L. *And Also Teach Them to Read: Y También Enséñeles a Leer.* Westport: CT: Lawrence Hill, 1983.

Holst, J. D. *Social Movements, Civil Society, and Radical Adult Education.* Westport, CT: 2002.

Holst, J. D. "Globalization and Education Within Two Revolutionary Organizations in the United States of America: A Gramscian Analysis." *Adult Education Quarterly,* 2004, *55*(1), 23–40.

Holst, J. D. "Globalization and the Future of Critical Adult Education." In S. Merriam, B. Courtney, R. Cervero, and G. McClure (Eds.), *Global Issues and Adult Education: Perspectives from Latin America, Southern Africa, and the United States.* San Francisco: Jossey-Bass, 2006, pp. 41–52.

Holst, J. D. "The Pedagogy of Ernesto Che Guevara." *International Journal of Lifelong Education,* 2009, *28*(2), 149–173.

hooks, b. *Teaching to Transgress: Education as the Practice of Freedom.* New York: Routledge, 1994.

Horkheimer, M. *Critical Theory: Selected Essays.* New York: Continuum, 1995.

Horton, M. *The Long Haul: An Autobiography.* New York: Doubleday, 1990.

Horton, M., and Freire, P. *We Make the Road By Walking: Conversations on Education and Social Change.* Philadelphia: Temple University Press, 1990.

Houle, C. O. *The Design of Education* (2nd Ed.). San Francisco: Jossey-Bass, 1996.

Howe, I. *Socialism and America*. New York: Harcourt, Brace and Jovanovich, 1986.

Jarvis, P. "Globalization, Citizenship and the Education of Adults in Contemporary European Society." *Compare*, 2002, *32*(1), 5–19.

Johnson-Bailey, J., Tisdell, E. J., and Cervero, R. M. "Race, Gender and the Politics of Professionalization." In E. Hayes and S.A.J. Colin III (Eds.), *Confronting Racism and Sexism*. New Directions for Adult and Continuing Education, No. 61. San Francisco: Jossey-Bass, 1994, pp. 63–76.

Kane, L. *Popular Education and Social Change in Latin America*. London: Latin America Bureau, 2001.

Kassam, Y. "Introduction." In Y. Kassam and K. Mustafa (Eds.), *Participatory Research: An Emerging Alternative Methodology in Social Science Research*. New Delhi: Society for Participatory Research in Asia, 1982, pp. 1–6.

Katsiaficas, G. (2004). "Seattle Was Not the Beginning." In E. Yuen, D. Burton-Rose, and G. Katsiaficas (Eds.), *Confronting Capitalism*. Brooklyn, NY: Soft Skull Press, 2004, pp. 3–10.

Kegan, R. *In Over Our Heads: The Mental Demands of Modern Life*. Cambridge, MA: Harvard University Press, 1994.

King, M.L.K. Jr. (n.d.). *Leadership Training Program and Citizenship Schools*. Atlanta, GA: SCLC National Office.

King, P. M., and Kitchener, K. S. *Developing Reflective Judgment: Understanding and Promoting Intellectual Growth and Critical Thinking in Adolescents and Adults*. San Francisco: Jossey-Bass, 1994.

Knowles, M. S. *The Modern Practice of Adult Education*. (2nd Ed.). New York: Cambridge, 1988.

Knox, A. B. *Helping Adults Learn*. San Francisco: Jossey-Bass, 1986.

Labouvie-Vief, G. "Beyond Formal Operations: Uses and Limits of Pure Logic in Life-Span Development." *Human Development*, 1980, *23*, 141–161.

Langenbach, M. *Curriculum Models in Adult Education*. Malabar, FL: Krieger, 1988.

Lavaca Collective, The. *Sin Patron: Stories from Argentina's Worker-Run Factories*. (K. Kohlstedt, Trans.). Chicago: Haymarket Books, 2007.

Lave, J. *Cognition in Practice*. New York: Cambridge University Press, 2003.

Lave, J., and Wenger, E. *Situated Learning: Legitimate Peripheral Participation*. Cambridge: Cambridge University Press, 1991.

Lawson, K. H. *Philosophical Concepts and Values in Adult Education*. Milton Keynes, England: The Open University Press, 1979.

Leiss, W., Ober, J. D., and Sherover, E. "Marcuse as Teacher." In K. H. Wolff and B. Moore, Jr. (Eds.), *The Critical Spirit: Essays in Honor of Herbert Marcuse.* Boston: Beacon Press, 1967, pp. 421–426.

Lens, S. *Radicalism in America.* New York: Thomas Y. Crowell, 1969.

Lewis, A., and Klein, N. (2007). "Foreword." In The Lavaca Collective, *Sin Patron: Stories from Argentina's Worker-Run Factories* (K. Kohlstedt, Trans.). Chicago: Haymarket Books, 2007.

Lindeman, E.C.L. *The Meaning of Adult Education.* Montreal: Harvest House, 1961. (First published by New Republic, 1926).

Loewen, J. W. *Lies My Teacher Told Me: Everything Your American History Textbook Got Wrong.* New York: Touchstone Books, 1995.

Luxemburg, R. "Reform or Revolution." In M. A. Waters (Ed.), *Rosa Luxemburg Speaks.* New York: Pathfinder Press, 1970. (Original work published 1900), pp. 51–128.

Luxemburg, R. *Reform or Revolution.* New York: Pathfinder, 1973.

Maguire, P. *Doing Participatory Research: A Feminist Approach.* Amherst, MA: The Center for International Education, University of Massachusetts, 1987.

Mandela, N. *Long Walk to Freedom.* New York: Little, Brown and Company, 1994.

Mansbach, A. "On Lit Hop." In J. Chang (Ed.), *Total Chaos: The Art and Aesthetics of Hip-Hop.* New York: Basic Books, 2006, pp. 92–101.

Marable, M. "Alain Locke, W.E.B. Du Bois, and the Crisis of Black Education during the Great Depression." In R. J. Linneman (Ed.), *Alain Locke: Reflections on a Modern Renaissance Man.* Baton Rouge: Louisiana State University Press, 1982, pp. 63–76.

Marcuse, H. *One-Dimensional Man.* Boston: Beacon, 1964.

Marcuse, H. "Repressive Tolerance." In R. P. Wolff, B. Moore, and H. Marcuse, *A Critique of Pure Tolerance.* Boston: Beacon Press, 1965, pp. 81–123.

Marcuse, H. *An Essay on Liberation.* Boston: Beacon Press, 1969.

Marcuse, H. *Five Lectures.* Boston: Beacon Press, 1970.

Marcuse, H. *Counterrevolution and Revolt.* Boston: Beacon Press, 1972.

Marcuse, H. *The Aesthetic Dimension: Toward a Critique of Marxist Aesthetics.* Boston: Beacon Press, 1978.

Maruatona, T. "Adult Literacy Education and Empowerment in Africa: Problems and Prospects." In S. B. Merriam, B. C. Courtenay, and R. M. Cervero (Eds.), *Global Issues and Adult Education.* San Francisco: Jossey-Bass, 2006, pp. 344–355.

Marx, K., and Engels, F. *The Manifesto of the Communist Party.* (S. Moore, Trans.). New York: International Publishers, 1948.

Marx, K. *Economic and Philosophical Manuscripts.* (T. B. Bottomore, Trans.). In E. Fromm (Ed.), *Marx's Concept of Man.* New York: Frederick Ungar, 1961.

Marx, K. *Capital, Vol. I.* (S. Moore, and E. Aveling, Trans.). New York: International Publishers, 1967. (Originally published in 1867)

Matte Pérez, C. *Silabario* (2nd Ed.). Santiago, Chile: Ediciones Millalonco, 2004.

McGary, H. "Alienation and the African American Experience." In J. P. Pittman (Ed.), *African-American Perspectives and Philosophical Traditions.* New York: Routledge, 1997, pp. 282–296.

McIntyre, A. *Participatory Action Research.* Thousand Oaks, CA: Sage, 2007.

McKnight, J. S. (2009). "Twenty-First Century Community Education: Using Web-Based Tools to Build on Horton's Legacy." Paper presented at the 50th Annual Adult Education Research Conference. Chicago: Dept. of Adult Education, National-Louis University, pp. 224–229.

McLaren, P. *Life in Schools: An Introduction to Critical Pedagogy in the Foundations of Education* (3rd Ed.). White Plains, NY: Longman, 1997.

McLaren, P. *Che Guevara, Paulo Freire, and the Pedagogy of Revolution.* Lanham, MD: Rowman and Littlefield, 2000.

Meeropol, M. "A Radical Teaching a Straight Principles of Economics Course." In T. Mills and B. Ollman (Eds.), *Studies in Socialist Pedagogy.* New York: Monthly Review Press, 1978, pp. 131–145.

Merriam, S. B., and Brockett, R. G. *The Profession and Practice of Adult Education: An Introduction.* San Francisco: Jossey-Bass, 2007.

Merriam, S. B., Caffarrella, R., and Baumgartner, L. *Learning in Adulthood* (3rd Ed.). San Francisco: Jossey-Bass, 2007.

Merriam, S., Courtney, B., Cervero, R., and McClure, G. (Eds.). *Global Issues and Adult Education: Perspectives from Latin America, Southern Africa, and the United States.* San Francisco: Jossey-Bass, 2006.

Merriweather-Hunn, L., Manglitz, E., and Guy, T. C. "Who Can Speak for Whom? Using Counter-Storytelling to Challenge Racial Hegemony." In *Proceedings of the 47th Adult Education Research Conference.* Minneapolis: Department of Adult Education, University of Minnesota, 2006, pp. 244–250.

Mezirow, J., and Associates. *Fostering Critical Reflection in Adulthood: A Guide to Transformative and Emancipatory Learning.* San Francisco: Jossey-Bass, 1990.

Mezirow, J., and Associates. *Learning as Transformation: Critical Perspectives on a Theory in Progress.* San Francisco: Jossey-Bass, 2000.

Miles, A. *Integrative Feminisms.* New York: Routledge, 1996.

Miller, V. *Between Struggle and Hope: The Nicaraguan Literacy Crusade.* Boulder, CO: Westview Press, 1985.

"Mississippi Freedom School Curriculum—1964: A Bib to the Teacher." *Radical Teacher*, 1991, *40*, 6–34.

Mitra, A. "Training and Skills Development for Decent Work in the Informal Sector: Case Studies from South India." In M. Singh (Ed.), *Meeting Basic Learning Needs in the Informal Sector: Integrating Education and Training for Decent Work, Empowerment and Citizenship.* Dordrecht, The Netherlands: Springer, 2005, pp. 155–182.

Mojab, S. "The Power of Economic Globalization: Deskilling Immigrant Women through Training." In R. M. Cervero, and A. L. Wilson (Eds.), *Power in Practice: Adult Education and the Struggle for Knowledge and Power in Society.* San Francisco: Jossey-Bass, 2001, pp. 23–41.

Mojab, S. "From the 'Wall of Shame' to September 11: Whither Adult Education?" In P. Kell, S. Shore, and M. Singh (Eds.), *Adult Education @ 21st Century.* New York: Peter Lang, 2004, pp. 3–19.

Morrell, E. "Rebel Musics: African Diaspora Culture and Critical Literacy Pedagogues." In C. M. Payne and C. S. Strickland (Eds.), *Teach Freedom: Education for Liberation in the African-American Tradition.* New York: Teachers College Press, 2008, pp. 222–234.

Mulenga, D. "Reflections on the Practice of Participatory Research in Africa." *Convergence*, 1999, *32*(1–4), 33–46.

Nadler, L. *Developing Human Resources.* Houston: Gulf, 1970.

Nelson, T. *Old Man: John Brown at Harper's Ferry.* Chicago: Haymarket Books, 2009.

Neruda, P. *Let the Rail Splitter Awake and Other Poems.* New York: International, 1988.

Neufeldt, H. G., and McGee, L. *Education of the African American Adult.* New York: Greenwood Press, 1990.

Newman, M. *Socialism: A Very Short Introduction.* New York: Oxford University Press, 2005.

Newman, M. *Teaching Defiance: Stories and Strategies for Activist Educators.* San Francisco: Jossey-Bass, 2006.

Nyerere, J. K. *Freedom and Unity.* New York: Oxford University Press, 1968.

Oduaran, A. "Globalization and Lifelong Education: Reflection on Some Challenges for Africa." *International Journal of Lifelong Learning*, 2000, *19*(3), 266–280.

O'Hearn, D. *Nothing But an Unfinished Song: Bobby Sands, the Irish Hunger Striker Who Ignited a Generation.* New York: Avalon, 2006.

Olivera, O. *¡Cochabamba! Water War in Bolivia.* Cambridge, MA: South End Press, 2004.

Ollagnier, E. "Training." In L. M. English (Ed.), *International Encyclopedia of Adult Education* (pp. 618–622). New York: Palgrave Macmillan, 2005.

Outlaw, L. T. Jr. *On Race and Philosophy.* New York: Routledge, 1996.

Ozanne, J. L., Adkins, N. R., and Sandlin, J. A. "Shopping (for) Power: How Adult Literacy Learners Negotiate the Marketplace." *Adult Education Quarterly*, 2005, *55*(4), 251–268.

Parks Daloz, L. A., Keen, C. H., Keen, J. P., and Daloz Parks, S. *Common Fire: Lives of Commitment in a Complex World.* Boston, MA: Beacon Press, 1996.

Patten, T. H., Jr. *Manpower Planning and the Development of Human Resources.* New York: Wiley, 1971.

Patterson, W. L. (Ed.). *We Charge Genocide.* New York: International, 1970.

Payne, C. "Ella Baker and Models of Social Change." *Signs: Journal of Women in Culture and Society*, 1989, *14*(4), 885–889.

Payne, C. M. *I've Got the Light of Freedom: The Organizing Tradition and the Mississippi Freedom Struggle.* Berkeley, CA: University of California Press, 1995.

Peery, N. *Entering an Epoch of Social Revolution.* Workers Press: Chicago, 1993.

Peery, N. *The Future Is Up to Us: A Revolutionary Talking Politics with the American People.* Chicago: Speakers for a New America, 2002.

Peery, N. *Black Radical: The Education of an American Revolutionary.* New York: The New Press, 2007.

Peres, K., and Raab, K. *Tear Down the Wall at Verizon.* Washington, DC: Communication Workers of America, 2007.

Peters, J. M. "Reflections on Action Research." In B. A. Quigley and G. W. Kuhne (Eds.), *Creating Practical Knowledge Through Action Research.* New Directions for Adult and Continuing Education, No. 73. San Framcisco: Jossey-Bass, 1997, pp. 63–72.

Peterson, E. A. "Creating a Culturally Relevant Dialogue for African American Adult Educators." In T. C. Guy (Ed.), *Providing Culturally Relevant Adult Education: A Challenge for the Twenty-First Century.* New Directions for Adult and Continuing Education, No. 82. San Francisco: Jossey-Bass, 1999, pp. 79–92.

Picher, M-C. "Democratic Process and the Theater of the Oppressed." In S. Hayes and L. Yorks (Eds.), *Arts and Societal Learning: Transforming Communities, Socially, Politically, and Culturally.* New Directions for Adult and Continuing Education, No. 116. San Francisco: Jossey-Bass, 2007, pp. 79–88.

Poor People's Economic Human Rights Campaign. (n. d.a). *Leadership School.* Retrieved September 8, 2008, from www.economichumanrights.org/about/uofpoor/LeadershipSchool.htm

Poor People's Economic Human Rights Campaign. (n. d.b). *Our Vision.* Retrieved September 8, 2008, from www.economichumanrights.org/about/about.html

Project South. *Today's Globalization.* Atlanta, GA: Author, 2002.

Putnam, R. D. *Bowling Alone: The Collapse and Revival of American Community.* New York: Simon and Schuster, 2001.

Putnam, R. D. *Democracies in Flux: The Evolution of Social Capital.* New York: Oxford University Press, 2004.

Quigley, B. A. "The Role of Research in the Practice of Adult Education." In B. A. Quigley and G. W. Kuhne (Eds.), *Creating Practical Knowledge Through Action Research.* New Directions for Adult and Continuing Education, No. 73. San Francisco: Jossey-Bass, 1997, pp. 3–22.

Ransby, B. *Ella Baker and the Black Freedom Movement: A Radical Democratic Vision.* Chapel Hill, NC: The University of North Carolina Press, 2003.

Rappaport, B. "Toward a Marxist Theory of Practice and Teaching." In T. Mills and B. Ollman (Eds.), *Studies in Socialist Pedagogy.* New York: Monthly Review Press, 1978, pp. 275–290.

Raven, L. "The Afro-Aesthetics of Hip-Hop Poetics: Hip-Hop Education as Youth Activism." Unpublished paper, Department of Organization, Leadership and Development, Teachers College: New York, 2008.

Reed, T. V. *The Art of Protest.* Minneapolis: University of Minnesota Press, 2005.

Robeson, P. *Here I Stand.* Boston: Beacon Press, 1958.

Robeson, P. *Paul Robeson Speaks: Writings, Speeches, Interviews, 1918–1974.* (Ed. P. S. Foner). New York: Brunner-Mazel, 1978.

Rocco, T. S., and Gallagher S. J. "Straight Privilege and Moral/izing: Issues in Career Development." In R. J. Hill (Ed.), *Challenging Homophobia and Heterosexism: Lesbian, Gay, Bisexual, Transgender, and Queer Issues in Organizational Settings.* New Directions for Adult and Continuing Education, No. 112. San Francisco: Jossey-Bass, 2006, p. 29–40.

Sandlin, J. A. "Culture, Consumption, and Adult Education: Refashioning Consumer Education for Adults as a Political Site using a Cultural Studies Framework." *Adult Education Quarterly*, 2005, 55(3), 165–181.

Sassen, S. *Globalization and Its Discontents.* New York: The New Press, 1998.

Schied, F. M. *Learning in Social Context: Workers and Adult Education in Nineteenth Century Chicago.* DeKalb, IL: L.E.P.S. Press, 1993.

Schied, F. M., Carter, V. K., and Howell, S. L. "Silent Power: HRD and the Management of Learning in the Workplace." In R. M. Cervero and A. L. Wilson (Eds.), *Power in Practice: Adult Education and the Struggle for Knowledge and Power in Society.* San Francisco: Jossey-Bass, 2001, pp. 42–59.

238   REFERENCES

Schmitt-Boshnick, M. Spaces for Democracy: Researching the Social Learning Process." *Proceedings of the 36th Annual Adult Education Research Conference.* Edmonton, Alberta: Canada, 1995, pp. 293–298.

Sheared, V. "Giving Voice: Inclusion of African American Students' Polyrhythmic Realities in Adult Basic Education." In T. C. Guy (Ed.), *Providing Culturally Relevant Adult Education: A Challenge for the Twenty-First Century.* San Francisco: Jossey-Bass, 1999, pp. 33–48.

Sheared, V., Johnson-Bailey, J., Colin, S.A.J., Peterson, E. and Brookfield, S. D. *Handbook of Race and Adult Education.* San Francisco: Jossey-Bass, 2010.

Shiva, V. *Earth Democracy.* Cambridge, MA: South End Press, 2005.

Shor, I., and Freire, P. *A Pedagogy of Liberation.* Westport, CT: Bergin & Garvey, 1987.

Simon, R. I., Dippo, D., and Schenke, A. *Learning Work: A Critical Pedagogy of Work Education.* Westport, CT: Bergin and Garvey, 1991.

Singh, M. "Introduction." In M. Singh (Ed.), *Meeting Basic Learning Needs in the Informal Sector: Integrating Education and Training for Decent Work, Empowerment and Citizenship.* Dordrecht, The Netherlands: Springer, 2005, pp. 1–21.

Sinnott, J. M. *The Development of Logic in Adulthood: Postformal Thought and Its Applications.* New York: Springer-Verlag, 1998.

Sork, T. J., and Welock, B. A. "Adult and Continuing Education Needs a Code of Ethics." In M. W. Galbraith and B. Sisco (Eds.), *Confronting Controversies in Challenging Times.* New Directions for Adult and Continuing Education, No. 54. San Francisco: Jossey-Bass, 1992, pp. 115–122.

Southern Christian Leadership Conference (SCLC). (n. d.). *Citizenship Workbook.* Atlanta, GA: Author.

Sternberg, R. J. *Successful Intelligence.* New York: Plume, 1997.

Sternberg, R. J. *Wisdom, Intelligence and Creativity Synthesized.* Cambridge, UK: Cambridge University Press, 2003.

Sternberg, R. J. (Ed.). *The International Handbook of Intelligence.* New York: Cambridge University Press, 2004.

Sternberg, R. J., and Jordan, J. A. (Eds.). *A Handbook of Wisdom: Psychological Perspectives.* Cambridge, UK: Cambridge University Press, 2005.

Subgroup of the Leadership Development and Current Issues Committee. (1964, March 21–22). *Subgroup report.* (SNCC Papers Reel 39, 451–454).

Sue, D. W., Bucceri, J., Lin, A. I., Nadal, K. L., and Torino, G. C. "Racial Micro-Aggressions and the Asian American Experience." *Cultural Diversity and Ethnic Minority Psychology,* 2007, *13*(1), 72–81.

Sutherland, E. (Ed.). *Letters from Mississippi.* New York: McGraw-Hill, 1965.

Taylor, E. W. "Analyzing Research on Transformative Learning Theory." In J. Mezirow and Associates, *Learning as Transformation: Critical Perspectives on a Theory in Progress.* San Francisco: Jossey-Bass, 2000.

Tennant, M., and Pogson, P. *Learning and Change in the Adult Years: A Developmental Perspective.* San Francisco: Jossey-Bass, 2002.

Tennessee Industrial Renewal Network (Producer). *From the Mountains to the Maquiladoras* [Motion picture], 1993. (Available from the Highlander Research and Education Center, 1959 Highlander Way, New Market, TN 37820.)

Thompson, J. L. "The Concept of Training and its Current Distortion." *Adult Education,* 1976, *49*(3), 146–153.

Thompson, J. L. *Learning Liberation: Women's Response to Men's Education.* Beckenham, UK: Croom Helm, 1983.

Thompson, J. L. "Learning, Liberation and Maturity: An Open Letter to Whoever's Left." *Adult Learning,* 1993, *4*(9), 244.

Torres, C. A. "Participatory Action Research and Popular Education in Latin America." In P. L. McLaren and J. M. Giarelli (Eds.), *Critical Theory and Educational Research.* Albany, NY: SUNY Press, 1995, pp. 237–255.

Torres, R. M. *De Alfabetizando a Maestro Popular: La Post-alfabetización en Nicaragua* [From Literacy Teaching to the Popular Teacher: Post-literacy Education in Nicaragua]. Managua, Nicaragua: INIES, 1983.

Tough, A. M. *The Adult's Learning Projects.* Toronto: Ontario Institute for Studies in Education, 1971.

Tuhiwai Smith, L. *Decolonizing Methodologies: Research and Indigenous Peoples.* London: Zed Books, 1999.

Vetter, M. A. *Violeta Parra: Canto a La Diferencia—Un Estudio De La Obra De Violeta Parra En El Contexto De La Lucha de Clases en Chile* (Unpublished master's thesis). Northern Illinois University, DeKalb, Illinois, 2000.

Vetter, M. A. "Education in Social Movements: A Cultural-cognitive Approach." Paper presented at the meeting of the Latin American Studies Association (LASA), Dallas, Texas, 2003.

Vogler, J. "The Rise of the Penguins." *NACLA Report on the Americas,* 2007, *40*(1), 51–52.

Wainwright, H. *Reclaim the State: Experiments in Popular Democracy.* London: Verso, 2003.

Waldron, M. W., and Moore, G.A.B. *Helping Adults Learn: Course Planning for Adult Learners.* Toronto: Thompson, 1991.

Watson, C. *Management Development Through Training.* Reading, MA: Addison-Wesley, 1979.

Welton, M. "Social Revolutionary Learning: The New Social Movements as Learning Sites." *Adult Education Quarterly,* 1993, *43*(3), 152–164.

West, C. *Prophesy Deliverance: An Afro-American Revolutionary Christianity.* Philadelphia: The Westminster Press, 1982.

West, C. *The Cornel West Reader.* New York: Basic Books, 1999.

White, B. J., and Madara, E. J. *The Self-help Group Sourcebook: Your Guide to Community and Online Support Groups.* Denville, NJ: Saint Clare's Health Services, 2002.

Wigmore, D. "Identifying Problems Collectively: Mapping." In J. Slaughter (Ed.), *A Troublemakers Handbook 2.* Detroit: Labor Education and Research Project, 2005a, pp. 79–81.

Wigmore, D. "Mapping for Organizing." In J. Slaughter (Ed.), *A Troublemakers Handbook 2.* Detroit: Labor Education and Research Project, 2005b, pp. 14–15.

Williams, R. *The Long Revolution.* Harmondsworth, UK: Pelican, 1965.

Williams, R. *Marxism and Literature.* New York: Oxford University Press, 1977.

Wilson, A. L., and Hayes, E. R. (Eds.). *Handbook of Adult and Continuing Education.* San Francisco: Jossey-Bass, 2000.

Wright Mills, C. *The Sociological Imagination.* New York: Oxford University Press, 1953.

X, Malcolm. *Malcolm X Speaks.* New York: Pathfinder, 1989.

Youngman, F. *Adult Education and Socialist Pedagogy.* London: Croom Helm, 1986.

Youngman, F. *The Political Economy of Adult Education and Development.* London: Zed Books, 2000.

Zibechi, R. "Subterranean Echoes: Resistance and Politics 'Desde el Sótano.'" *Socialism and Democracy,* 2005, *19*(3), 13–39.

Zweig, M. *The Working Class Majority: America's Best Kept Secret.* Ithaca, NY: ILR Press, 2000.

NAME INDEX

SUBJECT INDEX

A

Absolute surplus value, 136

Act Up, 161

Action: affirmative action, 47, 199; Che Guevara on learning in, 65; Citizenship Schools use of principles and, 74–75; radical training relationship between principle and, 71–72

Action research. *See* Participatory action research

Adult development: cognitive, psychological, and sociocultural models of, 44; critical theory to teach, 57–62; for democratic socialism preparation, 48–49; Marxist approach to, 49; postformal operations of, 44–45; a radical approach to conceptualizing, 49–57; reframed in normative pursuit of true democracy, 43; SDL (self-directed learning) process of, 45; teaching for radical, 57–62

Adult Education: Foundations of Practice (Darkenwald and Merriam), 68

Adult education: African American context of, 209–216; Basic American Negro Creed influence on, 211; debate over distinctions between training, 69–70; functions of

radical aesthetics in, 152–165; globalization context of, 139–143; new and changing challenges faced by, 216–221; as part of movement to realize democracy, 5–9, 25–26; radical development, 49–62; reconsidering concepts of, 2–3; SDL (self-directed learning) and learner control of, 38–40; traditional purpose and responsibilities of, 2–3; workplace learning within, 18. *See also* Radical adult learning

Adult Education (Bryson), 2, 3

Adult education programs: goals of, 95–99; issues to consider for planning, 86–88; planning criteria for evaluating, 99–106; principles of planning, 88–95

Adult Education Quarterly, 23

Adult Education Research Conference, 53, 208

Adult educators: City Colleges of Chicago (CCC) union of, 84–85; codes of ethics for, 88; educator-activist notion of, 116–117; examples of worker-oriented training by, 77–84; Jane Thompson's "open letter to whoever's left" to, 218; Marcuse's criticism of repressive tolerance taught by, 191–195; morality of coercion used by,

intersection of White supremacy ideology and, 17, 26, 40, 47, 109, 200, 202; learning liberation from, 26–32; SDL for establishing socialist alternatives to, 40–41; Soviet Union's practice of state, 52; systematic exploitation of, 14; transformative adult learning theory to explain ideology of, 34–35, 143–144; understanding internal relations of, 134; unquestioning celebration of, 4; workplace critical reflection and critique of, 36–37. *See also* Ideology

"Las Casitas del Barrio Alto" (song), 156

Centro de Investigaciones y Estudios de la Reforma Agraria, 79

"Check Your School" survey, 173

Chicano/Mexican American movement (1960s–1970s), 157

Chilean cultural movement, 151–152

Chilean Popular Unity Government, 165, 179

Citizenship School Teacher Training, 74

Citizenship Schools: origins of, 65–66, 71; principles and actions used in, 74–75; radical training in, 72–75, 180–181

Citizenship Workbook (SCLC), 181

City Colleges of Chicago (CCC), 84–85

Civil Rights Congress, 89

Civil rights Movement: as culmination of polarization process, 220; examples of participatory research in, 179–182; as historical process

of social change, 92; ideological conditioning on racism no longer being an issue, 199; love and empathy motivations of the, 90; Malcolm X's disapproval of nonviolence of, 92; origins of the, 66; radicalized learning facilitating the, 24, 75, 180; voter registration training during, 71, 72–73, 182; "We Shall Overcome" anthem of, 154–155. *See also* African American Freedom Movement; United States

Civil society decline, 48

The Clash (punk bank), 146

Clydeside shipbuilding sit-in (Scotland), 37

Coalition of Immokalee Workers (CIW), 98, 99, 105, 140, 142, 219

Codes of ethics, 88

Collective forms development, 52–56

Collective identity development, 50–51

Collective movement development, 52–56

Collectives of Popular Sandinista Education (CEPS), 78–79

College Republicans (University of Wisconsin-Madison), 157–158

Commando (Reitz), 21

Commission of Professors of Adult Education, 88

Common Fire (Parks Daloz, Keen, Keen, and Daloz Parks), 48

Communist Party of South Africa, 25

Communist Party USA (CPUSA), 173–174, 214, 217

Computer course (Zimbabwe), 129–130

development leading to discussion of, 48–49; examining radical adult learning in context of, 16–20; fairness in, 7–8, 11–14; four societal requirements of, 7–9; inclusive, 8–9, 14–16; meeting basic survival needs, 7, 9–10; standing against White supremacy ideology, 205; understanding power and building, 126–127. *See also* Socialism

Democratic Socialists of America, 41

Desegregation, 47

Developing agency, 51–52

Development. *See* Adult development

Differences: acknowledging individual, 13–14; confronting diversity, 205–206; creativity for ensuring fairness in spite of, 8, 12–14; inclusion in spite of, 8–9, 14–16. *See also* Diversity

Discipline learning principle, 91–92

Dispossessed: Basic American Negro Creed impact on, 211; does work begin with pressing demands of, 100; does work build organization exercising power by, 104–105; does work build political independence of, 103–104; does work develop skills and knowledge of, 105–106; does work facilitate understanding by the, 100–102; does work facilitate understanding of local and broader interconnectedness, 102–103

Diversity: confronting differences and, 205–206; dismantling privilege in context of, 206–216;

ideological detoxification related to, 201–205; practicing liberating tolerance of, 199–201; questioning the accuracy of celebrating narrative of, 190–191; repressive tolerance of, 27–28, 109–110, 191–199. *See also* Differences

Do the Right Thing (film), 153–154

Dorchester Center (Georgia), 73

Dusk of Dawn (DuBois), 210–211

E

Ebonics language, 159

Echo in My Soul (Clark), 73

Economic and Philosophical Manuscripts (Marx), 18

Education as the Practice of Freedom (Freire), 175

Educator-activist notion, 116–117

Edutainment (KRS-One), 150

Empathy, 90–91

Empowerment through art, 156–159

The End of History and the Last Man (Fukuyama), 218

ESL for Action (Auerbach and Wallerstein), 102

Ethnic cleansing, 45–46, 110

Eurocentric philosophy, 193

European-American Collaborative Challenging Whiteness (ECCW), 207

Evaluation. *See* Program evaluation criteria

Everyday Face of Globalization, 142

F

Fairness: as central to socialist ideal, 7; creativity to ensure, 8, 12–14; of democratic socialists society, 7–8; how to ensure, 11–12

"Haters Page" (Marcuse home
  page), 191
Health care ideology, 30–31
Hegemony: Che Guevara's goal
  for service, 94; teaching that
  illuminates power and, 118–120.
  See also Authority
Highlander Folk School, 38, 65–66,
  72, 74, 154–155, 180
Highlander Research and
  Education Center, 102–103
Hip-hop culture, 149–151, 154,
  159, 208
Hmong refugees, 164
Holocaust, 110
Home Depot, 135
Homophobia, 52
Honesty learning principle, 92–93
House on Un-American Activities
  Committee (HUAC), 166, 167
Human resource development
  (HRD), 93, 133
Hurricane Katrina, 95

I

Ideal speech situation, 62
Ideological detoxification, 201–205
Ideological manipulation:
  capitalism and, 4, 14, 26–32,
  36–37, 40–41; contemporary
  adult learning to resist, 31–32;
  critical reflection to resist, 23,
  31–32, 35–37; health care,
  30–31; self-directed learning
  to resist, 23, 31–32, 37–41;
  transformative learning to
  resist, 23, 32–35
Ideology: Basic American Negro
  Creed, 211; racism, 16, 45–46,
  199, 206; repressive tolerance
  used to promote, 109–110;
  transformative adult learning

theory explaining formation
  of, 34–35; "war of liberation,"
  46; Whitestream, 193. *See also*
  Capitalism; White supremacy
  ideology
Immigrant rights marches
  (2006), 219
Immigrant rights movement, 94
Immigrant workers, 93–94, 102–103
Immigration waves, 93–94
Inclusion: as democratic socialist
  society quality, 8–9, 15;
  recognizing differences and
  embracing, 14–16
*International Dictionary of Adult and
  Continuing Education* (Jarvis), 68
*International Encyclopedia of Adult
  Education* (English), 32, 66, 68
*International Journal of Lifelong
  Education,* 23
International Labor Organization,
  139
International Monetary Fund,
  129, 218
International Socialist
  Organization, 41
"The Internationale" (socialist
  anthem), 112
Internationalism, 89–90
Internationalist curriculum,
  112–113
Intrinsic motivation, 90–91
Iraq invasion (2003), 28, 46, 118
Irish Republican Army's (IRA)
  Bobby Sands hunger strike, 164

J

Johns Island voter registration, 71

K

Kenwood Academy, 150
Kmart, 135

to, 48–49; socialism approach to, 9–10

Street slang, 159

Student Nonviolent Coordinating Committee (SNCC), 66, 103, 106, 180

Student-centered learning, 116–117

Studies in Continuing Education, 23

Studies in the Education of Adults, 23

Subgroup of the Leadership Development and Current Issues Committee, 181

Sweet Honey in the Rock, 147, 151

T

Taco Bell Boycott workshop, 142

The Take (documentary), 82

Tales of Manhattan (film), 168

Teachers College (Columbia University), 2

Teaching: critical theory used in, 57–62; political issues of women, 59; for radical adult development, 57–62; as radical form, 114–117; as radical function, 111–114; self-criticism, honesty, and truth used in, 92–93. *See also* Adult educators; Adult learning; Radical teaching

Teaching Defiance (Newman), 1, 183

Tennessee Industrial Renewal Network, 102

Theory of consciousness, 60

Theory-practice dialectic of learning, 122–124

Tolerance: practicing liberating, 14, 199–201; repressive, 27–28, 109–110, 191–199

"The Tragedy of the Commons" (Hardin), 48

Training: and adult education in era of globalization, 139–143;

Che Guevara's exploration of learning in, 64–65; debate over distinctions between education and, 69–70; defining and debating, 67–71; downgrading attitude toward, 66; examples of radical, 71–84; voter registration, 71, 72–73; worker-oriented, 77–84

"Training by Corporations" (*Handbook* 1934), 68

"Training Leaders for Citizenship Schools: Outline of Training Workshop" (Highlander Folk School), 180

"Training" (Ollagnier), 66

Transformation adult learning: capitalism ideology explained by, 34–35, 143–144; challenging ideological manipulation through, 31–32; definition of, 32; globalization and, 143–144; radical development through, 56–57; research focus on, 23. *See also* Perspective transformation

Truth principle, 92–93

Truth and Reconciliation Commission (South Africa), 29

Turin factory councils, 37

U

UAW Local 879, 132–133

UAW/Ford MnSCU Training Center, 130

Ujamaa (African socialism), 49

Umkhonto we Sizwe group (Spear of the Nation) [South Africa], 20–21

UNESCO Krupskaya Prize for Literacy, 80

United Auto Workers, 140

United Nations, 89–90, 179